FASCISM

FASCISM

Comparison and Definition

Stanley G. Payne

The University of Wisconsin Press

Published 1980

The University of Wisconsin Press
114 North Murray Street
Madison, Wisconsin 53715

The University of Wisconsin Press, Ltd.
1 Gower Street
London WC1E 6HA

First printing

Printed in the United States of America

For LC CIP information see the colophon

ISBN 0-299-08060-9

Contents

Preface

The purpose of this book is not to provide another description of fascism but to wrestle with some basic problems of definition and comparison. The general bibliography on fascism is extensive, especially in the areas of Germany and Italy, and there are a number of works that provide descriptions of the principal fascist movements. What is wanting in this literature, however, is a systematic review, however brief, that endeavors to define characteristics and make distinctions on a broadly comparative basis. It is to this enterprise that the present book is addressed. This study is therefore not designed as a catch-all history of fascism for the introductory student, though I hope that with the use of other works discussed in the bibliography it may be read with profit by students of fascism at all levels.

It is logical and natural that study and commentary on the fascist-type movements have frequently generated as much heat as light. Forces that promoted a world-historical disaster are hard to view with scientific detachment, but my endeavor has been to disengage this analysis as much as possible from political emotions and overt moralizing.

I owe a special debt to some of my friends and colleagues in fascist studies—particularly George L. Mosse, A. J. Gregor, and Juan J. Linz—though we naturally do not agree on every point of interpretation. Thanks are also due to Mary Maraniss of the University of Wisconsin Press, who for the second time in only a few years has edited a book for me with skill and diligent discretion.

STANLEY G. PAYNE

Madison, Wisconsin
March 1979

FASCISM

1

What Do We Mean by *Fascism?*

The unprecedented disaster that was World War I swept away much of the basis of nineteenth-century liberalism and opened an era of revolution and political conflict more intense than any seen before or after. One of the major new revolutionary forces, Russian Communism, was a direct development of nineteenth-century European Marxist and Russian revolutionary theory. The other major new radical force unleashed by World War I—fascism—was newer and more original, for it was a direct product of the war itself. Neither a fascist party nor a fascist doctrine existed as such before 1919. Communism, however, was by and large rejected by the European left and for the next generation confined as a regime to Russia. Italian Fascism,[1] founded in 1919, was followed by imitations and parallel or somewhat analogous movements in many other European lands. Fascism largely

1. In this study the names of the Italian Fascist Party and its immediate antecedents, members, and components will be capitalized, while the terms *fascism* and *fascist* used in a broader and more generic sense will not.

seized control in Italy after 1922, to be followed a decade later by German Nazism. Powerful forces apparently similar in character gained strength in east-central Europe and in Spain by the 1930s, so that many historians refer to the entire generation before World War II as the fascist era in Europe. Yet the extension of the adjective to describe an entire period in European history has led to confusion as much as to clarity or understanding, for what the concept gained in scope was quickly lost in precision.

Fascism is probably the vaguest of contemporary political terms. This may be because the word itself has no implicit political reference, however vague, as do democracy, liberalism, socialism, and communism. To say that the Italian *fascio* (Lat. *fasces*, Fr. *faisceau*, Sp. *haz*) means "bundle" or "union" cannot tell us much. Some of the most common informal definitions of the term seem to be "violent," "brutal," and "dictatorial," but if those were the primary points of reference communist regimes would probably have to be categorized as the most fascist. Definition bedeviled the original Italian Fascists from the beginning, since they developed a formal codified set of doctrines only ex post facto, some years after Mussolini came to power, and then only in part. The problem is compounded by the fact that whereas nearly all communist parties and regimes prefer to call themselves communist, most of the political movements in interwar Europe commonly termed fascist did not in fact use that name for themselves. The problems of definition and categorization that arise are so severe it is not surprising that some scholars prefer to call putative fascist movements by their specific individual names alone without applying the categorical adjective. Still others deny that any such general phenomenon as fascism or European fascism—as distinct from Mussolini's Italian Fascism—ever existed.

If fascism is to be studied, it has first to be identified, and it is doubtful that can be done without some sort of working definition. Such a definition, or better, description, must be derived from empirical study of the interwar European movements. It must be of course to a certain extent a theoretical construct or abstraction, since no single movement of the group under observation would necessarily be found to have announced a program or self-description couched in the exact terms of this definition. Nor would such a hypothetical definition be intended at all to imply that the individual goals and characteristics identified were necessarily in every item unique to fascist movements, for most items might be found in one or more other species of political movement. The contention would be rather that *taken as a whole* the definition would describe what all fascist movements had in common without trying to describe the unique characteristics of each group. Finally, for reasons to be discussed later, the definition might refer only to interwar European fascist movements and not to a presumed category of fascist regimes or systems.

Any definition of common characteristics of fascist movements must be used with great care, for fascist movements differed from each other as significantly as they held notable new features in common. A general inventory of their distinctive characteristics is therefore useful, not as a full and complete definition of such movements in and of themselves, but only as an indication of the chief characteristics that they shared which distinguish them (in most respects, but not absolutely) from other kinds of political forces.

The problems involved in reaching an inductive set of characteristics may be illustrated by reference to the most clear-cut previous effort to establish a criterial definition of generic fascism: the six-point "fascist minimum" postulated by Ernst Nolte.[2] It consists of a set of negatives, a central organization feature, a doctrine of leadership and a basic structural goal, expressed as

> antimarxism
> antiliberalism
> anticonservatism
> the leadership principle

---

2. Nolte, *Die Krise des liberalen Systems und die faschistischen Bewegungen* (Munich, 1968), 385.

> a party army
> the aim of totalitarianism.

This typology correctly states the fascist negations, but postulates three primary characteristics derived especially from German National Socialism that cannot in such a simple formulation be correlated with other varieties of a broader political species.[3]

The common characteristics of fascist movements had to do with a new set of common negations, aspects of a new formal style, somewhat novel modes of organization, and in varying ways or degrees a new orientation in political culture and ideology, though always with very fundamental differences in the specific character of these new forms and ideas. Thus in order to arrive at a criterial definition applicable to all the interwar fascist movements *sensu strictu*, it seems appropriate to identify (a) the fascist negations, (b) common points of ideology and goals, and (c) special common features of style and organization.[4]

The descriptive typology in table 1 is suggested merely as an analytic device of limited scope for purposes of comparative definition. It does not propose to establish a rigidly reified category, but a loose wide-spectrum description that can identify a variety of differing allegedly fascist move-

3. H.-J. Puhle has criticized Nolte for ignoring the economic dimension of a fascist typology and suggests several basic modifications. He would replace *antimarxism* with *antisocialism* and give the general definition a more conservative slant by dropping *anticonservatism* altogether. Puhle specifies corporatism as the fascist economic doctrine, further stipulating "support of the capitalist economic order by respecting its relative basic autonomy" while exercising totalitarian political control. *Politische Agrarbewegungen in kapitalistischen Industriegesellschaften* (Göttingen, 1975), 278.

It seems to me that Puhle is correct in calling attention to the economic sphere and in modifying the concept of an anticonservatism pure and simple that was equivalent to fascism's antiliberalism and antimarxism, yet goes too far in giving fascism a conservative slant. Concerning antisocialism, there are too many different kinds and concepts of socialism to characterize fascism as fundamentally antisocialist.

4. The idea of a tripartite definition was first suggested to me by Professor Juan Linz in a conversation at a conference in Bergen, Norway in June 1974. The specific content is my own.

Table 1
TYPOLOGICAL DESCRIPTION OF FASCISM

A. The Fascist Negations:
Antiliberalism
Anticommunism
Anticonservatism (though with the understanding that fascist groups were willing to undertake temporary alliances with groups from any other sector, most commonly with the right)

B. Ideology and Goals:
Creation of a new nationalist authoritarian state based not merely on traditional principles or models
Organization of some new kind of regulated, multiclass, integrated national economic structure, whether called national corporatist, national socialist, or national syndicalist
The goal of empire or a radical change in the nation's relationship with other powers
Specific espousal of an idealist, voluntarist creed, normally involving the attempt to realize a new form of modern, self-determined, secular culture

C. Style and Organization:
Emphasis on esthetic structure of meetings, symbols, and political choreography, stressing romantic and mystical aspects
Attempted mass mobilization with militarization of political relationships and style and with the goal of a mass party militia
Positive evaluation and use of, or willingness to use, violence
Extreme stress on the masculine principle and male dominance, while espousing the organic view of society
Exaltation of youth above other phases of life, emphasizing the conflict of generations, at least in effecting the initial political transformation
Specific tendency toward an authoritarian, charismatic, personal style of command, whether or not the command is to some degree initially elective

ments while still setting them apart from other kinds of revolutionary or nationalist movements. Individual movements might then be understood to have possessed further beliefs, characteristics, and goals of major importance to them that did not contradict the common features but were simply added to them or went far beyond them.

The term fascist is used not for the sake of convention alone but because the Italian movement was the first significant force to exhibit those characteristics (or at least most of them) as a new type and was for long the most influential ideologically. It constituted the type whose ideas and goals were the most easily generalized, particularly when compared with racial National Socialism.

The nature of the fascist negations seems clear enough. As "latecomers" (in Linz's phrase), the post-World War I radical nationalist movements that we call fascist had to clear new political and ideological space for themselves, and were unique in their hostility to all the main established currents, left, right, and center. This basic attitude was complicated, however, by the need to find political allies in the drive for power. Since such movements emerged mostly in countries with established parliamentary systems and sometimes relied disproportionately on the middle classes, there was no real question of their coming to power through revolutionary civil war, as have key Leninist regimes. Though fascists in Italy and Romania established short-lived tactical alliances with the right-center (and in Portugal with the anarchist left), their most common allies lay on the right, particularly on the radical authoritarian right, and Italian Fascism as a semicoherent entity was partly defined by its merger with one of the most radical of all right authoritarian movements in Europe, the Italian Nationalist Association (ANI). Such alliances sometimes necessitated tactical, structural, and programmatic concessions. The only two fascistic leaders who actually rose to power, Hitler and Mussolini, began their governments as multiparty coalitions, and Mussolini, despite the subsequent creation of an officially one-party state, never fully escaped the pluralist compromise with which he had begun. Moreover, since the doctrines of the authoritarian right were usually more precise, clear, and articulate—and often more practical—than those of the fascists, the capacity of the former for ideological and programmatic influence was considerable. Nonetheless, the ideas and goals of fascists differed in several fundamental respects from those of the new authoritarian right (as will be discussed in more detail below), and the intention to transcend right-wing conservatism as well as liberalism and marxism was firmly held, though not always clearly realized in practice.

Much of the confusion and ambiguity surrounding the interpretation of fascist movements stems from the fact that only in a few instances did they succeed in passing to the stage of governmental participation, and only in the case of Germany were the full implications of a fascist doctrine—in the form of its most radical variant—carried out by a regime in power. It is thus difficult to generalize about fascist systems or the fascist doctrine of the state, since even the Italian variant was seriously compromised. All that can be established with clarity is that fascist aspirations concerning the state were unique in not being limited to traditional authoritarian doctrine such as monarchy or corporatism but positing a new radical secular system, normally republican and authoritarian. Yet to specify the aim of full totalitarianism, as has Nolte, seems unwarranted, for unlike Leninism, fascist movements never projected a state theory with sufficient centralization and bureaucratization to make complete totalitarianism possible. This problem will be treated in greater detail in subsequent chapters.

No point remained less clear in the doctrines of most fascist movements than economic structure and goals. To make fascism synonymous with corporatism is obviously incorrect, since only a minority of Italian Fascists espoused corporatism before Mussolini's compromise with the monarchy and the fusion with the Nationalists. More important, the most radical and developed form of fascism, German National Socialism, explicitly rejected formal corporatism (in part because of its pluralism). Conversely, the frequent contention of Marxist writers that the aim of fascist movements was to prevent economic changes in class relationships is not borne out by the movements themselves, but since no fascist movement ever fully completed the elaboration of a fascist economic system the point remains theoretical. What the fascist movements did have in common was the aim of a new

structure and functional relationship for the social and economic systems, eliminating the autonomy (or in some proposals, the existence) of large-scale capitalism, altering the
nature of social status, and creating a new communal or re-
ciprocal productive relationship. This was given a variety of
names, and its precise articulation was more often than not
left unclear.

Fascism is said to have been imperialist by definition, but
this is not entirely clear from a comparative reading of the
programs of diverse fascist movements. Most were indeed
imperialist, but all types of political movements and systems
seem to have produced imperialist policies, while several
fascist movements had little interest in and even rejected
new imperial ambitions. All, however, sought a new order
in foreign affairs, a new relationship or set of alliances with
respect to contemporary states and forces, and a new status
for their nation in Europe and the world.

Fascist ideology and culture deserve more attention than
they normally receive, for fascist doctrine, like all others,
stemmed from ideas, and the ideas of fascists had distinct
philosophical and cultural bases, despite frequent assertions
to the contrary. Fascist philosophical ideas are often said to
stem from opposition to the Enlightenment or the "ideas of
1789," when as a matter of fact they are a direct byproduct of
aspects of the Enlightenment and were derived specifically
from the modern, secular, Promethean concepts of the eighteenth century. The essential divergence of fascist ideas from
certain aspects of modern culture probably lies more precisely in fascist antimaterialism and its emphasis on philosophical vitalism and idealism and the metaphysics of the will.
Fascist culture, unlike that of the right, was in most cases
secular but, unlike that of the left and to some extent of the
liberals, was based on vitalism and idealism and the rejection of economic determinism, whether of Manchester or
Marx. The goal of metaphysical idealism and vitalism was
the creation of a new man, a new style of culture that
achieved both physical and artistic excellence and that prized

courage, daring, and the overcoming of previously established limits in the growth of a superior new culture that engaged the whole man. Fascists hoped to recover the true sense of the natural and of human nature—a basically eighteenth-century idea—on a higher and firmer plane than the reductionist culture of modern materialism and prudential egotism had yet achieved. The free natural man of developed will and determination would be able to transvalue and go beyond himself and would not hesitate to sacrifice himself for the sake of those ideals. Such modern formulations rejected nineteenth-century materialism, but did not represent anything that could be called a reversion to the traditional moral and spiritual values of the western world before the eighteenth century. They represented a specific attempt to achieve a modern, normally atheistic form of transcendence, and not, in Nolte's phrase, any "resistance to transcendence."

The novel atmosphere of fascist meetings struck many observers during the 1920s and 30s. All mass movements employ symbols and various emotive effects, and it might be difficult to establish that the symbolic structure of fascist meetings was entirely different from other revolutionary groups. What seemed clearly distinct, however, was the great emphasis on meetings, marches, visual symbols, and ceremonial or liturgical rituals, given a centrality and function in fascist activity that went beyond that found in the left revolutionary movements. The goal was to envelop the participant in a mystique and community of ritual that appealed to the religious as well as the merely political.

Most fascist movements did not achieve true mass mobilization, but it was nonetheless characteristic that such was their goal, for they always sought to transcend the elitist parliamentary cliquishness of poorly mobilized liberal groups or the mere sectarian exclusiveness and reliance upon elite manipulation often found in the authoritarian right. Together with the drive for mass mobilization went one of the most characteristic features of fascism, its attempt to militarize politics to an unprecedented degree. This was done by making militia groups central to the movement's organization and by using military insignia and terminology in reenforcing the sense of nationalism and constant struggle. Party militia were not invented by fascists but by the extreme left and radical right (e.g., Action Française), and in a country such as Spain the predominant "shirt movements" practicing street violence were those of the revolutionary left. However, the initial wave of central-European fascism was disproportionately based on World War I veterans and their military ethos. In general, the party militia played a greater role and were developed to a greater extent among fascists than among the left groups.

This was related to the positive evaluation of violence and struggle in fascist doctrine. All revolutionary mass movements have initiated and practiced violence to a greater or lesser degree, and it is probably impossible to carry violence to greater lengths than have some Leninist regimes, practitioners of, in the words of one Old Bolshevik, "infinite compulsion." The only unique feature of the fascist relationship to violence was the theoretical evaluation by some fascist movements: that violence possessed a certain positive and therapeutic value in and of itself, that a certain amount of continuing violent struggle, along the lines of late nineteenth-century Social Darwinism, was necessary for the health of national society.

This in turn was related to yet another fundamental characteristic: the insistence on what is now termed "male chauvinism" and the tendency to exaggerate the masculine principle in all aspects of activity. All European political forces in the era of fascism were overwhelmingly led by and made up of men, and those that paid lip service to female equality in fact had little interest in it. Only fascists, however, made a perpetual fetish of the "virility" of their movement and its program and style, stemming no doubt in good measure from the fascist concept of the militarization of politics and the need for constant struggle. Like rightist and also some left groups, the fascist notion of society was organic,[5] but in that relationship the rights of the male were to enjoy predominance. No other kind of movement professed such complete horror at the slightest suggestion of androgyny.

Nearly all revolutionary movements make a special appeal to young people and are disproportionately based on young activists. By the 1920s even moderate parliamentary parties had begun to form their own young people's sections. Fascist exaltation of youth was unique, however, in that it not only made a special appeal to them but also exalted youth over all other generations without exception, and to a greater degree than any other force based itself on generational conflict. This no doubt stemmed in part from the lateness of fascism and the identification of the established forces, including much of the left, with leaders and members from the older, prewar generation. It also stemmed in part from the organic concept of the nation and of the youth as its new life force, and from the predominance of youth in struggle and militarization. The fascist cult of daring, action, and the will to a new ideal was inherently attuned to youth, who could respond in a way impossible for older, feebler, and more experienced and prudent, or more materialistic, audiences.

Finally, we can agree with Pareto and Michels that nearly all parties and movements depend on elites and leadership for their functioning, but some recognize the fact more explicitly and carry the idea to greater lengths. Strongly authoritarian leadership and the cult of the leader's personality are obviously in no way restricted to fascist movements, nor is it even true that all fascist movements enshrined, as Nolte suggests, the *Führerprinzip* of a single, all-powerful chief. Most fascist movements began on the basis of elective leadership—elected at least by the party elite—and this was true

5. The term *organic* will be used in this study in a general sense to refer to concepts of society in which the latter's various sectors are held to bear a structured relationship to each other that serves to define and delimit their roles and rights, taking precedence over the identities and rights of individuals.

even of the National Socialists. The Spanish version of the Führerprinzip, the theory and practice of *caudillaje*, was introduced by the nationalist right in the person of Franco and imposed on the fascists. There was nonetheless a general tendency to exalt the function of leadership, hierarchy, and subordination, deferring to the creative function of leadership more than to prior ideology or a bureaucratized party line.

THREE FACES OF AUTHORITARIAN NATIONALISM

Comparative analysis of fascist-type movements has been rendered more complex, and often more confused, by a common tendency to identify these movements with more conservative and rightist forms of authoritarian nationalism in the interwar period and after. The fascistic movements represented the most extreme expression of modern European nationalism, yet they were not synonymous with all authoritarian nationalist groups. The latter were pluriform and highly diverse, and in their typology extended well beyond or fell well short of fascism, diverging from it in fundamental ways.

The confusion between facist movements in particular and authoritarian nationalist groups in general stems from the fact that the heyday of fascism coincided with a general era of political authoritarianism that on the eve of World War II had in one form or another seized control of the political institutions of the majority of European countries. It would be grossly inaccurate to argue that this process proceeded independently of fascism, but neither was it merely synonymous with fascism.

It thus becomes crucial for purposes of comparative analysis to distinguish clearly between fascist movements per se and the nonfascist (or sometimes protofascist) authoritarian right. During the early twentieth century there emerged a cluster of new rightist and conservative authoritarian forces in European politics that rejected moderate nineteenth-century conservatism and simple old-fashioned reaction in favor of a more modern, technically proficient authoritarian system distinct from both leftist revolution and fascist radicalism. These forces of the new right may in turn be divided into elements of the radical right on the one hand and the more conservative authoritarian right,[6] as will be suggested below. (For suggested examples, see table 2.)

The new right authoritarian groups combated many of the same things that fascists opposed (especially liberalism and Marxism) and did stand for some of the same goals. Moreover, there were numerous instances of tactical alliances— usually temporary and circumstantial—between fascists and right authoritarians, and sometimes even cases of outright fusion, especially between fascists and the radical right, who always stood rather closer to fascists than did the more moderate and conservative authoritarian right. Hence the general tendency to lump the phenomena together, which has been reenforced by subsequent historians and commentators who tend to identify fascist groups with the category of the right or extreme right.[7] Yet to do so is correct only insofar as the intention is to separate all authoritarian forces opposed to both liberalism and Marxism and assign them the arbitrary label of "fascism" while ignoring the basic differences between them. It is a little like identifying Stalinism and Rooseveltian democracy because both were opposed to Hitlerism, Japanese militarism, and west-European colonialism.

Fascism, the radical right, and the conservative authoritarian right differed among themselves in a variety of ways. In philosophy, the conservative authoritarian right, and in many instances also the radical right, based themselves upon

6. These analytical distinctions bear some analogy to Arno J. Mayer's differentiation of the counterrevolutionary, reactionary, and conservative in his *Dynamics of Counterrevolution in Europe, 1870–1956* (New York, 1971). Yet as will be seen below, my criterial definitions differ considerably in content from Mayer's.

7. For example, John Weiss, *The Fascist Tradition* (New York, 1967). In a somewhat similar vein, Otto-Ernst Schüddekopf's *Fascism* (New York, 1973), which is distinguished primarily for being the best-illustrated of the volumes attempting to provide general treatment of fascism, also tends to lump various fascist and right authoritarian movements and regimes together.

Table 2
THREE FACES OF AUTHORITARIAN NATIONALISM

Country	Fascists	Radical Right	Conservative Right
Germany	NSDAP	Hugenburg, Papen, Stahlhelm	Hindenburg, Brüning, Schleicher, Wirtschaftspartei, etc.
Italy	PNF	ANI	Sonnino, Salandra
Austria	NSDAP	Heimwehren	Christian Socials, Fatherland Front
Belgium	late Rex, late VNV, Légion Nationale	Verdinaso	early Rex, early VNV
Estonia		Veterans' League	Päts
Finland	Lapua/IKL	Acad. Karelia Society	Mannerheim?
France	Faisceau; Francistes, PPF, RNP	AF, Jeunesses Pat., Solidarité Française	Croix de Feu; Vichy
Hungary	Arrow Cross, National Socialists	"Right Radicals"	Horthy, National Union Party
Japan	Nat'l Soc/some "Imperial Way"	"Japanists," some "Control"	Konoye/IRAA
Latvia	Thunder Cross		Ulmanis
Lithuania	Iron Wolf	Tautininkai	Smetona
Mexico	Silver Shirts	Cristeros/Sinarquistas	PRI
Poland	Falanga, OZN	National Radicals	Pilsudski, BBWR
Portugal	Nat'l Syndicalists	Integralists	Salazar/UN

Table 2 *continued*

Country	Fascists	Radical Right	Conservative Right
Romania	Iron Guard	National Christians	Carolists, Manoilescu
South Africa	Gray Shirts	Ossewa-Brandwag	National Union
Spain	Falange	Carlists, Renovación Española	CEDA
Yugoslavia	Ustasa, Zbor	Orjuna	Alexander, Stojadinovic

religion more than upon any new cultural mystique such as vitalism, nonrationalism, or secular neoidealism. Hence the "new man" of the authoritarian right was grounded on and to some extent limited by the precepts and values of traditional religion, or more specifically the conservative interpretations thereof. The Sorelianism and Nietzscheanism of core fascists was repudiated in favor of a more practical, rational, and schematic approach.

If fascists and conservative authoritarians often stood at nearly opposite poles culturally and philosophically, various elements of the radical right tended to span the entire spectrum. Some radical right groups, as in Spain, were just as conservative culturally and as formally religious as was the conservative authoritarian right. Others, primarily in central Europe, tended increasingly to embrace vitalist and biological doctrines not significantly different from those of core fascists. Still others, in France and elsewhere, adopted a rigidly rationalistic position quite different from the nonrationalism and vitalism of the fascists, while trying to adopt in a merely formalistic guise a political framework of religiosity.

The conservative authoritarian right was only anti-conservative in the very limited sense of having broken with the parliamentary forms of moderate parliamentary conservatism. It wished, however, to avoid radical breaks in legal continuity if at all possible, and normally proposed only a partial transformation of the system in a more authoritarian direction. The radical right, by contrast, wished to destroy the entire existing political system of liberalism root and branch. Even the radical right, however, hesitated to embrace totally radical and novel forms of authoritarianism, and normally harkened back to a reorganized monarchism or an eclectic neo-Catholic corporatism or some combination thereof. Both the radical and the conservative authoritarian right tempered their espousal of elitism and strong leadership by invoking traditional legitimacies to a considerable degree. The conservative authoritarian right preferred to avoid novelty as much as possible in forming new elites as in dictatorship, while the radical right was willing to go farther on both points, but not so far as the fascists.

The conservative authoritarian right usually, though not always, drew a clear distinction between itself and fascism, whereas the radical right sometimes chose deliberately to blur such differences. In the fascist vertigo that afflicted so much of European nationalism in the 1930s, however, even some sectors of the conservative authoritarian right adopted certain of the trappings and externals of fascism, though they neither desired nor would have been able to reproduce all the characteristics of generic fascism.

Though the conservative authoritarian right was slow to grasp the notion of mass politics, it sometimes managed to exceed the fascists in mobilizing mass support, drawing on broad strata of rural and lower-middle-class people. The radical right was normally the weakest of all three sectors in terms of popular appeal, for it could not compete with the fascists in a quasi-revolutionary cross-class mobilization campaign and could not hope for the backing of the broad groups of more moderate elements who sometimes supported the conservative authoritarian right. To an even greater degree than the latter, the radical right had to rely on elite elements of established society and institutions (no matter how much they wished to change political institutions), and their tactics were aimed at manipulation of the power structure more than at political conquest from outside that would draw on popular support.

Thus the radical right often made a special effort to use the military system for political purposes, and if worst came to worst it was willing to accept outright pretorianism—rule by the military—though mostly in accordance with radical right principles. The fascists were the weakest of these forces in generating support among the military, for the conservative authoritarian right might in moments of crisis expect even more military assistance than could the radical right—its legalism and populism could more easily invoke principles of legal continuity, discipline, and popular approval. Consequently efforts by both the conservative authoritarian right and the radical right to organize their own militia usually stopped short of paramilitary competition with the armed forces. By contrast, fascists sought only the neutrality or in some cases the partial support of the military while rejecting genuine pretorianism, realizing full well that military rule per se precluded fascist rule, and that fascist militarization generated a sort of revolutionary competition with the army. Hitler was able to make his power complete only after he had gained total predominance over the military. When, conversely, the new system was led by a general—Franco, Pétain, Antonescu—the fascist movements were relegated to a subordinate and eventually insignificant role. Mussolini, by contrast, developed a syncretic or polycratic system which recognized broad military autonomy while limiting that of the party.

Contrary to a common assertion, economic development was a major goal of groups in all three categories, though there were exceptions (perhaps most notably the early Portuguese Estado Novo). The fascists, as the most "modernizing" of these sectors, gave modern development greater priority (again with some exceptions), though depending on national variations, some radical right and conservative authoritarian groups also gave it major priority. Right radicals and conservative authoritarians almost without exception became corporatists in formal doctrines of political economy, but the fascists were less explicit and in general less schematic.

One of the major differences between fascists and the two rightist sectors concerned social policy. Though all three sectors advocated social unity and economic harmony, for most groups of the radical and conservative authoritarian rights this tended to mean freezing much of the status quo. The question of fascism and revolution will be taken up later, but suffice it to say that the fascists were in general more interested in changing class and status relationships in society, and in using more radical forms of authoritarianism to achieve that goal. The rightist sectors were simply more rightist—that is, concerned to preserve more of the existing structure of society with as little alteration as possible, except for promoting limited new rightist elites and weakening the organized proletariat.

The conservative authoritarian right was in general less likely to advocate an aggressive form of imperialism, for that in turn would imply more drastic domestic policies and incur new risks of the kind that such movements were primarily designed to avoid. The same, however, could not necessarily be said of the radical right, whose radicalism and pro-militaristic stance often embraced aggressive expansion. Indeed, elements of the radical right were frequently more imperialistic than the moderate or "leftist" (social revolutionary) elements within fascism.

As a broad generalization, then, the groups of the new conservative authoritarian right were simply more moderate and generally more conservative on every issue than were the fascists. Though they had taken over some of the public esthetics, choreography, and external trappings of fascism by the mid-1930s, the style of the conservative authoritarian right emphasized more direct conservative continuity and its symbolic overtones were more recognizably traditional.

The radical right, on the other hand, often differed from fascism not by being more moderate or more conservative in the positive sense but by being more rightist. It was tied more to the existing elites and structure for support, however demogogic its propaganda may have sounded, and was unwilling to accept fully the cross-class mass mobilization and implied social, economic, and cultural change demanded by fascism. In some respects, with regard to violence, authoritarianism, militarism, and imperialism, however, the radical right was just as extreme as the fascists, and it was in these respects that the radical right was primarily distinguished from the conservative authoritarian right. Such differences will become easier to grasp in the concrete examples discussed in subsequent chapters.

2

Some Historical Antecedents of Authoritarian Nationalism in Europe

SOURCES OF RIGHT AUTHORITARIANISM

At first glance it might be assumed that the origins of the twentieth-century authoritarian right lay in the first reactions to the eruption of liberal and leftist forces during the French Revolution and its aftermath. While there are undeniable links between the new authoritarian right of the late nineteenth and early twentieth centuries and those forces of traditionalism, neolegitimism, and reaction that preceded them by a hundred years, major differences also exist. The reactionary movements of the early nineteenth century tended to be simply and directly traditionalist, and aimed at avoiding the development of modern urban, industrial, and mass society rather than transforming it, whereas by the latter part of the century the new rightist groups had achieved much greater sophistication, and tried in their own way to come to terms with modern social, cultural, and economic problems.

22

The emergence of the new forms of right authoritarianism was a long, often-slow and complex, process, for liberal parliamentarianism seemed on its way to an almost complete victory in formal institutions by the last decades of the century. Though certain major exceptions to liberalism might be found in the constitutional structures of Russia and Germany, the main challenges to liberalism after 1870 appeared to come from the socialist, anarchist, and populist left rather than from new forms of rightism. So complete was the intellectual and theoretical triumph of liberalism in the formal culture of many European countries that moderate liberals and conservatives at first sometimes groped helplessly for new concepts or doctrines of a more authoritarian structure of government to cope with their problems.

The roots of the new forms of the authoritarian right in the late nineteenth and early twentieth centuries may be found in at least four different areas: the growth of corporatist doctrine, primarily in Catholic circles, and the ambiguous development of certain new forms of political Catholicism; the transformation of moderate or conservative liberalism, by degrees, in an overtly authoritarian direction, especially in southern Europe; the transformation of previously traditionalist antiliberal and monarchist forces in various countries from the Latin west to Russia; and the emergence of an instrumental, modernizing, and imperialist new kind of radical right in Italy.

Growth of Corporatist Doctrines

By far the greatest confusion in the interpretation of these developments has stemmed from the efforts to conceptualize the movement toward corporatism both with respect to its origins and also its structure. The organization of various sectors of society into distinct "corporations," partly autonomous and partly state-regulated, dates from Roman times, and various partial systems of limited autonomy and self-regulation within a broader framework of government authority and limited representation were a common feature of the Middle Ages, particularly in local city states but also to some degree within larger kingdoms. The beginnings of modern corporatism stem from the early nineteenth century in reaction to the individualism, social atomization, and new forms of central state power arising from the French Revolution and modern liberalism. The first ultraright corporative ideas, prominent mainly in Germany (but also in France), proposed a partial return to the medieval estates system under a more authoritarian government. Purely reactionary or semireactionary, corporatism should, however, be distinguished from some of the Catholic doctrines that developed in the middle and later nineteenth century and were directed toward reducing the powers of government, providing for social group autonomy with less concern for strictly economic and political issues. The difference here, at least in part, is that between what later corporatists called "societal" (socially autonomous) and "state" (government-induced and controlled) corporatism. Yet another strand of corporatist or semicorporatist thought developed toward the end of the nineteenth century among moderate and conservative liberals in reaction to the atomistic and invertebrate, conflict-oriented character of purely individualistic liberalism. This was the "solidarist" school of Léon Bourgeois in France, paralleled by minor echoes in other countries and to some extent by the "juridical" corporatist school of Anton Menger in Austria.

By the beginning of the twentieth century, however, there was a growing convergence among conservative and rightist exponents of corporatism toward state rather than societal corporatism, even though abstract formal doctrines tended, even more perhaps than revolutionary leftist theories, to disguise the degree of compulsion and authoritarianism under which the proposed new system would operate.

The best succinct working definition of what is meant in the twentieth century by most doctrines of corporatism has been provided by Philippe Schmitter:

> Corporatism can be defined as a system of interest representation in which the constituent units [i.e., social and eco-

nomic sectors] are organized into a limited number of singular, compulsory, noncompetitive, hierarchically ordered and functionally differentiated categories, recognized or licensed (if not created) by the state and granted a deliberate representational monopoly within their respective categories in exchange for observing certain controls. . . .[1]

From Conservatism and Conservative Liberalism to Moderate Neoauthoritarianism

Aside from corporatism, the other source for the early development of a moderate authoritarian right lay in the slow trend toward an authoritarian orientation among the more conservative elements of late-nineteenth-century liberalism and semiliberalism. The chief expressions of "authoritarian liberalism" were to be found in central Europe, mainly Germany and Italy, but also perhaps in Hungary, with specific manifestations in Portugal and Spain. One aspect of this tendency may be found first in Germany, where the political system had never become fully liberal anyway. Bismarck, in his last year as chancellor (1889–90), began to consider seriously reducing even further the extent of liberal prerogatives, cutting back the parliamentary franchise and other civil rights. Authoritarian constitutionalism became increas-

---

1. Philippe C. Schmitter, "Still the Century of Corporatism?" in F. Pike and T. Stritch, eds., *The New Corporatism* (Notre Dame, 1974), 85–131. Schmitter's article also offers a useful background discussion on nineteenth-century corporatism, as does Howard Wiarda's unpublished article "Corporatist Theory and Ideology: The Latin American Development Paradigm."

The main studies of corporative ideas in nineteenth-century Germany and France are Ralph H. Bowen, *German Theories of the Corporative State* (New York, 1947), which covers the years to 1919; and Matthew H. Elbow, *French Corporative Theory, 1789–1948* (New York, 1953). These two studies treat both Catholic doctrines of societal corporatism and more secular theories of state corporatism. Among the latter ideas, see Elmer Roberts, *Monarchical Socialism* (New York, 1913).

A roughly corresponding work on Italy is Carlo Vallauri, *Le radici del corporativismo* (Rome, 1971), mainly but not exclusively devoted to Catholic theories of societal corporatism, which tended not to emphasize the economic or political dimensions.

ingly influential among German conservatives in the years before World War I.

Reversion to a more authoritarian liberalism first became a serious option for Italy when it had to face the beginning of political democratization and mass politics after the Milan riots of 1898. The chief proponent of this position, Sidney Sonnino, summed it up in the slogan *Torniamo allo Statuto* ("Back to the Statute," the Statute being the original and unamended restrictive liberal charter of Piedmont in 1848), but the Sonninian formulae as represented by the Pelloux government of 1898–1900 were ultimately rejected by the crown itself. They were nonetheless kept alive, albeit somewhat covertly, during the Giolittian reform era, and began to come to the fore in the Salandra-Sonnino government of 1914–16 that plunged Italy into World War I as part of the process of bolstering a more moderate and conservative authoritarian alternative.

As the liberal systems of southern Europe became more democratic, conflictive, and unmanageable, there were mounting demands for a moderately authoritarian alternative, even if no more than a temporary "cincinnatian" dictatorship. Invocation of emergency powers by the Habsburg crown might, for example, be considered one example of such procedure, but a broader step was taken in this direction during the decomposition of the Portuguese parliamentary monarchy, when João Franco was given power by the crown to rule temporarily by decree in 1907–8. As distinct from limited "decree powers" recognized by the Third Republic in France, for example, or the emergency authority of the Habsburg crown, Franco's dictatorship could not be legitimized by the Portuguese constitutional system and it operated on the dubious authority of the crown alone. Franco personified one variant of the new "managerial" trend in conservative liberalism, one of his mottoes being *pouca política, muita administração*. In the decade after World War I, other variants of this "authoritarian liberal" trend, only marginally associated with legitimate constitutional powers, appeared throughout southern Europe.

Neomonarchist Authoritarianism

Though most of the new rightist, neo-authoritarian groups of the early twentieth century were in one sense or another monarchist (with a very few exceptions), one type of new right force made the monarchy itself a major focus of authoritarian nationalism, unlike moderate Catholic corporatists or the more liberal authoritarians. The prime exemplar of specifically neomonarchist authoritarian nationalism was the Action Française, founded in 1899. Its core principles of legitimist monarchy and corporate representation under a neo-traditionalist state were not in themselves novelties, for they had formed part of the basis for traditionalism throughout the past century.

The uniqueness of the Action Française was that it provided a new synthesis of all the nineteenth-century traditionalist ideas that converted monarchism from a dynastic principle into a complete system of "integral nationalism." This rested not merely or even primarily on the traditional patrimonial kingdom but on the nation as an organic whole, of which the monarchy was head. In attempting a new monarchist system on the basis of nationalism, Charles Maurras and the other ideologues of the party went beyond traditional royalism in the direction of a new, sophisticated, ideologically developed nationalism. Their cultivation of style and esthetics, combined with a seemingly up-to-date, often deftly rendered, elitist propaganda espousing the most extreme and shrill new tones, made the Action Française *the* nationalist party of early twentieth century France. It struck a more radical note with its broad use of anti-Semitism, and mention is sometimes made of the "Camelots du Roi," the militant young street groups of the movement, as the first prefascist "shirt movement" of radical European nationalism. In fact, the Action Française never aspired to develop a "movement militia" in the style of Fascism or Nazism—which were far removed from its own style—just as it never aspired to become a full-scale, organized political party. Political gangs of a fairly elementary sort that might occasionally engage in street violence were not entirely unprecedented in southern Europe. Only after 1917 were they transformed into mass militia forces, and that process was not initiated by the ultraright Action Française.

Though officially Catholic, the attitude of most of the movement's leaders to religion was utilitarian and theologically skeptical, yet another way in which they differed from most traditional legitimists. Maurras and Léon Daudet were themselves more interested in spiritualism and magic than in Christian theology. Their pragmatic approach led to their condemnation by the Papacy in 1925.

The political economy of the Action Française, such as it was, was corporatist, derived in large measure from the nineteenth-century doctrines of René de la Tour du Pin. A socioeconomic program was not in fact worked out in detail until Firmin Baconnier undertook the task in the 1920s, but that was no more than a rehash of Catholic corporatist ideology. The Action Française could never have been called a modernizing nationalist movement. Its chief historian has judged that the function of the Action Française was "to furnish the Right with an ideology with which it could mask its lack of positive program or purpose in what was largely an obstinate—and often effective—holding action against change."[2] Though a few fumbling efforts were made to consider cooperation with anarchosyndicalists against the centralized, liberal republican state, the rigid neotraditionalist confines of the movement eventually prompted many activist younger members, such as Valois, Bucard, Darnand, Rebatet and Brasillach, to leave for more radical forces sometimes developed in imitation of Italian Fascism.

Abroad, the greatest influence of the Action Française might be found in Spain and Portugal, particularly in the latter country, where a neomonarchist party Integralismo Lusitano was organized, largely in imitation, under the new

2. Eugen Weber, *Action Française* (New York, 1962), 530. See also Edward Tannenbaum, *Action Française* (New York, 1962); René Remond, *La Droite en France* (Paris, 1963); Armin Mohler, *Die französische Rechte* (Munich, 1958); and Samuel M. Osgood, *French Royalism since 1870* (The Hague, 1970).

Portuguese republic after 1910. Spanish Carlism, which had emerged in the nineteenth century as one of the most powerful traditionalist forces in southern Europe, later evolved in the early twentieth century in a direction somewhat analogous to the Action Française, though much more fervently Catholic.

Some analogy might also be found in Russia, with the emergence of the Union of the Russian People in 1905. The URP of course altogether lacked the style and sophistication of an association like the Action Française, and equally lacked the conceptual rigor and modernizing thrust of the new Italian Nationalists (to be discussed below). It was a more elementary formation whose short life and limited development make it hard to categorize in western terms. The URP combined authoritarian monarchism and a vague corporatism with some effort at mass mobilization and new social reform. It emphasized violent strong-arm squads (the Black Hundreds) more than did the new west-European rightist groups, and was extreme in its semiracial anti-Semitism and support of the new style of Russian nationalist imperialism.[3] It perhaps resembled von Schönerer's Austrian Pan-Germanism (which will be mentioned in the next section) more than it did any other west-European movement, and so in some respects foreshadowed the new semirevolutionary and partially collectivist nationalism more than the class-based west-European extreme right.

Emergence of an Instrumental, Modernizing Radical Right

Proposals for moderate or neomonarchist authoritarianism were exceeded by more extreme demands for a new modern form of authoritarianism that would promote domestic modernization and violent national expansion.

3. Hans Rogger, "Was There a Russian Fascism?—The Union of Russian People," *Journal of Modern History* (hereafter cited as *JMH*) 36.4 (December 1964): 398–415; and "Russia," in Hans Rogger and Eugen Weber, eds., *The European Right* (Berkeley, 1965), 443–500. Further data may be found in J. J. Brock, Jr., "The Theory and Practice of the Union of the Russian People, 1905–1907" (Ph.D. diss., University of Michigan, 1972); and D. C. Rawson, "The Union of the Russian People, 1905–1907" (Ph.D. diss. University of Washington, 1971).

The most sophisticated and clear-cut of the new radical right groups evolving from conservative liberalism was the Italian Nationalist Association, founded in 1910. At first a conflicting assemblage of democratic, moderate, and radical authoritarian nationalists, it achieved relative ideological unity when Alfredo Rocco's doctrine of the authoritarian corporate state was adopted in 1914. Unlike Catholic corporatists, who theoretically strove to minimize the role of the state, Rocco held statism to be the only logical, consistent, and scientific approach to modern political organization. He claimed to derive much of his theory from German doctrines of the juridical state, which held that human rights were not inherent but resulted from the self-limitation of sovereign state power.

The divisiveness of parliamentary party politics and the social strife and underdevelopment besetting the Italian economy were all to be overcome by the organization of a corporate state. This would replace parliament by a corporate assembly representing economic interest groups and regulated by a state with predominant power. Its function would be to achieve social harmony, promote economic modernization, and make of Italy a strong, imperial country. Though his enemies often termed Rocco's corporate state reactionary, he distinguished it from that of Catholic conservatives as not being based on archaic blueprints of medieval estates but, rather, planned to promote modern industrial coordination to build a new, modern society. Yet though the ANI's goals were modernizing they were not revolutionary, in that the existing sovereignty of the Italian crown and the general class structure were to be largely preserved through authoritarian means while the technology and industrial potential of the society as a whole were being transformed.

Perhaps the most radical aspect of Rocco's program lay in its ultimate goal, which was to strengthen Italy for modern war and imperial expansion. These the Nationalists held to be necessary and indeed, from a kind of social Darwinist viewpoint, inevitable. They were the first political group in Italy to organize on their own to meet the revolutionary left in violent confrontation, and it was the Nationalist militia—

the Sempre Pronti ("Always Ready")—that first responded to leftist violence with physical assaults on the left in Bologna in July 1919, before the minuscule new Fascist movement was ready or willing to do so.[4]

A partial analogy of a more crude but even more radical sort—though less directed toward modernization—may be found in the transformation of elements of the old German Conservative Party and the new German Landowners' League (Bund der Landwirte) in the 1890s. Forsaking earlier principles of ultraconservative legalism, the new German radical right turned toward overtly authoritarian politics on the basis of demagogic new mass mobilization, racialism, and racial anti-Semitism. Striving to foster particular interests within a new authoritarian racial nationalist framework, the new German radical right also eagerly promoted militarism and imperial expansion.[5]

4. The only general study is Alexander J. De Grand, *The Italian Nationalist Association and the Rise of Fascism in Italy* (Lincoln, Nebr., 1978). Briefer introductions are given by Francesco Leoni, *Origini del nazionalismo italiano* (Naples, 1965) and *La stampa nazionalista* (Rome, 1965); Raffaele Molinelli, *Per una storia del nazionalismo italiano* (Urbino, 1966); and Wilhelm Alff, "Die Associazione Italiana Nazionalista von 1910," in Alff's *Der Begriff Faschismus und andere Aufsätze zur Zeitgeschichte* (Frankfurt, 1971), 51–95. Paolo Ungari, *Alfredo Rocco e l'ideologia giuridica del fascismo* (Brescia, 1963), provides an excellent presentation of Rocco's ideas. The other main Italian Nationalist ideologue has been studied by Ronald Cunsolo in "Enrico Corradini and Modern Italian Nationalism, 1896–1923" (Ph.D. diss., New York University, 1962); and Monique de Taeye-Henen, *Le Nationalisme d'Enrico Corradini et les origines du fascisme dans la revue florentine "Il Regno" (1903–1906)* (Paris, 1973). Links with big business are scrutinized in R. A. Webster, *Industrial Imperialism in Italy, 1908–1915* (Berkeley, 1975).

5. The main study is Hans-Jürgen Puhle, *Agrarische Interessenpolitik und preussischer Konservativismus im wilhelmischen Reich 1893–1914* (Bonn, 1975). See also Puhle's *Von der Agrarkrise zum Präfaschismus* (Wiesbaden, 1972) and "Radikalisierung und Wandel des deutschen Konservatismus vor dem ersten Weltkrieg," in G. A. Ritter, ed., *Deutsche Parteien vor 1918* (Cologne, 1973), 165–86.

There were a variety of efforts to mobilize anti-Semitic and racial right-nationalist groups in the Second Reich on a broader popular basis; they all failed. See R. S. Levy, *The Downfall of the Anti-Semitic Political Parties in Imperial Germany* (New Haven, 1975); P. G. J. Pulzer, *The Rise of Political Anti-Semitism in Germany and Austria* (New York, 1964); and Richard Massing, *Rehearsal for Destruction* (New York, 1967).

PRECURSORS OF REVOLUTIONARY, SEMICOLLECTIVIST NATIONALISM

Apart from right-wing monarchist and corporatist forms of authoritarian nationalism, new kinds of more radical egalitarian and semicollectivist movements emerged near the end of the nineteenth century, primarily in France and in Austria-Bohemia. These anticipated some of the main postulates of the movements that became Fascism and Nazism, particularly the latter. Hence they have sometimes been identified as forms of prefascism, a vague and eclectic concept that tends to reify and exaggerate a number of at best only partially connected phenomena.

France

New political tendencies have normally been found earlier in France than almost anywhere else in the world. Of all European polities, that of France moved most rapidly through the early phases of democratization and conflict overloading, and thus the Second Empire of Louis Napoleon (1851–70) became the first modern syncretic, postliberal national authoritarian regime, preceding all others by more than half a century. Hence the concept found in some quarters of "Bonapartism" as the "first fascism."

Here one must specify carefully what is being referred to. What first inspired a Marxist theorist to make the comparison[6] was Marx's own analysis of Louis Napoleon's regime as the product of a new phase of social conflict producing an authoritarian system no longer primarily dependent on a single social class—that is, a dictatorship that was politically autonomous and self-perpetuating, however buttressed

6. The comparison was apparently first made by August Thalheimer in 1930. His essays have been partially reprinted in *Faschismus und Kapitalismus*, ed. W. Abendroth (Vienna, 1967), 19–38; and in *Texte zur Faschismusdiskussion*, ed. R. Kühnl (Reinbek, 1974), 14–29. The concept has been further elaborated by Gustav A. Rein, *Bonapartismus und Faschismus in der deutschen Geschichte* (Göttingen, 1960).

by the backing of wealthy elites and broader lower-middle-class sectors.[7] While this is probably a correct description of much of the political basis of the Second Empire, it might also be equally descriptive of the main features of communist regimes and a variety of other dictatorial systems, and hence could scarcely refer to anything discretely "fascist."

The Second Empire was extraordinarily eclectic, a remarkable mixture of conservatism, clericalism, classic Bonapartist authoritarianism, and electoral neoliberalism, accompanied by mass propaganda and economic modernization. Though it anticipated certain individual features of twentieth-century dictatorships, the Second Empire was in fact a precocious syncretistic product of the mid-nineteenth century lacking several of the most novel qualities of the more radical twentieth-century regimes. Its state structure was basically that of a traditional form of empire, unlike Nazi Germany or the Soviet Union. It never proposed a very novel, much less collectivist, sort of economic system or an original regulatory structure, though several kinds of ideas were toyed with. The Second Empire's political culture was almost as much scientific-rationalist as that of most contemporaries, and it never attempted a party movement, much less a new political militia. Louis Napoleon was about as squeamish as most of his contemporaries about the use of violence, and though a caesarian or pretorian figure, strove to legitimize himself as much as possible in traditional terms. His Bonapartism relied directly on the military while seeking to accommodate conservative and traditionally religious forces. His regime for the most part preserved existing class relationships while striving to promote economic modernization through largely orthodox means. Insofar as Bonapartism in France was the precursor of any particular state system, it would seem more related to several of the right-wing, primarily nonfascist systems of the interwar period, which were sometimes similarly

7. Karl Marx, *The Eighteenth Brumaire of Louis Bonaparte* (New York, 1970). See M. Rudel, *Karl Marx devant le Bonapartisme* (Paris, 1960).

pretorian-led and proclerical, retained pseudo-liberal formulae, and tried to promote economic modernization without mass mobilization of new state economic systems.[8]

The authoritarian interlude in modern French government occurred very early, probably because of the precocity of social mobilization and modern social conflict in France. Its overthrow did not come as the result of domestic rebellion but, as in the case of nearly all institutionalized modern European authoritarian systems, of foreign military defeat. After 1870 France moved slowly and uncertainly into stable liberal democratic government, and managed [largely] to institutionalize most of its attendant forms and values before the new collectivist, semirevolutionary nationalism could fully develop.

Nonetheless, it was indeed in France that new forces of semirevolutionary nationalism with egalitarian and collectivist overtones first emerged, even though the new context of vigorous liberal democratic institutions, combined with strong government, stunted their growth. The first examples would be the agitation of Paul Déroulède's League of Patriots and the Boulangist movement of the 1880s. One of the main motivations for a revolutionary nationalism—status deprivation—weighed upon France after 1870, and the French left, still at that time quite nationalist and not Marxist, felt defrauded by the Third Republic, just as sectors of the nationalist left were to feel in central-European countries after World War I. Boulangism and the League of Patriots expressed a new kind of nationalism that was at the same time authoritarian, contemptuous of parliamentary democracy; and directed toward the masses. It sought to harmonize the interests of diverse classes with promises of new economic regulations that appealed especially to small shopkeepers and the lower middle classes, but it also mobilized

8. The best brief critique of the Fascism/Bonapartism thesis is Jost Dülffer, "Bonapartism, Fascism and National Socialism," *Journal of Contemporary History* (hereafter cited as *JCH*), 11.4 (October 1976); 109–28. On the politics and structure of the Second Empire, see Theodore Zeldin, *The Political System of Napoleon III* (Oxford, 1958).

urban workers and promoted labor organization.[9] It propounded a new charismatic caesarism to break the bonds of
existing parties. A central motif was national vengeance,
based on a doctrine of neomilitarism and a mystique of discipline and death rooted in the national soil and people's culture.[10]

Despite a novel combination of ideas and tendencies, it
would also be a mistake to label Boulangism a categorical
prefascism. For one thing, such an inflated concept would
give Boulangism more coherence than it had in fact. The
Boulangist movement was compounded of supernationalist
révanchards, political radicals who wanted no party parliament but a more plebiscitary form of direct government with
strong elective presidential leadership, neo-Bonapartist
peasants yearning for a strong patriotic leader, revolutionary
Blanquists seeking direct action and violent overthrow of the
bourgeois republic, social nationalists of the patriotic left,
and authoritarian royalists of the patriotic right. Despite domestic discontents and national status deprivation, French
society was in general reasonably contented and successful
in the 1880s and 90s, not the soil for a mass-mobilizing movement to establish deep enough roots for a violent overthrow
of the system. Finally, both Boulanger and Déroulède were
men of the nineteenth century who had only a limited toler-
ance for violence.

A somewhat more coherent kind of nationalist radicalism
was the new concept of "national socialism," which also appeared earlier in France than anywhere else. Perhaps its first
proponent was a quixotic adventurer, the Marquis de Morès,
whose radical Parisian circle, Morès et ses Amis, tried to

9. Cf. P. H. Hutton, "Popular Boulangism and the Advent of Mass Politics
in France," *JCH* 11.1 (January 1976): 85–106.
10. The key study is Zeev Sternhell, *La Droite révolutionnaire 1885–1914*
(Paris, 1978), 15–127. See also Sternhell, "Paul Déroulède and the Origins of
Modern French Nationalism," *JCH* 6.4 (October 1971): 46–71; and *Maurice
Barrès et le nationalisme français* (Paris, 1972). Adrien Dansette, *Le Boulangisme*
(Paris, 1947), is superseded by Frederic H. Seager, *The Boulanger Affair* (Ith-
aca, N.Y. 1969).

combine extreme nationalism with limited economic socialism, racism, and direct action. Its small strong-arm gangs
were more violent and determined than those of the rightist
Action Française, for from the beginning they were willing
to employ maximal force, including murder. Another novelty, compared with the subsequently more restrained and
elitist action of the Action Française, was Morès's effort, limited though it was, to employ racist antisemitism as a means
of popular mobilization among common people.[11]

Morès does not seem to have employed the formal label
national socialism, and the concept was evidently first advanced under the phrase *socialist nationalism* by Maurice Barrès during the electoral campaign of 1898. In Bohemia, the
Czech National Socialist Party was founded that same year,
followed by the French National Socialist Party of François
Biétry (which failed to gain support) in 1903 and the German
Workers Party of Bohemia, which also adopted the banner of
national socialism, in 1904. Biétry's National Socialist Party
was the political expression of an anti-Marxist trade union
movement, the Fédération Nationale des Jaunes de France,
and propounded national syndicalism (that is, trade union-
ism), worker profit-sharing, and a strong authoritarian state
with a corporative assembly.[12] It was thus statist but only
semicollectivist.

The most salient intellectual proponent of the new national
socialism was Maurice Barrès, whose political career and
ideas (primarily the latter) have recently attracted considerable scholarly attention.[13] The mystique that Barrès devel-

11. D. J. Tweton, *The Marquis de Morès* (Fargo, N. Dak., 1972); and R. F.
Byrnes, "Morès, the First National Socialist," *Review of Politics* 12.3 (July
1950): 341–62.

12. See Sternhell, *Droite révolutionnaire,* 245–317; George Mosse, "The
French Right and the Working Classes: Les Jaunes," *JCH,* 7.3–4 (July-October 1972): 185–208; and Eugen Weber, "Nationalism, Socialism and Nation-
al-Socialism in France," *French Historical Studies* 2.3 (Spring 1962): 273–307.

13. In addition to the work by Sternhell, there is Robert Soucy, *Fascism in
France: The Case of Maurice Barrés* (Berkeley, 1972); and, less satisfactorily, C.
S. Doty, *From Cultural Rebellion to Counterrevolution: The Politics of Maurice
Barrès* (Athens, Ohio, 1976).

oped of *la terre et les morts* (the national soil and the dead) was derived in considerable measure from the Déroulède doctrines, but in his formulation tried to combine the search for energy and a vital new style of life with national rootedness and a sort of Darwinian racism. Barresian national socialism differed from Action Française doctrines in its stress on economic radicalism and its reliance on intuition and emotion (theoretically rejected by the monarchist rationalists). While rejecting traditional Christian and clerical anti-Jewishness, Barrès vigorously espoused a modern racial anti-Semitism, whose unifying and mobilizing potential he quickly grasped.[14] He also propounded hero worship and charismatic leadership, and yet despite his effort to achieve a new semirevolutionary kind of nationalism, Barrès at no time fully overcame a lingering conservatism. Failing to generate broad support, he later lapsed into traditionalism and a sort of fatalism that largely ignored his earlier advocacy of radical vitalism and willpower.

Austria and Bohemia

The first continuous, moderately successful national socialist parties emerged in Habsburg Bohemia after the turn of the century. The pioneer of a radical and aggressive kind of social nationalism in the Austrian world, however, was the pan-German publicist and agitator Georg Ritter von Schönerer. Schönerer's shrill racial nationalism, which invoked a high degree of militarism and imperial expansion, differed from that of the right radicals of the early twentieth century in its precocious and vigorous espousal of intranational egalitarianism, democratic voting rights, and extensive social reforms. The impact of Schönerer's original "Linz Program" of 1882 on both radical nationalist and socially progressive politics was considerable. For that reason, despite Schönerer's lack of political skill, his inability to mobilize an effective following, and the bellicose primitivism and blood-

14. Zeev Sternhell, "National Socialism and Antisemitism: The Case of Maurice Barrès," *JCH* 8.4 (October 1973): 47–66.

lust of his main goals, he is frequently counted among the fathers of central-European national socialism.[15]

Indeed, though some of the Austro-Bohemian national socialists later looked to Schönerer as one of their main precursors, both the Czech National Socialists and Austro-Bohemian German Workers Party were born as democratic, radically reformist and socially progressive movements. The Czech party never entirely lost this orientation, and went on to play a significant role in interwar Czech politics.

The original German Workers Party (DAP) was a radical democratic movement organized among German-speaking blue collar industrial workers in the Sudetenland of Bohemia. Though nationalist, it was not racist, imperialist, or militarist, and advocated that standing armies be replaced with national militias. It demanded the democratization of political and social institutions, and the "national socialism" that it came to formally espouse within a few years proposed some drastic changes, including the socialization or nationalization of big business enterprises. It differed from Marxist socialism in advocating a common socialism for all working and producing sectors of national society, whether worker, peasant, lower-middle-class, middle-middle-class, or intellectual, and in pressing for a mixed socialism within the particular framework of interests and possibilities of the nation.

By 1913, however, the DAF had become seriously infected with pan-German racialism and imperialism. It adopted an anti-Semitic position and was increasingly shrill and bellicose. By the end of World War I it had expanded into a National Socialist German Workers Party (NSDAP) for both Bohemia and Austria, retaining its cross-class orientation and program of partial socialism as a "labor association of all producers" (*Gewerkschaft aller Schaffenden*).[16]

---

15. The best book on Schönerer is A. G. Whiteside, *The Socialism of Fools* (Berkeley, 1975). On the permutation of cultural attitudes into radical nationalism in Austria, see W. J. McGrath, *Dionysian Art and Populist Politics in Austria* (New Haven, 1974).

16. Whiteside's *Austrian National Socialism before 1918* (The Hague, 1962) is the most useful account.

THE CULTURAL CRISIS OF 1890-1914

The expansion of right authoritarian nationalism, and especially the growth of the more revolutionary new forms of collectivist nationalism, seem to have been especially encouraged by the new ideas and cultural emphases fostered by
changes in thought within central Europe, in particular, during the generation 1890-1914.

The term *cultural crisis of 1890-1914* admittedly refers to an
abstract concept focusing a series of new attitudes, theories,
and changes in sensibility that appeared in certain areas of
thought and culture, and afflicted some countries a good deal
more than others. For Europe as a whole there was not necessarily a generalized cultural crisis in this period, but in the
larger continental countries, and particularly in central Europe, changes in attitude among much of the cultural elite
were striking.

It is generally accepted among cultural historians that by
the end of the nineteenth century a mood of rejection toward
dominant values of the preceding generation was setting in.
Faith in rationalism, the positivist approach, and the worship of materialism came under increasing fire. Hostility toward bureaucracy, the parliamentary system, and the drive
for "mere" equality accompanied this spirit of rejection.

In philosophy the age of Bentham and Comte was succeeded by that of Nietzsche and Bergson. Neoidealism and
new theories of vitalism and *Lebensphilosophie* replaced rationalism, pragmatism, and materialism. The process took diverse forms. Heterodox Marxists seeking a new sense of community and social development embraced ethics (contrary to
their master's teaching) and the importance of moral education in society, and this later tended to reenforce the organic
theories of nationalists. Conversely, proponents of vitalism
and life philosophy emphasized the futility of conventional
ethics and morality and the affirmation of direct action, force,
or at the very least subjective practical experience.

This was paralleled by the rediscovery of the unconscious
and the focus on the nonrational in the new psychology, led
by Freud. New theories of crowd psychology (LeBon) and of

revolutionary propaganda and mobilization (Sorel) relied on the manipulation of emotion, the irrational and subconscious, stressing the primordial function of myth among the masses.

The old mid-nineteenth-century scientism had at first seemed to encourage liberalism, democracy, and egalitarianism; the new scientism encouraged doctrines of race, elitism, hierarchy, and the glorification of war and violence. By the late nineteenth century Social Darwinism was in full vogue and had encompassed a variety of scientific fields and social theories. This was marked in the new anthropology and the new zoology, particularly pseudoscientific extrapolations therefrom. New racial doctrines and categories exerted wide appeal. They ranged from reasonably serious studies of "scientific racism" down to the most vulgarized and nonsensical notions of racial differences and hierarchies passed off as demonstrated scientific fact. The determinism of biological heredity exerted widespread influence, and leading scientists who propagated Social Darwinist doctrines, such as the zoologist Ernst Haeckel in Germany and the psycho-physiologist Jules Soury in Paris, were widely read. Haeckel's *Welträtsel* (*Riddle of the Universe*, 1899) had enormous sales, and the German Monist League that he founded in 1904 enjoyed extensive membership and broad influence. It stressed the need for a cultural, not a socioeconomic, revolution to develop the race through a strong authoritarian state.[17]

By the beginning of the new century, a search for the unity of nature was attracting more and more followers. In the German-speaking world (and to a lesser degree in some other areas), this meant a quest to associate the ideal and the physical, the cultural and the material, the spiritual realm with biology, and nature with society, so that the ultimate unity

17. Daniel Gasman, *The Scientific Origins of National Socialism: Social Darwinism in Ernst Haeckel and the German Monist League* (New York, 1971). Certain exaggerations in this work are corrected in Alfred Kelly, "Wilhelm Bölsche and the Popularization of Science in Germany" (Ph.D. diss. University of Wisconsin, 1975). Earlier French parallels are detailed in Sternhell, *Droite révolutionnarie*, 146–76.

and hidden essence of "nature" might be revealed. Such tendencies strongly reenforced the conceptualization and appeal of nationalism, for they exalted biogroup identity and placed a new value on organic relations within societies and on nations as whole units. This in turn reenforced a growing stress on order, authority, and discipline rather than individualism or self-indulgence, for only through stronger authority could organic relations be buttressed and biogroup identity more fully affirmed. All of this contributed mightily to the spirit of 1914 and the great slaughter that ensued.

Pseudoscientific and cultural attitudes were paralleled and stimulated by new sociological and political theories of elitism and "leaderism." Bureaucracy and routine were increasingly decried; even so sober and rationally analytic a sociologist as Max Weber could look to a kind of charismatic leadership as the main alternative to the stultification of government by bureaucratic mediocrity. In Italy, particularly, the new "sociological tradition" represented especially by Mosca and Pareto subjected the parliamentary system to scathing criticism and affirmed the necessary dominance of elites in all political and social systems.[18] Many lesser-known scholars and theorists advanced or supported similar doctrines in other lands.

By the time of World War I, the shift in attitudes, ideas, and sensibilities resulted in a very different climate among much of the European elite than had prevailed during most of the nineteenth century. The new cultural mood would not fully run its course until 1945, with the end of the era of World Wars in Europe. In the meantime, it contributed to the proliferation and acceptance of new doctrines of authoritarian nationalism, whether of the rightist or revolutionary varieties.

18. Armand Patrucco, "Italian Critics of Parliament, 1890–1918" (Ph.D. diss. Columbia University, 1966); and A. James Gregor, *The Ideology of Fascism* (New York, 1969), 1–139.

3

The Fascist and National Socialist Movements

ITALIAN FASCISM

It was for long commonly held that the the doctrines of Italian Fascism could not be systematically discussed because neither movement nor regime possessed a coherent ideology. Yet neither the fact that the Fascist Party never achieved a fully unified formal ideology nor that the Mussolini regime failed to follow or enforce a completely unified ideological system is novel in radical politics. Though an exact and elaborate codification of doctrine was never achieved, it is now becoming recognized that Italian Fascism did function on the basis of a reasonably coherent set of ideas.

Fascism was created by the nationalization of certain sectors of the revolutionary left, and the central role in its conceptual orientation was played by revolutionary syndicalists who embraced extreme nationalism. Revolutionary syndicalists, especially in Italy, were frequently intellectuals or theorists who had come out of the Marxist and Socialist party matrix but had struggled to transcend limitations or errors that they believed they found in orthodox Marxism. They espoused direct action and a qualified doctrine of violence,

42

but tried to reach beyond the narrow and cramped confines of the urban proletariat to broader mobilization of peasants and other modest sectors of producers.

By around 1910 most of the revolutionary syndicalists had given up Marxism, and as early as 1907 a few of them had begun to exploit the concept of the "proletarian nation" first developed by Enrico Corradini and some of the more right-wing nationalists. According to this idea, the true "class differences" lay not between social sectors *within* a backward, weak country like Italy but rather *between* the peoples of the developed, imperial, capitalist, "plutocratic" nations and the peoples of backward, exploited, and colonized lands. This attitude has become a key political concept of the twentieth century and was central to the thinking of Italian Fascists.

The leading revolutionary syndicalists who turned to nationalism, such as Sergio Panunzio and A. O. Olivetti, emphasized the broad function of syndical organization and education for all producing sectors of society. They were not devotees of "creative violence" and direct action for its own sake, though they believed that violence might be positive and therapeutic in certain instances. Sorelian-inspired doctrines of myth and emotional manipulation had little place in their schemes of national education.

Nor were the revolutionary syndicalists, permuted into "national syndicalists," fanatical proponents of narrow new authoritarian elites. They held that national syndicalism should create a broad new elite of creative working forces to serve as examples and leaders for the development of Italy. On the international level, they ardently supported the Italian effort in World War I to develop a revolutionary struggle that would alter the power balance in Europe and promote revolution or radical reform within most of the belligerent powers. They did not necessarily support Italian imperialism. In 1916 Panunzio published a lecture *Il concetto della guerra giusta—The Concept of the Just War* (just war as distinct from imperialist war)—and in 1920, as a Fascist, he brought out a booklet in support of the League of Nations.[1]

1. The best study of the transformation of revolutionary syndicalism into

While it is probably correct to say that Mussolini himself never possessed a fully developed and systematic political ideology in the period between his abandonment of Marxism and the formal codification of Fascist doctrine in the late 1920s, he did operate throughout the main part of his career on the basis of certain fundamental ideas or notions formed during the decade 1905–15. These had to do with the concept of leadership necessarily excercised by an elite, of the substitution of the influence of ideas, emotions, and the subconscious for mechanistic materialism or pure rationalism, and of the importance of mobilizing the broader masses (approached at least in part by crowd psychology), rather than strict class orientation.[2] Mussolini had considerable contact with the revolutionary syndicalists and their ideas, some of which he accepted, but he differed from the syndicalists in his more-categorically positive evaluation of violence and direct action and in the use of myth and symbols. By 1915 he had responded to the problem of the nonrevolutionary nature of the proletariat in Italy (or almost anywhere else) by substituting the idea of the revolution of the nation and the people.

The Futurists, led by Marinetti, were the third ideological influence in the founding of Fascism. They went as far "left" as the syndicalists or Mussolini in their rejection of old norms and existing institutions, and exceeded them in their virtually nihilistic exaltation of violence ("war the sole hygiene of nations," etc.) The Futurists were metaphysical motorcycle riders, fascinated by speed, power, motors, machines, and all the possibilities of modern technology, as indicated by many of their paintings. Beyond frequently

Fascist national syndicalism is David Roberts, *The Syndicalist Tradition and Italian Fascism* (Chapel Hill, 1979), but see also A. James Gregor's forthcoming study of Italian Fascist policy. Charles Bertrand, "Revolutionary Syndicalism in Italy, 1912–1922" (Ph.D. diss., University of Wisconsin, 1969), is a highly critical account of its deviation from Marxism.

2. The best account is Gregor's forthcoming study of Italian Fascist policy. See also his "The Ideology of Fascism," in G. L. Weinberg, ed., *The Transformation of a Continent* (Minneapolis, 1975), 3–46; and J. J. Roth, "The Roots of Italian Fascism: Sorel and Sorelismo," *JMH* 39.1 (March 1967): 30–45.

juvenile invocations of the destruction of all the old and the apotheosis of all the new, however, the Futurists also claimed to stand for broad processes of social transformation that would bring democratic enfranchisement and emancipation for all the lower classes, including voting rights for women[3] (a position also supported by Mussolini at least through 1927).

Out of this melange came the program of the founders of Fascism in 1919, calling for the installation of a republic in place of monarchy and for radically democratic, semisocialist reforms. In government, this would require decentralization of the executive and an elective, independent magistracy; in military affairs, the termination of obligatory military service, general disarmament, and the closing of arms factories; in economic structure, the suppression of joint-stock companies, confiscation of unproductive capital, excess war profits, and church properties, confiscation of land for associative cultivation by landless peasants, and in industry, a national syndical system of industrial management by syndicates of workers and technicians; and finally, in foreign affairs, the abolition of secret diplomacy and a new policy based on the independence and solidarity of all peoples within a general federation of nations.[4] This, of course, is not what is generally understood by "fascism."

The initial Fasci Italiani di Combattimento, founded in Milan in March 1919, were a failure. Their total support was limited to only a few thousand people, mainly national syndicalists and small groups of workers in Milan and Liguria, led by a handful of Mussolini socialists and by some nationalist enthusiasts of the *arditi* (special commando troops) of the old army and attended by Marinetti's Futurists. They failed to elect a single deputy in the 1919 elections.

The movement began to expand significantly only in the

3. Emilio Gentile, "La politica di Marinetti," *Storia Contemporanea* (hereafter cited as *SC*) 7.3 (September 1976), 415–38.
4. On the "founding Fascists," or *sansepolcristi*, see Renzo de Felice, *Mussolini il rivoluzionario* (Turin, 1965), 419–544. The first official program of the Fasci di Combattimento appeared in June and had already become more moderate in most respects. Ibid., 742–45.

autumn of 1920, following the great red scare prompted by the Socialist offensive in northern Italy earlier that year. The first fascism had been urban and largely national syndicalist; the expanded fascism of 1920–21 found its greatest support in the countryside of northern Italy, where land seizures and revolutionary strike activity threatened largeholders, small owners, and stable renters alike.[5] Though the eventual mass fascism of 1921, organized officially into the Italian National Fascist Pary of October 1921, had many of the same leaders and used much of the same language as the original Fasci di Combattimento, its social composition and political direction were considerably different.

It will probably never be possible to obtain a precise measurement of the social composition of Italian Fascism before the march on Rome,[6] but the best evidence indicates that it

5. Changes in the north-Italian countryside and the growth of rural Fascism are treated in Paul Corner, *Fascism in Ferrara 1915–1925* (Oxford, 1965); A. Roveri, *Le origini del fascismo a Ferrara 1918–1921* (Milan, 1974); Anthony Cardoza, "Agrarian Elites and the Origin of Italian Fascism: The Province of Bologna, 1901–1922" (Ph.D. diss., Princeton University, 1975); and Marco Bernabei, "La base di massa del fascismo agrario," *SC* 6.1 (March 1975): 123–56.

The main political account of this period is Roberto Vivarelli, *Il dopoguerra in Italia e l'avvento del fascismo (1918–1922)* (Naples, 1967). For the growth of the Fascist movement proper, the best studies are the Mussolini biography by De Felice, and Adrian Lyttelton's *The Seizure of Power* (New York, 1973). A standard early work is Angelo Tasca [A. Rossi], *The Rise of Fascism* (London, 1938). Of the several general histories of Fascism, the one that deals most directly with the diversity of currents within the party is Enzo Santarelli, *Storia del fascismo*, 3 vols. (Rome, 1973). There are numerous regional studies of early Fascism in Italian.

6. The principal statistics commonly cited for the social composition of the movement late in 1921 were those published by the official Fascist party paper, *Il Popolo d'Italia*, on November 8, 1921. The main categories presented were farm workers (24.3 percent), urban workers (15.4 percent), students (13 percent), landowners of all categories (12 percent), white-collar employees (9.8 percent), and professionals (6.6 percent). These statistics were quite incomplete, however, and accounted for little more than 70 percent of the membership claimed by the party at that time. See W. Schieder, "Der Strukturwandel der faschistischen Partei Italiens in der Phase der Herrschaftsstabilisierung," in W. Schieder, ed., *Faschismus als soziale Bewegung* (Hamburg, 1976), 69–96. Schieder wrestles with the problem of social bases but has little further light to shed on the early movement.

was formed mainly of the middle classes, especially the lower-middle classes of the countryside and the smaller towns, as an expression of radical—but no longer socially revolutionary—nationalism. Since Fascism had been founded to support the cause of the "revolutionary war" it had always invoked certain forms of violence, but the practice of violence on a sizable scale developed only late in 1920 and 1921, directed against the main subversive antinationalist force—the Socialists.

Use of assault *squadre* was integral in the Fascist drive to power, yet the notion that the PNF somehow invented political violence is lamentably superficial. The goal of some sort of paramilitary militia was inherent in the Jacobin tradition and was a major characteristic of the left in countries like Spain throughout the nineteenth century. The inventor of the "shirt movement" was indeed an Italian, but he was Garibaldi (of the Red Shirts), not Mussolini. By the close of the nineteenth century, organization of paramilitary youth groups was becoming increasingly frequent in parts of central Europe. Systematic deployment of a political militia—the Red Guards—was an innovation of Lenin and his Bolsheviks in 1917. Hence the notion that "the novelty of fascism lay in the military organization of a political party"[7] seems rather exaggerated. What the Fascists did was to imitate a common revolutionary style, including aspects of Bolshevist behavior and tactics. They added to it by creating a party uniform and a violent, military-sounding party rhetoric, but the "party-army" was not a Fascist invention.

By the autumn of 1921 the PNF had swollen to approximately 250,000 members, the largest mass party that Italy had yet seen. Generational differentiation was an important factor in recruitment. Fascism made its strongest appeal to younger members of the middle classes in the rural provinces of the north, and to younger members of the middle classes in general. As against the antinationalist Socialist revolution, it proposed an alternative revolution of a more authoritarian nationalist government, led by new elites and ad-

7. Lyttelton, *Seizure of Power*, 52.

vancing broad new national interests. Its economic program had become one of "productivism." The party still espoused a vague national syndicalism but increasingly deemphasized statist economics in favor of freeing national energies and reducing unproductive overhead. As early as September 1919 Mussolini had dropped his original antiimperialism, and by 1921–22 the party's radical nationalism had taken on increasingly imperalist overtones. By 1921 Mussolini as indispensable leader of the movement had espoused political compromise, accepting the principle of monarchy and limited collaboration with the governing liberal groups.

By 1921–22 there was understandable confusion about the "program" of the party. This was partly because of the normal obfuscation and compromises of a radical movement heading toward a share of power, but partly also because of extreme changes on practical points that could not be denied. For some, Mussolini heightened the confusion by insisting that the unity of the movement lay in dynamism and activism per se rather than in doctrine. The Fascist affirmation, common by 1921, that action preceded ideology and formed it had the effect of exaggerating the vitalistic and antirationalist impulses that provided the cultural background of Fascist politics, so that the enemies of Fascism soon claimed that the Fascists had no consistent ideas or doctrines at all. What they had in fact were certain consistent attitudes and cultural preconceptions, though something approaching a codified ideology would not be achieved until the late 1920s and even then would never be fully systematized.

In 1921–22 the party leadership was taking a fairly consistent new stand on economic policy, but one that varied considerably from the 1919 program. The goal was "productivism," but aspects of collectivism were now being dropped from immediate Fascist proposals in order to encourage capital investment. In many ways this made sound sense for the Italian economy—as has ultimately been recognized by one or two communist historians[8]—but strongly paralleled the

8. Mihaly Vajda, "The Rise of Fascism in Italy and Germany," *Telos* 12 (Summer 1972), 12, reprinted in A. James Gregor, *Interpretations of Fascism* (Morristown, N. J., 1974), 166–70.

position of moderate liberals and conservatives in the June 1922 program of the Parliamentary Economic Alliance (supported by the Fascists).[9] This would require further reduction of state expenditures to free productive forces, and a program of financial reform to improve the tax structure, reduce waste, and stimulate capital formation.[10] It was eminently practical but not revolutionary or in any way collectivist, which led to increased murmuring among party radicals.

Fascism had become, as Mussolini observed at the beginning, the great "antiparty," opposed to most of the old orthodoxies of left, right, and center, but it had also become the only new all-Italian party representative of diverse social and regional sectors and even diverse cultural attitudes. Thus it emerged as the only new national force not bound by class to either left or right, and the prime candidate for restoring order and unity to a divided country and providing new leadership.

Yet though Fascism was the only broad new national force and though it aspired to mass mobilization, drawing some limited support from workers and peasants, it never drew more than about 15 percent of the popular vote in a fair election.[11] It is true that the movement reached its peak of popularity probably in 1922–23 and became much stronger than at the time of the 1921 elections, and yet there was never any possibility of its becoming a majority party in Italian affairs. The other major forces—Socialists, liberals, and Catholics—retained a large share of their constituency, whereas the heresies, brash youthfulness, and violent style of the Fascists ultimately limited their appeal. Thus Mussolini could become prime minister only as head of a typical Italian parliamentary coalition, not as the leader of Fascism alone.

9. Roland Sarti, *Fascism and the Industrial Leadership in Italy 1919–1940* (Berkeley, 1971), 31.

10. A. James Gregor, "Un programma per la 'grande Italia,' " *Intervento*, no. 27 (May-August 1977), 91–104.

11. Because of the united list system in the last free election, that of 1921, it is impossible to determine the discrete party vote. The figure of 15 percent should in fact be considered a maximal, rather than a minimal, estimate.

Other Parties and Groups

Fascism was in varying degrees flanked by other forces of authoritarian nationalism that sometimes competed with it and sometimes were allied with it. The Nationalist Association (ANI) had developed a much more clear cut right-authoritarian corporatist ideology and suffered from no equivocations in supporting Social Darwinism, militarism, and imperialism. It had organized an armed militia in a few north-Italian cities well before the Fascists (February–March 1919) and had launched an assault on the Bologna Camara del Lavoro on July 15, 1919, the first instance of antileft violence. The Nationalists were acceptable to respectable institutions in a way that the Fascists were not, and some overlap in ANI and PNF membership was already evident by 1921, though rivalry continued until their fusion in February 1923.[12] ANI membership continued to grow in the postwar crisis but could never achieve the mass mobilization of the Fascists.

The other potential allies of Fascism were those liberals and Catholics who were inclined to accept a moderate degree of authoritarianism as a guarantee of social and institutional security. The right liberals had after all begun the violation of constitutional structure in 1915, when the Salandra-Sonnino government helped to engineer an Italian declaration of war against the wishes of parliament;[13] though later in 1922–23 Salandra drew back from the Fascists, who he realized would not just "tighten up" government institutions but replace them altogether.[14]

There was only one source of left nationalist competition for the Fascists, and it stemmed from the D'Annunzio–De Ambris band of progressivistic national corporatists who had come together in the Fiume enterprise of 1919–20. De

12. R. Ronzio, *La fusione del nazionalismo con il fascismo* (Rome, 1943); and De Grand, *Italian Nationalist Association*.

13. Brunello Vigezzi, *L'Italia dalla neutralitá all'intervento nella prima guerra mondiale* (Milan, 1965); Edgar R. Rosen, "Italiens Kriegseintritt im jahre 1915 als innenpolitisches Problem der Giolitti-Ära," *Historische Zeitschrift* 187.2 (April 1959): 289–363; and John A. Thayer, *Italy and the Great War* (Madison, Wis., 1964), 233–390.

14. Antonio Salandra, *Memorie politiche (1916–1925)* (Milan, 1951), 73–75.

Ambris's "Carta del Carnaro," a reasonably imaginative attempt at a representative and democratic kind of societal corporatism, momentarily exerted considerable influence on the Fascist national syndicalists, and some of them temporarily veered in the direction of D'Annunzio and De Ambris late in 1921 as Mussolini carried the party toward compromise with the right.[15]

GERMAN NATIONAL SOCIALISM

When most theorists of generic fascism refer to fascism they seem to mean, in fact, National Socialism. Of all the authoritarian nationalist movements in Europe during the interwar period, only Hitler's National Socialism achieved great power and dynamism, to become by itself a potentially world-historical force. The literature on Hitler and National Socialism is already vast but continues to grow rapidly, not merely in German and English but in other languages as well. Detailed and systematic historical description is now available of the main personalities, policies, and most of the key institutions of the Nazi Party and the Third Reich. The more material that is amassed, however, the more problematic certain fundamental questions of interpretation and taxonomy seem to become. Dilemmas of theory and analysis are the more acute in Germany because much of the interpretation of National Socialism is carried out not by empirical scholars but by ideologues, normally "Marxist," who have little interest in verifiable data but are primarily concerned to affix words or labels to National Socialism for their own political or ideological purposes.[16] Answers to ultimate questions of how

15. Michael A. Ledeen, *The First Duce* (Baltimore, 1977); Nino Valeri, *D'Annunzio davanti al fascismo* (Florence, 1963); and Ferdinando Cordova, *Arditi e legionari dannunziani* (Padua, 1969). De Ambris's final critique of Fascist state corporatism appeared in his posthumous *Dopo un ventennio di rivoluzione: Il corporativismo* (Paris, 1935).

16. Some of the problems involved in German Marxist theories of National Socialism and fascism are elucidated in A. G. Rabinbach, "Toward a Marxist Theory of Fascism and National Socialism," *New German Critique*, no. 3 (Fall 1974), 127–53.

National Socialism is to be defined or how National Socialism is to be understood will escape consensus.

Ideologically, though not structurally, post-1918 National Socialism built on the prewar movement. It is important to remember that National Socialism originally did stand for a certain concept of political economy that espoused partial collectivism and was reiterated in the founding Twenty-Five Points of Hitler's National Socialist German Workers' party (NSDAP) of 1920. This embraced partial collectivism, aimed primarily against big business, large landholdings, leading financial institutions, and major corporations and industrial concerns, whose strict regulation or nationalization was to be harmonized with small-scale individual ownership. In short, National Socialism originally stood for partial collectivism or a limited state socialism that would sustain a mixed economy, partly state or collective but mostly under private ownership. Other radical (and democratic) features, such as the replacement of the regular army with a people's militia, were retained in the first Hitler program. That such aims were not later carried out in the Nazi regime has no more nor less relevance than the observation that Lenin's original, highly demagogic revolutionary program of 1917 was not carried out under the Lenin-Stalin regime. Revolutionary movements normally (there are some exceptions, such as Castro) start on a broadly radical, demagogic platform and then work down to practicalities.

There are some rough equivalencies between early Fascism and early National Socialism in terms of economic goals and to some extent style, but the differences are equally striking. The NSDAP began as a new movement in Germany after 1919, despite its ideological precursor, and was led for the most part by individuals without strong previous political identity. It did not involve a kind of "Marxist heresy" or nationalization of sectors of the revolutionary left. It failed to mobilize as effectively as the Fascists during the postwar crisis, nor did it merely duplicate the social structure of Fascist support: the structure of German society was profoundly different from that of Italy, and the Nazis had more competition from well-organized nationalist groups to their right than did the Fascists.

In some respects the two movements soon acquired a similar style, developing fairly elaborate liturgical processes common to many revolutionary movements, and they also in a general way participated in the revolt against rationalism, positivism, liberalism, old-fashioned conservatism, Marxism, and internationalism. Like nearly all revolutionary movements, they placed a positive evaluation on the use of violence, and both relied heavily on war veterans in the early phases of recruitment.

At the same time, ideological and doctrinal differences were from the beginning profound. If the Fascists had a kind of intellectual method and general orientation, they arrived at a coherent Fascist ideology only with some difficulty. Conversely, the Nazis probably never achieved a fully rounded and developed ideology at all, but by the mid-1920s, before the growth of National Socialism as a mass movement, Hitler had developed a firmly held world view,[17] whose general implications for politics and government he acted upon tenaciously to the very end. Fascist antipositivism did not require the complete rejection of liberal/rational principles and pedagogical goals, which the Fascists proposed to synthesize with other values into a greater whole. Hitler, inspired by the romantic notions of *Völkisch* (racial-environmental) nationalism blended with pseudoscientific social Darwinism, totally rejected certain aspects of modern culture (even though, as will be discussed later, he relied heavily on other key features of modernity).

Before 1938 most Fascists had no concept of race and derided Nazi racism. Their doctrine of nationalism was cultural-environmental, not racial-environmental, and did not include anti-Semitism; Italian Jews were in fact proportionately overrepresented in the Fascist Party.[18] Similarly, certain sectors of Fascism were at first antiimperialist, and

17. Eberhard Jaeckel, *Hilter's Weltanschauung* (Middletown, Conn., 1972).
18. See Michael A. Ledeen, *Universal Fascism* (New York, 1972).

proponents of national liberation for the weaker and more-backward Mediterranean and Middle Eastern peoples. Some of the earliest Fascist theorists rejected social Darwinism and militarism, embracing international cooperation, a new post-liberal national syndicalist "ethical state," and the League of Nations. Fascism was sometimes conceived as harmonious with the interest of other peoples—at least at first.

Just as Fascist doctrine and culture embraced limited aspects of liberal principles on the one hand and "modern art" on the other (modern art in Italy meant, above all, Futurism, and leading Futurists were founding Fascists), so it reached as uneasy *modus vivendi* with Catholicism. By 1922 a wing of "Catholic Fascism" represented part of the incorporation of all ostensibly positive aspects of modern Italian culture. Admittedly, the coexistence of a Catholic Fascism with the more orthodox secular, violent, and revolutionary strains was uneasy, but it endured for some time, at least until the partial Nazification of the late 1930s. By contrast, any serious form of Catholic, Protestant, or Christian Nazism was obviously a contradiction in terms. Many nominal Christians voted for Hitler, but there was never any question of the party incorporating a religious variant. The subsequent effort to create a "German Christianity" required a complete break with all orthodox Christianity, something never required by syncretistic and semitolerant Fascism.

One of the most fundamental differences was that by about 1925–26, and in some respects already by 1922–23, the NSDAP had become incontestably the "Hitler movement,"[19] thoroughly subordinated to the myth-cult of the Fuehrer in a manner incomprehensible to Italian Fascism qua movement and never even fully achieved during the *ducismo* era of the 1930s. By contrast, Fascism was not at all created by Mus-

19. Hitler's self-transformation into absolute Fuehrer is treated in Albrecht Tyrell, *Vom "Trommler" zum "Führer"* (Munich, 1975), perhaps the best recent monograph on Hitler. The early NSDAP is studied in Georg-Franz Willing, *Die Hitler Bewegung* (Hamburg, 1962). The best general study of the Nazi party is Dietrich Orlow, *The History of the Nazi Party*, 2 vols. (Pittsburgh, 1969–73).

solini as a party or movement but grew up around or beyond him and by 1921–22 in some respects increasingly in opposition to him. One cannot speak of a Fascist leadership principle in the same terms as one speaks of the Nazi *Fuehrerprinzip*. For Mussolini, his own party became both the necessary vehicle of his success and potentially a major obstacle to his new regime, a contradiction not equally conceivable in Nazi Germany.

Mussolini formed a government coalition three and a half years after the start of the Fascist movement, whereas the same process took Hitler fourteen years. (Conversely, the Italian regime was not converted into a full dictatorship for nearly three years, something that took Hitler less than six months.) Beyond such chronological differences, however, the dynamics of the two movements did have something in common with respect to phases and sequences as well as the political relations involved. Both developed large-scale party militia for political violence, but nearly all radical and revolutionary parties of the period did that, and it would be difficult to show the uniqueness of the Fascists and Nazis save that they perhaps carried it to a greater extent and were rather more successful at it. Both movements toned down the radicalism of their socioeconomic propaganda—a common phenomenon among revolutionary groups of diverse stripes, though some go in the opposite direction and become more class-demagogical in less-developed countries. Both made compromises with conservative forces in the drive to power. After the failure of the Beer-Hall Putsch in 1923, Hitler learned what Mussolini had intuitively grasped from the beginning: in an organized central-European state with institutions still largely intact, a violent coup d'état or revolutionary insurrection was not feasible. A multiclass nationalist movement must come to power legally or not at all. The possibility of mobilizing a statistical majority was next to impossible, and so the only route to power lay through a compromise coalition, primarily with right-wing nationalists. The latter were the most likely allies, because they shared strong nationalist demands (though differing radically on some aspects of policy) and were opposed to both liberalism and the Marxian left.

There has been much debate on what the Nazi program, and the dominant interests behind Nazism really were during the drive to power. Related to this is the secondary but very important issue of to what extent the real programmatic goals and the true interests, if either are identifiable, were directly perceived by Nazi supporters. The Twenty-Five Points were never repudiated and always remained the party program, though the point that called for expropriation of big landed estates had been dropped by 1928. Through the mid-1920s the party had made a major effort to become indeed a national socialist German workers' party, just as its name indicated, by competing with Socialists and Communists for blue-collar support in the large north-German cities. This "leftist" tactic was abandoned by 1927–28 because of its scant success,[20] and during the last five years of its history as a movement National Socialism became more genuinely multiclass than ever, seeking to mobilize at least some support in almost every major sector of German society.

During this period it would be difficult to identify a precise program of any sort that was presented to the German people in consistent detail. The semisocialist aspects of National Socialism were normally downplayed, just as in an equivalent phase the collectivist dimensions of Fascist national syndicalism were similarly deemphasized. Hitler himself had no very precise ideas of political economy or structure, save that economics was not important in itself and must be subordinated to national political considerations.[21] Indeed, one could have found a wide variety of economic attitudes among Nazis during the last phase of mass mobili-

20. Two different treatments of this tactic and orientation, neither fully satisfactory, may be found in Reinhard Kühnl, *Die nationalsozialistische Linke 1925–1930* (Meisenheim am Glan, 1966); and Max Kele, *Nazis and Workers* (Chapel Hill, N.C., 1972).

21. The best summary of Hitler's attitudes toward economics is Henry A. Turner, Jr., "Hitlers Einstellung zu Wirtschaft and Gesellschaft vor 1933," *Geschichte und Gesellschaft*, no. 2 (1976), 89–117.

zation. Some were petit-bourgeois capitalists, a few favored big business, others espoused a semi-Italian or semi-Catholic corporatism, and some of the hard core retained the semi-socialist aspirations of the original national socialism. Ambiguity was, however, the essence of the leadership's strategy.

The same might be said of other policy goals. No precise theory of state dictatorship was presented save for the *Fuehrerprinzip*, and though all understood that a Hitler government would adopt a much more forceful foreign policy, what this would entail was purposely left vague. "National Socialism means peace" became a well-worn phrase in 1932, while anti-Semitic propaganda seems to have been slightly deemphasized, since it was less attractive to the broader masses.

The question of relationship to special interests is also somewhat complicated. There are basically three positions on this issue: (a) the classic vulgar Marxist explanation that Nazism was merely a tool of big business;[22] (b) the position of the revisionists, especially Henry A. Turner, Jr.,[23] who endeavor to show that Hitler and big business had relatively little to do with each other and that the latter mainly supported right-wing authoritarianism; and (c) that of the counter-revisionists,[24] who are sometimes too sophisticated to invoke fully the complete vulgar Marxist approach, but endeavor to demonstrate contacts between the Nazi leadership and big business that were extensive and at least to some extent determinant. That is to a considerable degree an argu-

22. The major recent spokesman has been Eberhard Czichon. See his *Wer verhalf Hitler zur Macht?* (Cologne, 1967).

23. "Big Business and the Rise of Hitler," *American Historical Review* (hereafter cited as *AHR*) 75 (1969): 56–70; and Turner's other articles in his *Faschismus und Kapitalismus in Deutschland* (Göttingen, 1972).

24. Dirk Stegmann, "Kapitalismus and Faschismus in Deutschland 1929–1934," *Beiträge zur Marxischen Theorie*, no. 6, (Frankfurt, 1976), 19–91; and Ulrike Horster-Philipps, "Grosskapital, Weimarer Republik und Faschismus," in G. Hardach and Reinhard Kühnl, eds., *Die Zerstörung der Weimarer Republik* (Cologne, 1977), 38–141. A lucid recent summary is provided by James Pool and Suzanne Pool, *Who Financed Hitler* (New York, 1978), which tends to support Turner.

ment about motives and intentions, partially reasoned by inference and difficult to resolve by clear-cut empirical evidence. High-level contacts between Hitler and other Nazi leaders and big businessmen or agents did take place; in the last phase of the Nazi drive for power substantial contributions were made. Nonetheless, Turner is evidently correct that the right authoritarians, not the Nazis, were the main party of big business, and the counter-revisionists have failed to prove that big business "bought" Hitler any more than that the seventy million gold marks paid by the Imperial German Government to the Bolsheviks to finance the Russian Communist revolution "bought" Lenin. That the Marxist interpretation is incorrect is however greatly to be regretted, for if German big business had managed to buy Hitler there would probably have been no general agreement for war and the world might be a better place today.

Just as the program was often vague, ambiguous, and multiform, so the composition of National Socialist membership and voting support has often been misconstrued. The most thorough of many studies of Nazi voting support in the major elections of 1930–32 finds little evidence of unusually strong support from the middle classes. Germany was to a large degree a middle-class country by 1930, and the middle classes provided significant support for a wide variety of movements, including the Socialists. Careful investigation has shown that in the major cities they supported the Nazis only in approximate proportion to the general middle-class share of the population. Unusually heavy support was not found among the urban middle classes but among the rural farmers and small-town middle classes and among the urban upper classes.[25] Thus one must be very careful about the

25. These conclusions are drawn from an unpublished book-length study by Richard Hamilton of McGill University, who has conducted the most systematic and detailed analysis. The most elaborate development of the theory of Nazism as the revolutionary conservatism of the Mittelstand is Gerhard Schulz's *Aufstieg des Nationalsozialismus* (Berlin, 1975). The interpretation offered by H. A. Winkler, *Mittelstand, Demokratie und Nationalsozialismus* (Cologne, 1970), is somewhat more subtle, for he grasps that the Nazis were not themselves the Mittelstand as such and did not represent it,

Table 3
OCCUPATIONAL STRUCTURE OF THE NSDAP, 1923, 1930, 1933,
AND 1935 (by percentages)

	1923	1930	1933	1935	Proportion of Gainfully Employed German Population
Workers (including skilled)	19.7 (8.5)	26.3	32.5	32.1	46.3
White collar	12.9	24.4	20.6	20.6	12.4
Civil servants	6.6 ⎫ =7.7 ⎫ =6.5			9.4	3.9
Teachers	⎭ ⎭			3.6	0.9
Students (University)	4.2	1.0	1.2		
Professions	3.1 ⎫				1.0
Business	16.2 ⎬ =18.9	17.3	20.2		3.9
Handicraft	21.3 ⎭				4.7
Farmers	10.4	13.2	12.5	10.7	10.0
Pensioners		1.9	1.6		
Women	1.1	3.6	4.1		
Others	4.5	3.4	3.5	3.4	16.9
	100.0	100.0	100.0	100.0	100.0

Source: Peter Merkl, "Comparing Fascist Movements," in Stein U. Larsen et al., eds., *Who Were the Fascists?* (Oslo/Bergen, forthcoming), based upon information in Michael H. Kater, "Zur Soziographie der frühen NSDAP," and Wolfgang Schaefer, *NSDAP: Entwicklung und Struktur der Staatspartei des Dritten Reiches.*

hoary interpretation of Nazism as a quintessentially middle-class operation.

The Nazi Party membership was itself somewhat dispro-portionately middle-class, but it became increasingly "prole-tarian" in social composition as it expanded into a mass movement. By the time that Hitler came to power, one-third

---

but did rely increasingly on manipulating certain sectors of the Mittel-stand—particularly in rural areas—and later defrauding it. The relative weakness of the Nazi vote among women and the unemployed is treated in R. J. Evans, "Women and the Triumph of Hitler," *JMH* 48.1 (March 1976); and R. I. McKibbin, "The Myth of the Unemployed: Who Did Vote for the Nazis?" *Australian Journal of Politics and History* 15.2 (August 1969): 25–69.

On the agrarian appeal in nationalist myth, Klaus Bergmann, *Agrarroman-tik und Grossstadtfeindlichkeit* (Meisenheim am Glan, 1970).

of the members of his party were blue-collar workers. If to that figure is added all other employees, craftsmen, and farm laborers, over half the membership were nonprofessional workers and employees without capital and only a minority were bureaucrats, professional intelligentsia, and capital-possessing elements. The most heavily blue-collar section of the movement was the Storm Troopers (SA); a recent study has shown that at this phase of maximal expansion in 1932–34 the SA was at least two-thirds blue-collar in its social composition.[26] By comparison, the only statistics that we have on the Italian PNF in a similar period (1921), though much less complete and presumably less accurate than the Nazi figures, indicate a much lower blue collar membership (15.4 percent) but a large minority of agricultural laborers (24.3 percent). These statistics naturally reflect the much more rural and nonindustrial structure of Italian society, which in turn makes any exact comparison somewhat unrealistic.

At any rate, such a morphology renders quite dubious the interpretation advanced by Wolfgang Sauer and others that the NSDAP represented a movement of "losers" in the modernization process. White collar employees, state bureaucrats, and teachers are winners, not losers, in twentieth-century employment patterns. It is possible to make out blue collar workers as losers, following the main phase of industrialization, but in that case it would be the Socialist and Communist parties that represented movements of "losers." The clearest losers might have been the small rural elements, but their representation within the NSDAP membership was only proportionate to their share of German society as a whole, though they bulked disproportionately large among Nazi voters. The only political sectors clearly relying on pre-industrial strata and appeals were the radical right monarchists and nationalists, who lost out completely to the Nazis.

26. C. J. Fischer, "The Occupational Background of the SA's Rank and File Membership during the Depression Years, 1929 to mid-1934," in Peter D. Stachura, ed., *The Shaping of the Nazi State* (London, 1978), 131–59.

Age differentiation—the generational revolt of those who came of age in World War I and soon afterward—seems to explain the Nazi Party membership as well as any other single factor.[27]

Right Authoritarian Competitors of National Socialism

National Socialism developed as the most radical branch of a multiform patriotic movement that first mushroomed in the wake of German defeat after 1918. More than one hundred different nationalist parties, groups, and societies have been identified. A few of them paralleled the national socialist aspirations of the Nazis but most were distinctly to their right. For as long as ten years, some of them were also much stronger and more numerous.

The most immediate precursor of right authoritarian nationalism in Germany emerged during World War I, specifically in the Fatherland Party organized by Admiral von Tirpitz and Wolfgang Kapp in 1917–18. Its organizers hoped to develop a broad patriotic association uniting all classes behind a militarist and imperialist program under strong leadership, while carefully avoiding any alteration of domestic class relations.[28] It disappeared with German defeat.

The chief paramilitary representatives of the patriotic movement were the Free Corps bands of 1919–20,[29] a chronological and to some extent spiritual parallel of the *arditi* veterans who led the first Italian *squadre* or the Fiume adventurers

27. On this factor in the NSDAP and other movements, see the discussion by Peter Merkl, "Comparing Fascist Movements," in Stein U. Larsen et al., eds., *Who Were the Fascists?* (forthcoming).
Concerning Nazi youth and student support, see Peter D. Stachura, *Nazi Youth in the Weimar Republic* (Santa Barbara, Calif., 1975); and Michael S. Steinberg, *Sabers and Brown Shirts: The German Students' Path to National Socialism* (Chicago, 1977).
28. G. E. Etue, Jr., "The German Fatherland Party" (Ph.D. diss., University of California, Berkeley, 1959).
29. R. G. L. Waite, *Vanguard of Nazism* (Cambridge, Mass., 1954); and James M. Diehl, *Paramilitary Politics in Weimar Germany* (Bloomington, Ind., 1978).

of d'Annunzio. The main German veterans' association under the Republic was the Stahlhelm, a mass organization more moderate than some of the most radical nationalists but nonetheless not a mere veterans' interest group in the conventional sense. It was in fact a parapolitical organization working for the overthrow of the republic, which the Stahlhelm wanted to see replaced by a more authoritarian nationalist system.[30] More rightist and less offensive in style and behavior than the Nazis, it was also—at least for part of the time—Mussolini's preferred German authoritarian nationalist movement.[31]

The main right nationalist group was the German Nationalist People's Party (DNVP), a radicalized authoritarian outgrowth of the old Conservative Party of the Second Reich. The DNVP emerged in the immediate postwar years as the main German conservative group, with a broad federal following in the first postwar elections. As the Weimar Republic stabilized, however, the DNVP lost support and was in the process of being reduced to a socially somewhat archaic traditional conservative force of aristocrats and east-German farmers. It assumed, at first, a rather moderate conservative position under the Republic, though never wholly accepting the new democratic system,[32] but was radicalized after 1928 under the leadership of the press lord Alfred Hugenburg.[33] From that point on the DNVP moved steadily to a radical right authoritarian position, aiming to replace the Republic with a permanently authoritarian, preferably monarchist, system. During the German political crisis, the DNVP was intermittently allied with the Nazis, and in fact assisted in

30. Volker R. Berghahn, Der Stahlhelm (Düsseldorf, 1966).

31. K.-P. Hoepke, Die deutsche Rechte und der italienische Faschismus (Düsseldorf, 1968).

32. Hans Booms, Die Deutschkonservative Partei (Düsseldorf, 1954); Werner Liebe, Die Deutschnationale Volkspartei, 1918–1924 (Düsseldorf, 1956); Lewis Hertzman, DNVP: Right-Wing Opposition in the Weimar Republic, 1918–1924 (Lincoln, Nebr., 1963).

33. John A. Leopold, Alfred Hugenburg (New Haven, 1978).

bringing Hitler to power—but this was proving fatal even before 1933, as the party lost a large part of its voting support to the Nazis.[34]

More moderate tendencies toward nationalist authoritarianism could be found in other mainline parties. Elements of the Catholic Center (Brüning, Papen, etc.) aimed to replace the republic with a more authoritarian monarchist system, albeit as gently and legally as possible. Indeed, the main moderate liberal party, Stresemann's German People's Party (DVP), virtually broke up during the depression. One of its first offshoots (formed in the 1920s), the Business Party (Deutsche Wirtschaftspartei), took a corporatist and authoritarian line. The same thing happened to much of the Democratic Party, German's main progressive liberal group. It was largely replaced by the new "State Party" (Deutsche Staatspartei), which worked for a moderate authoritarian state in cooperation with one of the main nationalist (and at least moderately authoritarian) youth groups, the Jungdeutscher Orden.[35]

Some efforts were made during 1931–32 to create a kind of right liberal, or at least only moderately authoritarian, nationalist Sammlungspartei or unity party out of the more moderate elements of the DNVP and various other center-right parties and splinters. Big business representatives such as the "Keppler circle," interested in an authoritarian nationalist alternative, were little attracted to the kind of reactionary aristocratic and agrarian right authoritarianism represented by Hugenburg. They preferred an alternative with more modern social and economic content, and eventually

34. Attila Chanady, "The Disintegration of the German National People's Party," *JMH* 39.1 (March 1967): 65–91; and F. Hiller v. Gärtringen, "Die Deutschnationale Volkspartei," in E. Matthias and R. Morsey, eds., *Das Ende der Parteien: 1933* (Düsseldorf, 1960), 543–652.

35. See the studies in the Matthias and Morsey volume; Karl D. Bracher, *Die Auflösung der Weimarer Republik* (Villingen, 1964); and on the Business Party, M. Schumacher, *Mittelstandsfront and Republik: Die Wirtschaftspartei, Reichspartei des deutschen Mittelstandes 1919–1933* (Düsseldorf, 1972).

were willing to deal with the more socially moderate, business-oriented elements among the Nazis, a willingness skillfully manipulated by Hitler.

Proponents of the "conservative revolution" in German cultural and social life should also be counted among the moderate authoritarian nationalists. The conservative revolution's advocates never developed a political movement of any significance. Their spokesmen were mainly writers and theoreticians, organized in small groups and cultural circles, who hoped to restore traditional values through organic and corporative relationships that would transcend capitalist economics and liberal parliamentarianism. Their orientation was *bündisch* (literally "fascist" in a verbally cognate—though not political—sense, since the term refers basically to banding together in vital, organic association) and honored especially the function of leadership. Yet the "conservative revolutionaries," despite their yearning for a radically different organic and corporative society, were relatively moderate in their relationship to politics and in fact frequently apolitical. Unlike the more radical authoritarian right and the Nazis, they tended to reject militarism (and to some extent imperialism) and were comparatively mild in the use of racial myths.[36]

There was also an authoritarian nationalist left that stood well to the left of the more socialistic Nazis. Its main expression was the small National Bolshevist group headed by Ernst Niekisch that proposed the combination of state eco-

36. The background of this and other forms of German nationalist thought is treated in George L. Mosse, *The Crisis of German Ideology* (New York, 1964). On the conservative revolutionaries themselves, see Mosse's "The Corporate State and the Conservative Revolution in Weimar Germany," in his *Germans and Jews* (New York, 1970), 116–43; James M. Rhodes, "The Conservative Revolution in Germany" (Ph.D. diss., Notre Dame University, 1969); Armin Mohler, *Die konservative Revolution in Deutschland 1918–1922* (Stuttgart, 1950); K. von Klemperer, *Germany's New Conservatism* (Princeton, 1957); Herman Lebovics, *Social Conservatism and the Middle Classes in Germany, 1914–1933* (Princeton, 1969); and Kurt Sontheimer, *Anti-demokratisches Denken in der Weimarer Republik: Die politischen Ideen des deutscher Nationalismus zwischen 1918 und 1933* (Munich, 1962).

nomic socialism with intense German nationalism and German cultural tradition.[37]

Outside the regular party structure altogether stood the representative of a special kind of German pretorianism, General Kurt von Schleicher, head of the Political Office of the German army and the most active (if not exactly the most representative) general in politics during the last year of the Republic. Had Schleicher been successful in his leadership of the German government at the end of 1932, he would probably have headed a very moderate, essentially anti-Nazi form of nationalist authoritarianism that would have avoided a sharp break with the republican constitution and promoted a reflationary, reformist economic policy along Keynesian or New Deal lines to revive the economy and conciliate German society.[38]

The Victory of National Socialism

The triumph of National Socialism over the other German political forces in 1933 was so fateful for Germany and for the world, and in some respects so surprising for a country of Germany's level of culture and general development, that it has been subject to all manner of interpretations and explanations. Some of the most common may be summarized under the concepts of the accident theory, the agent theory, and the mass mobilization of frustrated nationalism theory.

The accident theory concentrates especially on the way in which Hitler became chancellor and emphasizes the "back stairs deal" aspect of his entry into the government. While the initial Hitler government was the product of a political intrigue, the accident theory fails to explain exactly why the key figures in German politics were willing to accept Hitler, and why such a general swing toward authoritarianism had occurred among so many center-right groups.

---

37. Louis Dupeux, *Stratégie communiste et dynamique conservatrice: Essai sur les différents sens de l'espression "National-Bolchévisme" en Allemagne, 1919–1933* (Paris, 1976); and O.-E. Schüddekopf, *Linke leute von Rechts* (Stuttgart, 1960).

38. Thilo Vogelsang, *Reichswehr, Staat und NSDAP* (Munich, 1962).

The agent theory is primarily of Marxist inspiration, but fails to demonstrate specifically just whose agent Hitler was and on exactly what terms. Moreover, it fails to explain why such a dynamic and determined agent as Hitler was required instead of more moderate and controllable figures such as those who had preceded him.

No single factor or simple interpretation can account for something so complex and momentous as the process that brought Hitler to power, but the mass mobilization of frustrated nationalism theory offers a broader understanding than either of the foregoing theories alone. Though Germany was an advanced industrial nation, its position in the modern world, when compared with other major industrial states, was highly anomalous. Germany was the newest of the major industrial powers and by far the lowest in international status. No other country remotely comparable to Germany's size, productivity, and achievement lacked an empire, much less equal status in international affairs. The humiliation of 1918 had been followed by a remarkable concatenation of national crises unparalleled in any other country. The postwar revolutionary crisis of 1919–20 was followed by the French invasion, great inflation, and minor revolutionary insurrections of 1923, followed in turn by the great depression. Moreover, all these crises could easily be interpreted as having been forced upon Germany by foreign diplomatic, military, and economic pressures (accompanied by Russian-inspired efforts at internal subversion). The degree of status deprivation and national disorientation was without precedent for a country at Germany's level.

If Germany had an advanced economy and technology and a sophisticated educational system, the same could not be said for her political culture. Responsible parliamentary democracy came only in 1919 as a product of defeat and humiliation, and its psychological and behavioral acceptance was never completed during the 1920s. Moreover, German culture had been more deeply affected by the cultural and intellectual crisis of 1890–1914 than that of any other country, and the disposition to turn to racial, authoritarian, and extreme nationalist remedies was undeniably greater than in any advanced country.

Hitler built the largest political force in Germany, and by the rules of the democratic game had the right to form a government. With a left divided between democratic socialists and Stalinist communists and a center-right thoroughly splintered, no viable alternative seemed possible. In a sense, National Socialism had become the only *national* party drawing support from a broad variety of social classes and geographic regions.

Then, too, it must be remembered that Hitler did not campaign on a platform of beginning World War II in 1939 and cremating Jews. During the mass electoral drives of 1930–32 the more shrill and extreme forms of anti-Semitism were toned down, and despite *Mein Kampf*, Hitler's international aims were made more reassuring. A common slogan in 1932 was "National Socialism means peace," for only a strong, resolute and united Nazi government could defend and restore German interests without being plunged into another disastrous war.

The circumstances of social and economic crisis in the German depression do not alone account for Hitler's rise to power, for other countries suffered almost as much and did not succumb to radical dictatorships. Rather, the social and economic consequences of the depression occurring in a country of Germany's peculiar historical and cultural circumstances made National Socialism possible.

Timing and luck were also involved, and to this extent the accident theory cannot be entirely dismissed. It was not possible to sustain a movement of such tensions and demagogical contradictions as National Socialism for a long period. The Nazi vote was already dropping sharply by the end of 1932. If the general quality of German leadership had not been so poor, Hitler might well have been resisted one more year. There were indications that by the end of 1933 the National Socialist groundswell might have decisively receded.

4

The Mussolini and Hitler Regimes

THE MUSSOLINI REGIME

Phases

A major obstacle to any definition of Italian Fascism is the problem of differentiating between different phases both of the movement and of the regime. Emphases and orientation shifted considerably from one phase to the next, and valid generalizations are difficult to establish. During the first phase, from the March on Rome to the beginning of 1925, the regime was a largely constitutional continuation of coalition government. The second phase was that of the construction of the dictatorship from 1925 to 1929. It was followed by three years of comparative nonactivism and consensus, from 1929 to 1932. There ensued a period of active foreign policy and continued consensus at home from 1933 to 1936. This was succeeded by the years of autarchy and semi-Nazification (1936–40), followed by the war (1940–43) and finally by the puppet regime of Salò (1943–45).

Though the second phase brought the construction of the first durable institutionalized and semipluralist new authoritarian system in Europe since the age of Louis Napoleon, all of the first three phases involved a process of controlling and purging the Fascist movement itself in the interest of a semi-pluralist new system. A largely fictive refascistization came somewhat belatedly, more and more under the influence of National Socialism. After Mussolini had finally been overthrown by a combination of Fascist moderates and the non-Fascist right, his last government attempted a formal return to national syndicalist radicalism, but drew breath only as a German puppet.

Structure

Though the Fascist Party was able to present certain doctrines and ideas of national syndicalism that could form the basis for an alternate political system, it did not have a clear-cut political theory for a new state, and Mussolini assumed office as prime minister without any specific plan for a new system, dictatorial or otherwise. Expressing the divergences, Giuseppe Bottai said that "The Fascisms [in their pluralist diversity] marched on Rome. . . . [but now] in Rome we have to found [a unified] Fascism."[1] Though Mussolini immediately cracked down on the more extreme sectors of the nationalist left (D'Annunzians) and internationalist left (Communists), one of his major problems was how to cope with and coordinate the Fascist Party itself. A Grand Council was quickly instituted as ruling organ of the party under Mussolini's control (December 1922), and then he acted to reaffirm the supremacy of state prefects over district party leaders (January 1923) and transformed the *squadristi* into an official state militia, the MVSN (January 1923), partly under regular military control. The right-wing Nationalists then merged fully with the Fascists (February 1923), giving a more rightist, though not necessarily conservative, cast to the movement.

Mussolini gained the opportunity to dominate the political situation fully only with the elections of April 1924, in which

1. Lyttelton, *Seizure of Power*, 151.

the Fascist coalition won about 70 percent of the seats. The murder of the Socialist deputy Matteotti two months later by squadristi (following the murder of a secondary Fascist leader in Rome by opposition activists) revived strong opposition and placed Mussolini at the crossroads, where he was faced with the alternative of devising a clear-cut permanently institutionalized authoritarian system or resigning power.

Elaboration of the first choice was not such a simple or likely development as it has sometimes seemed to later commentators. Before the 1920s, modern political theory had no precise doctrine of permanent authoritarian rule, the only existing theories being short-term constructs of "Cincinnatian" dictatorship (temporary emergency rule by decree) and the vague transitional "dictatorship of the proletariat," the ill-defined Marxist version of the Cincinnatian doctrine. Right-wing theorists who strove for a more elitist or authoritarian system before the 1920s normally turned to some traditional institutional buttress such as monarchy. During the 1920s a variety of attempts to establish more authoritarian nationalist regimes were made in southern and eastern Europe but had great difficulty sustaining themselves, in part for lack of a clear new theory or strategy for institutionalizing a permanent authoritarian structure. All three of the first attempts at a kind of dictatorship in the other south-European countries (Pimenta de Castro in Portugal, 1915; Primo de Rivera in Spain, 1923–30; Pangalos in Greece, 1926) failed completely. The Kemalist regime did survive in Turkey, but as the first third-world "guided democracy" it still paid lip service to the theory and structure of parliamentary liberalism; though it functioned like a more unified and successful version of the Chinese Kuomintang.

The Fascist Party itself was profoundly divided over doctrine and tactics, the only real unity stemming from the de facto leadership of the *Duce* himself. The most coherent theoretical position was that of the national syndicalists (Panunzio, Olivetti, Grandi, Rossoni), who did possess a new doctrine of social and economic organization that might be extended to a new form of organic political organization as well. There were the moderates and "revisionists," led by Giuseppe Bottai and Massimo Rocca, who in varying ways wanted to fit Fascism into the existing Italian constitutional system as a new elite and tutelary force. There were the *squadristi* radicals, led by Roberto Farinacci and his like, who were vague about national syndicalism and complex structural proposals but simply wished to impose a one-party dictatorship based on force and elitism, an "empty revolution" rather like that of a South American strong man. Then there were elements of the new Fascist right, led by ex-Nationalists like Rocco and Mario Carli, who wished to establish an authoritarian corporative system of government and economic regulation under the monarchy, to create a strong new state that could expand an imperial Italy.[2] Numerous individual variants appeared within and between these general groupings of opinion.

Of these attitudes, the only orientations that contained the germs of a workable new institutional system were those of the (formerly left-wing) national syndicalists and the right-wing former Nationalist corporatists of Rocco. What Mussolini did, beginning in 1925, was to develop an ad hoc new corporative authoritarian system based on an unsteady fusion of their ideas, together with a controlled application of the one-party ambition of the Fascist radicals.

Parliament was transformed and Italian government turned into a one-party system, but at the same time a careful purge and transformation of the party itself was carried out. The PNF was brought under state bureaucratic control rather than vice versa, and by the beginning of 1927 party rolls had been reduced by nearly 25 percent (down to 600,000), though by the end of that year a mostly bureaucratized membership was permitted to expand once more. By that point the new mass bureaucratic Fascist Party was mostly composed of

2. See especially Gentile, 253–415. The best biography of a Fascist *gerarca* is G. B. Guerri, *Giuseppe Bottai, un fascista critico* (Milan, 1976).

lower-middle- and middle-class people (about 75 percent), increasingly in the employ of the state, while the worker-peasant proportion declined to about 15 percent. Over 200,000 of the most radical, the most idealistic, and the most thuggish had been eliminated, and the party had become a bureaucratic instrument at the service of the state.

The guiding figures in the institutional transformation were not so much the original Fascists as the top Nationalists such as Rocco (minister of justice) and Luigi Federzoni (minister of the interior). In 1926 the formation of a national syndicalist system comprising thirteen global syndicates for the regulation and representation of all the major areas of national economic activity was begun, with workers and employers to be represented organically in different branches of general national syndicate groupings. A ministry of corporations was soon created, and the thirteen national syndicates were later replaced by twenty-two corporations in 1934.

Edmondo Rossoni, leader of the Fascist worker syndicates, tried to maintain a national association of Fascist labor under the national syndicalist system, but he was soon undermined by party rivals, the Fascist right, and business interests. Late in 1928 there occurred the *sbloccamento* (unblocking) of the Fascist worker syndicates, henceforth restricted to the local and regional level, while the national industrialists' confederation (Confindustria) was permitted to retain its central structure alongside the state syndical/corporative system. Though the common interpretation that Fascist corporatism was a capitalist system pure and simple is exaggerated, there seems little doubt that in the early years particularly, the national syndicalist/corporate system worked more to the advantage of capital than labor.

In 1928 the Fascist Grand Council was made the highest deliberative organ of government, with authority to pass on all major laws and constitutional changes. In 1928, on the expiration of the first Mussolini-controlled congress, elections to parliament were made indirect and corporative through a process controlled by the state and the party. Ten years later the corporative parliament was replaced by a new Chamber of Fasces and Corporations that formalized the corporative structure of nominal representation.[3]

The Totalitarian State

In 1925 Mussolini and Giovanni Gentile, Italy's most prominent academic philosopher and a leading abstract theorist of Fascism, began to use the term *totalitario* to refer to the structure and goals of the new state. Aspiring to an organic unity of Italian society, economic activity, and government, the new state was to achieve total representation of the nation but would also exercise total guidance of national goals. Thus was born, somewhat vaguely, the original concept of "totalitarianism."

The paradox of all this is that serious analysts of totalitarian government now recognize that Fascist Italy never became totalitarian. In the decade following the establishment of Mussolini's system, the Leninist dictatorship in the Soviet Union was ruthlessly transformed by Stalin into a complete state socialist system of almost total de facto dictatorial control over the economy and all formal institutions. A few years later, the dynamic power lust of Hitler's regime in Germany, with its efficient police, militarist power, concentration camp system, and eventual extermination policies in conquered territory appeared to create a noncommunist National Socialist equivalent of the Stalinist system of control. These two have provided the dominant models of what political analysts, particularly between 1940 and 1960, tended to call totalitarianism. Mussolini's Italy bore little resemblance to either one.

It is important first of all to understand what was really implied by the vague concept of the totalitarian state used by Mussolini, Gentile, and Rocco. This terminology was derived in part from the theory of the "ethical state" developed

3. The basic work on the development of the system is Alberto Acquarone, *L'organizzazione dello stato totalitario* (Turin, 1965). See also Alberto Acquarone and M. Vernassa, eds., *Il regime fascista* (Bologna, 1974).

by Gentile and also by the national syndicalist ideologue Panunzio. The theory posited a tutorial state with greater authority than the old liberal regime to develop the resources of the entire people and realize the higher ("ethical") aspirations of the nation, a Rousseau-derived ambition that has become increasingly common in the twentieth century. Yet though the cruder Mussolini formulation indicated that nothing was to be developed beyond the scope of a superstate that would in one sense or another (never precisely defined) be all inclusive, there was never the slightest proposal, nor so far as we know the slightest intention, of developing a complete police system with direct control over all institutions. None of these theorists proposed full state control over all Italian institutions in practice. Rocco, as minister of justice, did speak of the overriding authority of the new state over other institutions, but seemed to be referring primarily to spheres of conflict rather than to a practical bureaucratic structure for applying government intervention to all avenues of Italian life on a daily basis. In practice, Fascist "totalitarianism" referred to the preeminent authority of the state in areas of conflict, not to total—or in most cases even approximate—day-by-day institutional control. Nonetheless, though there can be little debate that this was the actual nature of the Mussolinian state, it is also true that the "totalitarian" theory of the preeminent state and its "ethical" demands did provide a concept of broader state power that might become greatly expanded in practice. The hypothetical possibility always remained—a concern for leftists and conservatives alike—that the Mussolini dictatorship might eventually become more radical and expansive.

In practice, it might be described as a primarily political dictatorship that presided over a pluralistic or semipluralistic institutional system. Victor Immanuel III, not the Duce, remained constitutional head of state. The PNF itself had become almost concretely bureaucratized and subservient to the state itself. Though worker interests were effectively regimented, big business, industry, and finance retained extensive autonomy, in the early years particularly. The armed forces enjoyed at least equal autonomy and were mostly left to their own devices, though by no means exclusively. The Fascist party militia was placed under general army control, though it in turn enjoyed a semiautonomous existence when made part of the regular military institutions.[4] The pre-Mussolini judicial system was left largely intact and partially autonomous as well. The police continued to be directed by state officials and were not taken over by party leaders as in Nazi Germany, nor was a major police elite created as in Germany and Soviet Russia. Though a new political police (OVRA) was formed in 1932, political prisoners in Mussolini's Italy were numbered in the hundreds—never amounting to more than a few thousand—rather than in the tens and hundreds of thousands as in Nazi Germany or the millions as in Stalin's Russia. The Lateran Treaty of 1929 established a modus vivendi with the Catholic Church that continued to function[5] despite the church-state conflicts of the early 1930s. There was never any question of bringing the church under overall subservience to the regime, as in Germany, much less the near-total control that has often existed in Russia. Sizeable sectors of Italian cultural life retained rather extensive autonomy, and there was no major state propaganda-and-culture ministry until the German example was belatedly taken up in 1936.[6] As twentieth-century dictatorships go, the Mussolini regime was neither sanguinary nor particularly repressive.

Fascism came to power on the basis of a kind of tacit compromise with established institutions, and Mussolini was never able fully to escape the constraints of that compromise. "Totalitarianism" remained a possible vague threat for the future, but throughout the Fascist regime it was just a word.

4. See Alberto Acquarone, "La milizia volontaria nello stato fascista"; and Giorgio Rochat, "Mussolini e le forze armate"; both in Il regime fascista, 85–132.

5. See Richard A. Webster, The Cross and the Fasces (Stanford, 1960); Sandro Rogari, Santa Sede e Fascismo (Bologna, 1977); and Pietro Scoppola, "La Chiesa e il fascismo durante il pontificato di Pio XI," in Il regime fascista, 195–232.

6. See Philip V. Cannistraro, "Mussolini's Cultural Revolution," JCH 7.3–4 (July-October 1972): 115–40; and La fabbrica del consenso: Fascismo e mass media (Bari, 1975).

The regime was so little integrated and so unsystematic that Norman Kogan has doubted that there was even anything that could be called a Fascist state.[7]

Yet the Mussolini regime did achieve historical significance on one level, for it was the first effectively institutionalized authoritarian non-Marxist regime that achieved enough structural coherence, whatever the limitations involved, to endure for a full generation or more. It was defeated, but unlike the governments of Primo de Rivera and Pangalos it did not collapse of its own weight. Thus by the 1930s it had become a sort of model or example for a new kind of syncretistic, semipluralist dictatorship at least theoretically based on a single state party, the first of more than a score of such regimes to establish itself on a secure basis.

"Universal Fascism"

By the time that the depression struck, the regime was securely established, and to some extent had even managed to codify a formal Fascist ideology in several official publications of the late 1920s.[8] Yet an underlying malaise persisted, and young Fascists in particular lamented the limitations of the "Fascist revolution" and the failure to achieve a new Fascist culture. These persistent complaints stemmed from the contrast between official doctrines of vitalism, elite leadership, and organic nationalist corporatism and the failure of the regime to carry out a thorough transformation of Italian life or anything approaching a full institutional revolution.

The dilemma was equally severe for Mussolini himself, since he lacked both a clear policy and the necessary political self-confidence for anything approaching a "Fascist revolution." Weakening of the party within Italy was the direct consequence of his own policies. Between 1929 and 1933 Mussolini dismissed most of his ablest ministers and some of the best Fascist party administrators, such as the honest and efficient Augusto Turati (fired in 1931), who Mussolini

7. Norman Kogan, "Fascism as a Political System," in S. J. Woolf, ed., *The Nature of Fascism* (London, 1968), 11–18.

8. Gregor, *The Ideology of Fascism*, 140–240.

himself admitted was the most effective secretary the party ever had. "The development of the regime during 1929–33 showed Mussolini's determination not to allow any stable governing elite to crystallize."[9] The party had swollen to 1,000,000 by 1932, and, after later regulations automatically extended membership to most civil servants and teachers, to 2,600,000 by 1939. Evisceration and mass bureaucratization of the Fascist party thus proceeded *pari passu,* so that the larger the party grew the less of a guiding elite it became. This made it clear that the Fascists themselves would never make a revolution, and Mussolini became almost resigned to the fact that a Fascist society could at best only emerge a generation or so later after training a new generation of Italian youth in public schools. Yet since PNF propaganda facilities remained moderate at best and indoctrination in schools was considerably less than thorough, the delay promised to be long indeed.

In these circumstances both the Duce and some of the young party leaders developed growing interest during the depression years in the expansion of Fascism at home, but even more abroad, as part of a broad new European pattern of national rejuvenation in which Italy would have set the first example. Such aspirations were not new, and had been voiced by several party leaders and publicists in the late 1920s, but were developed with a new urgency after 1930.

It may be a mistake to date the attempt to expand a specifically Fascist political influence abroad from any single year, for Mussolini was always inclined from time to time to support useful or parallel movements or forces in other countries. From about 1930, however, a more direct effort was made to promote what he looked upon as foreign fascisms, culminating in the initiatives to cultivate "universal fascism" in 1933–35 and never entirely disappearing until the end of the regime.

The attempt to achieve a universal fascism, a sort of fascist international, was part of the general expansion of Italian foreign policy that began in 1933. This is normally explained as

9. Lyttelton, *Seizure of Power,* 430.

Mussolini's need to respond to the economic miseries of the depression. In fact, the depression was no worse in 1933–34 than earlier and no more severe in Italy than in other countries of approximately similiar structure. A partial recovery had already been carried out before mobilization for the Ethiopian campaign, and no major rearmament program was ever adopted.

The activist policy was more likely prompted by two other, different incentives. One was the stagnation of the Fascist revolution at home in a political and cultural sense, resulting in a restlessness among young Fascist militants and a conviction on the part of Mussolini that only grand national policies conducted by himself really counted. It seemed almost as if the more Mussolini's confidence in domestic Fascism diminished, the greater became his inflated sense of personal power and self-esteem. Lacking the tools for a further transformation at home, he sought power and prestige abroad, not unlike Communist regimes in the 1970s. Thus Mussolini does indeed seem to have been propelled outward by domestic factors, but they were probably more political than economic.

The second new factor, at least equally decisive, was the disruption of the European power balance by the emergence of the Hitler regime in Germany. For the first time since the March on Rome, new space was opening up for a more completely independent and active Italian policy.

Despite Mussolini's initial applause for the victory of "German fascism," the National Socialist regime soon came to be appreciated as a dangerous, possibly fatal, new rival in the politics of nationalist/imperialist Europe. During the first year of the Hitler government relations cooled considerably and by mid-1934, with the Nazi assassination of the Austrian premier and the apparent threat of German expansion southward, reached a point of major tension and name-calling. Brickbats seem to have been wielded with especial frequency and vigor by the Fascists. National Socialism was variously and simultaneously denounced as racist, militarist, imperialist, pagan, ruthlessly authoritarian, anti-Christian, anti-European, and opposed to the individual spirit and western culture. There were few epithets used by western liberals aganst Nazis that were not applied by Fascists, who also coined special slurs of their own, denouncing the Nazis, for example, as a "political movement of pederasts." By contrast, the Fascists distinguished their system and doctrine from that of the Nazis by pointing to their freedom from racism and anti-Semitism, their (supposed) reconciliation of the individual and the collective, their intimate association with European culture and symbiosis with Catholicism.[10]

The effort to create a fascist international foundered on some of these same differences. In the late 1920s Fascist writers had sometimes pointed out that a cooperative international of radical nationalist movements like their own was an essential contradiction in terms. So it proved to be. Fascists in charge of relations with the fraternal parties found it very difficult to define adequately the content of *fascist*, and the main attempt at forming a fascist international in 1934 collapsed in large measure over the issues of racism and anti-Semitism.[11]

Autarchy and Modernization

In recent years considerable debate has been stimulated, particularly by A. J. Gregor, about the Mussolini regime's economic policy and the rate or degree of economic modernization in Italy during the Fascist period.[12] Related to this is the question of "capitalist domination," dear to Marxist commentators, as contrasted with state control or fascist collectivism.

10. Some of the best anti-Nazi invective has been collected by D. Mack Smith, *Mussolini's Roman Empire* (New York, 1977), 44–58. See also Mussolini's remarks as quoted by his would-be Austrian counterpart, in E. R. von Starhemberg, *Between Hitler and Mussolini* (London, 1942), 164–68.

11. In April 1935 at the last recorded meeting of the commission created by the Montreux conference, the formal declaration rejected "any materialistic concept which exalts the exclusive domination of one race over others." Ledeen, *Universal Fascism*, 123–124.

12. A. James Gregor, "Fascism and Modernization: Some Addenda," *World Politics* 26.3 (April 1974): 370–85; his *The Fascist Persuasion in Radical Politics* (Princeton, 1974); and his forthcoming book on Fascist policy. This approach was suggested to some extent by Franz Borkenau in 1933 and is

The rightist compromise made by Mussolini and the official PNF is a perfectly obvious fact that requires no further elucidation. What must be kept in mind is that it was only a compromise, not a complete and permanent capitulation. While the regime largely accepted the right corporatist and capitalist program of the ANI during the 1920s and early 30s, the national syndicalist projects of semicollectivism and the recasting of Italian class structure were never entirely renounced.[13] The encouragement of private investment, which dominated Italian policy in the 20s, was considered by radical Fascists but a transitory phase.

By 1935, with the beginning of the Ethiopian war and the transition to a more state-controlled and autarchic policy, Mussolini emphasized greater government intervention. In an official statement on Fascist doctrine three years earlier, he had announced "This is the century of the collective, and hence the century of the state."[14] He momentarily frightened Italian industrialists in 1936 by announcing that the regime was about to begin partial nationalization of industry.

In fact, the Mussolini regime never generated one single complete and integrated economic program but switched back and forth between diverse policies. The Corporate State

employed tentatively in more recent work by the Hungarian communist historian Mihaly Vajda. It has been advanced by Italian scholars in Mario Abrate, et al., *Il problema storico del fascismo* (Florence, 1970); and Ludovico Garruccio [pseud.], *L'industrializzazione tra nazionalismo e rivoluzione* (Bologna, 1969). The productivist and modernizing goals of early Fascism have been pointed out by Roland Sarti, "Fascist Modernization in Italy: Traditional or Revolutionary?" *AHR* 75.4 (April 1970): 1029–45; and Edward R. Tannenbaum, "The Goals of Italian Fascism," *AHR* 74.4 (April 1969): 1183–1204. The relative autonomy of Mussolini's economic policy is in varying degrees recognized by Piero Melograni, *Gli industriali e Mussolini* (Milan, 1972); and Salvatore La Francesca, *La politica economica del fascismo* (Bari, 1972).

For some brief comparative considerations, see A. F. K. Organski, *The Stages of Political Development* (New York, 1965), and "Fascism and Modernization," in Woolf, ed., *The Nature of Fascism*, 19–41; and Mary Matossian, "Ideologies of Delayed Industrialization," in J. A. Kautsky, ed., *Political Change in Underdeveloped Countries* (New York, 1962).

13. See Roberts, *The Syndicalist Tradition*, 274–306.

14. In the article "Fascismo: Dottrina," signed by Mussolini in the 1932 edition of the *Enciclopedia Italiana*.

never emerged as a governing or planning body. Direct state investment in industry began as an emergency measure during the depression with the introduction of the IRI (Institute for Industrial Reconstruction) in 1933. By 1940, the IRI possessed 17.8 percent of the capital assets of Italian industry,[15] giving Italy the second largest state industrial plant in the world, yet this was not part of any coherent, organized plan for collectivism per se. After 1935, state intervention in the economy increased steadily, including a leniently applied 10-percent-capital-assets levy on corporations in 1937, but usually on an ad hoc basis. The collectivist schemes of the revolutionary national syndicalists were never directly applied.[16]

If we turn to the actual performance of the Italian economy, the results are somewhat mixed, though not unfavorable to the Mussolini period. Using the global statistics compiled by Angus Maddison,[17] Gregor notes that using the 1913 level as the norm, aggregate economic production had by 1938 risen to 153.8 in Italy compared with 109.4 in France and 149.9 in Germany. The aggregate index for output per worker in 1938, compared with the same 1913 base, stood at 145.2 for Italy, 136.5 for France, 122.4 for Germany, 143.6 for Britain, and 136.0 for the United States. Similarly, the aggregate index for output per man hour by 1938 was 191.1 for Italy, 178.5 for France, 137.1 for Germany, and 167.9 for Britain. Even though Italy's average rate of annual industrial growth in the depression years of 1.7 percent was less than Germany's and considerably less than Sweden's, it was only slightly below the west-European norm and stood well above the figure of minus 2.8 for liberal democratic France.[18] In these respects the overall performance was creditable, and indeed under

15. Sarti, *Fascism and the Industrial Leadership,* 123.

16. Some attention has been given the "socialist corporatism" rhetoric of Ugo Spirito and young Fascist radicals in the 1930s, but they had scant influence on policy, and suggested less of an alternative than is sometimes supposed. Cf. Silvio Lanaro, "Appunti sul fascismo 'di sinistra,' " in Acquarone and Vernassa, eds., *Il regime fascista,* 413–34.

17. Angus Maddison, *Economic Growth in the West* (New York, 1964), appendices A, E, H, I.

18. Derek Lomax, *The Inter-war Economy of Britain, 1919–1939* (London, 1970); and Pierluigi Ciocca, "L'economia nel contesto internazionale," in P.

Mussolini the value of industrial production exceeded that of agriculture for the first time (in 1933).

Nonetheless, the majority of economic historians tend to be critical of the Fascist period because the rate of development was higher just before 1913 and during the great post- . World War II boom after 1947.[19] They sometimes also point to the lowered rate of overall investment during the 1930s. Though these criticisms are technically correct, they overlook the major problems faced by the Mussolini regime in overcoming the dislocation of World War I and the general depression of the 1930s. The interwar period cannot be so simply compared with either the booms before World War I or after World War II, since the difficulties involved were rather more severe. Compared with other economies at similar stages of development, the Italian system performed reasonably well. The great Stalinist industrialization in Russia was achieved by catastrophic exploitation of the rural economy and hugely disproportionate human and economic investments—hardly a superior performance, since per capita So-

---

Ciocca and G. Toniolo, eds., *L'economia italiana nel periodo fascista* (Bologna, 1976), 36.

19. The most recent and systematic survey of the period by economic historians, edited by Ciocca and Toniolo and cited in the preceding note, concludes that "compared with the other leading countries of the capitalist world, the general performance of Italian industrial production in the period . . . appears not at all brilliant" (p. 155). This, as has been suggested, is a matter of judgment, since comparative global statistics are not so unfavorable. Moreover, the conclusion somewhat misses the point in that Italy was not then "a leading country of the capitalist world," and that was one of the things Fascism was all about. Finally, even Ciocca and Toniolo admit that Italian industry became considerably more modern in structure during the Fascist period, and made especially notable advances in chemicals and the mechanical industries.

The economic articles in *Il regime fascista* provide reasonably well-balanced assessments. Sober and empirical criticism is provided by Arnold Hughes and Martín Kolinsky, " 'Paradigmatic Fascism' and Modernization: A Critique," *Political Studies* 24.4 (December 1976): 371–96; while the studies in Guido Quazza, ed., *Fascismo e società italiana* (Turin, 1973), tend to be less objective.

viet income did not exceed the 1928 level until about 1953. Moreover, of the four industrial states that increased economic production rapidly in the late 1930s, three—Germany, Japan, and the Soviet Union—did so in large measure on a burgeoning military industrial complex. Despite Mussolini's blustering rhetoric about considering Italy "in a permanent state of war," he never made truly major investments in military production. Consequently Italy was not ready to participate in World War II, but the mixed economy of Italy was less distorted toward arms productions than that of other major industrial states. Since Fascism is normally excoriated for being militaristic, its lack of economic militarism presumably merits some degree of approbation. Only socialism—Russian, German, or Cuban style—permits a maximal degree of militarization, something precluded by the semi-autonomous, mixed economy of the Mussolini regime.

During the early 1930s Mussolini placed great emphasis on the *ridimensionamento* of Italy's socioeconomic structure, which aimed at controlling urbanization, improving environmental conditions, and keeping a large percentage of the rural population in the countryside. The critics hold this to be antimodernism, yet from the perspective of 1980 it would seem in some ways a remarkably sophisticated presentiment of the problems of twentieth-century urbanization and industrialization, long before social democrats got on the bandwagon. Fascists and Nazis were in fact among the first major environmentalists in twentieth-century politics, though they failed to achieve most of their stipulated goals.

The regime also carried out fundamental reorganization of the Italian banking system and the state's civil, commercial, and penal codes. These reforms have long survived fascism and formed part of the structure after 1945. Conversely, the predominance of the humanistic intelligentsia among the middle classes was not reduced during the Mussolini period in favor of technical experts, as occurred in both Nazi Germany and the Soviet Union. This is further evidence of the absence of a fascist cultural revolution, compared with the much more revolutionary and thorough-going structures of Germany and Russia.

Semi-Nazification and German Satellite

The downfall of the Mussolini regime was not caused by its repressiveness and unpopularity, nor by its allegedly inept, reactionary, or antimodern character. It was not very repressive as modern dictatorships go, was probably no more unpopular than the preceding oligarchic liberal regime, and as indicated above, was not remarkably reactionary or antimodern. It presided over an expanding economy, and before 1939 seemed no more inept than most governments. Rather, its downfall came as the result of Mussolini's adventurous foreign policy and alliance with Nazi Germany. This led to defeat in World War II and total destruction of the regime, though not of all its works, some of which were incorporated into the post-1947 "economic miracle."

In view of the profound differences between Mussolinian Italy and Hitlerian Germany and of the sharp enmity toward Nazism expressed by Fascists during 1934, it may be wondered just how this came about. The simple answer is a combination of fear and envy on the part of Mussolini. After 1937 he was convinced that Germany would soon become the dominant state in Europe and that Italy could best protect its interests by aligning itself to a large degree with the Hitlerian new order. To this must be added the extent of Mussolini's own megalomania by the late 1930s and his inflated sense of *ducismo*, constantly surrounded by yes-men, which caused him to lose perspective and believe that his personal decisions would produce victory.

The basic turning point occurred as early as 1935, when Mussolini rejected a reasonably generous settlement of east-African boundaries offered by France and Britain in favor of direct invasion of Ethiopia and military conquest. During the first decade of his regime, the Italian position regarding expansion had been ambivalent. On certain occasions it preached the conquest of a new Roman empire; on others it insisted that Italy could create a great new modern sphere of empire without conquering a single kilometer of new territory. Once Mussolini rejected moderate expansion within the existing European framework in favor of a "new order" empire, however, some sort of rapprochement or parallelism with Germany became logical.

It should be understood that at no time did Mussolini— even after signing the "Pact of Steel" (a full military alliance) with Germany in May 1939—intend to be involved in a major war in the near future. Neither Italian industry nor the armed forces were geared for prolonged, major engagement. Mussolini helped to promote the Munich settlement, tried to arrange a second Munich for Poland in August 1939, carefully avoided involvement in the first phases of World War II, and even secretly warned the Low Countries of the impending German onslaught in 1940. He never desired total German victory, realizing that that would leave Italy too dependent, and finally entered the conflict late in the day (June 1940), only to wage a "parallel war" and carve out an autonomous Italian zone in southern Europe that would also serve to protect it from Germany.[20] In the latter enterprise the regime failed completely. Italian debacles in Greece and North Africa reduced Italy to the role of mere satellite from 1941 on.

A superficial Nazification did occur in Italy after 1937, as among most European fascist movements in those years, but it lacked depth and substance and was mostly confined to gestures such as introduction of the goose step, renamed the *passo romano*. The most blatant aspect of Nazification was the introduction of the Fascist doctrine of racism in 1938, but this was partly a defensive policy based on cultural, not biological, criteria,[21] reflecting the extension of the Italian empire

20. For an introduction to Mussolini's policy in the war, see Harry Cliadakis, "Neutrality and War in Italian Policy 1939–1940," *JCH* 9.3 (July 1974): 171–90; and Renzo de Felice, ed., *L'Italia fra tedeschi ed alleati* (Bologna, 1973); and, on its background, Mario Toscano, *The Origins of the Pact of Steel* (Baltimore, 1967); and various articles in *Il regime fascista*. The standard work on the relations between Mussolini and Hitler is F. W. Deakin, *The Brutal Friendship* (New York, 1966).

21. Gregor, *Ideology of Fascism*, 241–82; and M. van Creveld, "Beyond the Finzi-Contini Garden: Mussolini's 'Fascist Racism,' " *Encounter* 42.2 (February 1974): 42–47.

deeper into black Africa[22] but also endeavoring to carve out a niche of equality for Italy in a German "Aryan" Europe. Its formal anti-Semitism marked an abrupt reversal of traditional Fascist policy,[23] even though the sanctions against Jews were mild by German standards.

The contradictions of Mussolini's policy reached a height during the war years. On the one hand, at least from 1937 on, he liked to emphasize the ideological nature of the association with Germany (and later the war effort) by underscoring the revolutionary mystique of the Nazis and Fascists fighting for a "faith" against the merely materialistic western plutocracies. (Nazis, of course, also liked to make the same point in comparing themselves with communists.) All the while, Mussolini strove ineptly to develop an autonomous Italian sphere of power that could protect Italy from its erstwhile ideological associate. Mussolini's suggestion to Hitler in 1943 that peace be made with the Soviet Union so as to concentrate on the war against the western democracies was perhaps not dictated by an ideological proclivity so much as by the immediacy of Anglo-American military pressure, much nearer than the Red Army.

The overthrow of the regime in 1943 was, as in the case of all fully institutionalized modern European dictatorships prior to post-Franco Spain, the product of external military defeat. The ouster of Mussolini was effected by an ad hoc coalition of the old right—monarchy, army and upper class—with whom Mussolini had had to compromise from the very be-

22. Gene Bernardini, "The Origins and Development of Racial Anti-Semitism in Fascist Italy," *JMH* 49.3 (September 1977): 431–53; and Luigi Preti, *Impero fascista, africani ed ebrei* (Milan, 1968). The most thorough study is Meir Michaelis, *Mussolini and the Jews* (New York, 1978).

23. Five of the 191 founders of the Fasci in 1919 were Jews, and of the nine Jews in parliament two years later, one was a Fascist. In 1938 there were 10,125 adult Jewish members of the PNF. See further, Renzo de Felice, *Storia degli ebrei italiani sotto il fascismo* (Turin, 1961).

Given Italy's exiguous Jewish population (a small fraction of one percent), these statistics may be read as indicating that Jewish support for and participation in Fascism was higher than the indices for the Italian population as a whole.

ginning, and a sizable group of the more moderate and responsible Fascist leaders.

The last phase of Fascism was essentially that of not even a German satellite but a mere German puppet. Establishment of a neo-Fascist Italian Social Republic (popularly known as the Salò regime, from the location of Mussolini's last official residence) nevertheless allowed the PNF, finally divested of its right-wing allies and compromises, to return during 1943–45 to its semirevolutionary origins. Deserted by the propertied and upper classes, residual Fascism declared for a proletarian and semisocialist nationalism to be based on the working classes of industrial northern Italy and the peasantry. The Salò regime introduced certain mechanisms for workers' councils and profit-sharing, together with increasing provision for direct nationalization. Mussolini first announced plans for the nationalization of industry early in 1944, but this was only decreed in the shadow of defeat in April 1945.[24]

It scarcely made any difference, for a defeated Fascism as puppet of Germany could not rally popular support. The territory of the Salò regime was controlled and administered by Germany in all the ways that really counted,[25] and Fascist socialization was only partially tolerated as a demagogical device. Throughout continental Europe Hitler preferred to deal with the orthodox right rather than fascisms, and in northern Italy German administration was concerned to maintain production and avoid disturbing the socioeconomic order any more than necessary. Growth of a large-scale armed resistance movement in northern Italy in 1944 demonstrated that Fascism had been decisively repudiated by the bulk of Italian opinion well before the end of the war. This was yet another fundamental way in which Italian Fascism differed from German National Socialism.

24. Sandro Setta, "Potere economico e Repubblica Sociale Italiana," SC 8.2 (June 1977): 257–87. For a general history, see Edmondo Cione, Storia della Repubblica Sociale Italiana (Rome, 1951).

25. E. Collotti, L'amministrazione tedesca dell'Italia occupata 1943–1945 (Milan, 1963).

THE HITLER REGIME

Speculation about and categorization of the Hitler regime has tended to revolve around rudimentary concepts of "capitalist domination" of its political economy or "totalitarianism." Probably neither one is literally very accurate.

As has been seen in chapter 3, neither Hitler nor the Nazi Party had a very precise doctrine of political economy. The so-called socialist or left sector of the party was not consistent in its economic radicalism, and its erstwhile leader, Gregor Strasser, had veered toward the right by 1932.[26] Hitler always rejected any full or systematic socialism—an "unfortunate term," as he put it—since it contradicted the principles of spontaneity, antibureaucratism, familialism, and competition that formed the basis of the Nazi world view. There were, however, other concepts of political economy among the party leaders when Hilter came to power. O.W. Wagener, sometime head of the political economy section of the party organization division, tried to lead an essentially conservative and middle-class kind of corporative organization, a *Ständesozialismus* geared to the preservation of the existing German class and economic structure. Walther Funk, a subsequent economics minister, headed up the right wing of the party and was the main representative of the interests of German big business within the organization. The Funk tendency hoped to avoid genuine corporatism as potentially too restrictive for big business, and promoted authoritarian *Planwirtschaft* (a limited planned economy) as the best solution to social and economic problems and the fitting framework for a major expansion of private industry.[27]

26. The best treatment will be found in Peter D. Stachura," 'Der Fall Strasser,' " in Stachura, ed., *The Shaping of the Nazi State*, (London, 1978), 88–130.

27. Probably the best analysis of these tendencies within the NSDAP will be found in Dirk Stegmann, "Kapitalismus und Faschismus in Deutschland 1929–1934," *Beiträge zur Marxischen Theorie*, no. 6 (Frankfurt, 1976), 19–91.

After coming to power, Hitler quickly quashed any expectations of a conservative, middle-class corporatism of the Wagener or conservative Catholic varieties. The extreme right-wing agrarian tendencies represented by Prussian right authoritarianism among Nazi allies such as Hugenburg similarly fell by the wayside. By 1934 it appeared that the Funk tendency had won out, and the policies of the pro-Nazi big business "Keppler circle" were in the ascendant (Keppler himself briefly serving as a German state secretary).[28]

This, too, was only temporary, for the first three years of the regime (1933–36) were devoted to economic recovery under a framework of limited state controls and regulations, thereby achieving what Arthur Schweitzer called "partial fascism."[29] That phase came to an end in 1936, when the main drive for rearmament began. If one employed Schweitzer's terminology, this would have presumably initiated "full fascism." In fact, no completely coherent model of political economy was ever introduced in Nazi Germany. Hitler's basic position was that National Socialism meant the subordination of the economy to national interest—*Gemeinnutz geht vor Eigennutz*—by whatever means, referring to collective interest rather than direct structural collectivization. Moreover, he boasted that there was no need to nationalize the economy since he had nationalized the entire population.

After 1936 the tendency was firmly toward ever more state regulation and control, a network of government *Zwangswirtschaft* (a forced or compulsion economy). This never took the form of a general program of state socialism or nationalization, but it progressively subordinated all sectors of the economy through controls, regulations, taxation, contracts, and allocation. During the first phase of the dictatorship the national pressure group associations of business and industry were broken up and replaced by territorial and functional

28. Ibid.
29. Arthur Schweitzer, *Big Business in the Third Reich* (Bloomington, Ind., 1964), 6 and *passim*.

administrative groups that were more convenient for the state. The accelerated cartelization that ensued also was conducted in conformity with state guidelines, so that the label "capitalist domination" ought more accurately to be inverted. The war accentuated these tendencies, which might as well be termed "military socialism" as anything else, representing in many respects a continuation of World War I controls and partial *Planwirtschaft.*

This did not amount to a completely new economic system, however, and no final model was developed. The Four-Year Plan of 1936–40 developed a few industrial projects of state capitalism (or state socialism, depending on the terminology preferred), but this was altogether secondary. More extreme Nazis, including a few SS leaders, speculated during the war about a partially state-socialist economy under a completed Nazi revolution once victory had been achieved, but one may cite quotations from Hitler on both sides of the issue. Late in the war he tried specifically to reassure industrialists that a triumphant National Socialism would *not* nationalize most German industry.[30] What would in fact have come with Nazi victory is a matter of speculation.

At any rate, the most systematic student of comparative fascist economics, Alan Milward, has judged as intrinsically inaccurate the contention of Marxist historians like Reinhard Kühnl and Eberhard Czichon that National Socialism "preserved the capitalist system." "The new [fascist] governments did not, contrary to Kühnl's hypothesis, 'preserve the capitalist system.' They changed the rules of the game so that a new system was emerging,"[31] The new system was never completed, as Milward goes on to observe, and meanwhile private ownership and private profit were upheld, though with increasing restrictions. Profits, in fact, increased,

30. See John Toland, *Adolf Hitler* (New York, 1976), 789.
31. Milward, "Fascism and the Economy," in W. Laqueur, ed., *Fascism: A Reader's Guide* (Berkeley, 1976), 399. Milward's three earlier books represent the most sustained comparative inquiry into National Socialist economics: *The German Economy at War* (London, 1965); *The New Order and the French Economy* (London, 1969); and *The Fascist Economy in Norway* (New York, 1972).

though their use and distribution were carefully regulated by the state.

Under Hitler, the German economic system remained a compound of primarily private ownership of property and capital operating under an ever-increasing and rigid structure of state regulations and controls.[32] Thus it is doubtful that a triumph by Hitler would have "saved German capitalism" in the conventional sense of such a phrase; German capitalism enjoyed much more autonomy and general power under liberal democracy both before and after Hitler. Rather, the reverse of such a notion would be more nearly true: what ultimately saved German capitalism was the defeat of National Socialism in the west by the Anglo-American capitalist powers, and the incorporation of West Germany into the American sphere of hegemony.

Just as Nazi Germany was not dominated by an economic elite, neither was it dominated by a social class. The NSDAP party leadership tended to be rather more middle-class in so-

32. Perhaps the clearest brief statement in English is Tim Mason, "The Primacy of Politics," in S. J. Woolf, ed., *European Fascism* (London, 1969), 165–95. Mason's interpretation originally appeared in the German journal *Das Argument* (8.6 [December 1966]: 473–93), which also printed E. Czichon's debate, "Der Primat der Industrie im Kartell der nationalsozialistichen Macht" (10.3 [April 1971]: 168–92) and Mason's rejoinder (Ibid., 193–209). For a discussion of economic policy in terms of Hitler's broader aims, see Norman Rich, *Hitler's War Aims*, 2 vols. (New York, 1973), I; and Klaus Hildebrand," "Le forze motrici di politica interna agenti sulla politica estera nazionalsocialista," *SC* 5.2 (June 1974): 201–22. The latter tends to agree with A. Kuhn, who terms National Socialism "an absolute contrast with capitalism" (*Das faschistische Herrschaftssystem und die moderne Gesellschaft* [Hamburg, 1973], 31). Thilo Vogelsang has concluded that "the economy, whose fundamentally capitalist structure was maintained," had become, for utopian objectives and even more for the imperial goals of the regime, a prisoner of the National Socialist state." *Die nationalsozialistische Zeit: Deutschland 1933 bis 1939* (Frankfurt/am Main, 1967), 75; quoted in Hildebrand, "Le forze motrici," 206.

Then there are those like the independent Marxist Rudolf Hilferding who have seen no difference between Russian totalitarian state ownership and German National Socialist state regulation and control. "The controversy as to whether the economic system of the Soviet Union is 'capitalist' or 'socialist' seems to me rather pointless. It is neither. It represents a *totalitarian state economy*, i.e., a system to which the economies of Germany and Italy are

cial background than the membership as a whole,[33] but since that is true of nearly all political movements, including many communist ones, it does not demonstrate anything conclusive. Hitler's concept of social revolution was essentially one of status transformation—the identity and values of a racial Volksgemeinschaft.[34] National Socialism no more achieved a complete, organic status revolution than the Soviet Union has achieved a classless society, but at the same time it must be recognized that Hitler did largely break the existing German class system. After 1933, or at least after 1936, no classes were specifically recognized as such. Corporatism was rejected as a model for German political economy precisely because it does tend to recognize different classes, specific interests, and autonomies. Hence trade unions were not replaced by national syndicalism but by a general German Labor Front (DAF),[35] and such autonomy as sectors of industry did enjoy was held not as a class right and privilege but as the functional prerogative of specific functional units on an industry-by-industry basis. General labor contracts did not exist, nor was a national *stand* of industrial entrepreneurs recognized. After 1936, no autonomous class, existing by and for itself (to use Marxian terminology), existed any longer in Germany.

The same kind of interpretation has nonetheless sometimes been applied to Nazi foreign policy and the German war effort, as though Hitler's megalomaniac and grandiose program of military expansion was motivated primarily by the petty desire to increase profits for German industry. Two factors are sometimes referred to in this regard: one is the depletion of Germany's economic resources in 1938–39,

drawing closer and closer." "State Capitalism or Totalitarian State Economy," *Modern Review* (June 1947): 266–71; reprinted in R. V. Daniel, ed., *The Stalin Revolution* (Boston, 1965), 94–97.

33. See the articles by H. A. Winkler and Hans Mommsen in Schieder, ed., *Faschismus als soziale Bewegung*.

34. David Schoenbaum, *Hitler's Social Revolution* (New York, 1966).

35. Timothy W. Mason, *Sozialpolitik im Dritten Reich* (Opladen, 1977), provides a full and critical account of labor policy.

which is held to have required a war of conquest at that point to make them good,[36] and the other is the participation of German industrial firms and cartels in the economic exploitation of conquered areas. The first argument, while correctly stating the situation of German finance and raw materials in 1939, confuses effect with cause. The condition of the German economy did not itself dictate war—there was no autonomous German economy at that point—but rather found itself in that state because Hitler had for three years been subordinating economic interests to the preparation for war. As far as the second argument is concerned, sectors of the German economy participated in the exploitation of conquered territory on much the same basis on which they operated at home, as subordinate individual units, not as dominant or fully autonomous ones. In the final analysis, this structure of things resulted from Hitler's reversal of Stalin's revolutionary priorities—revolutionary conquest abroad must precede the completion of revolution at home. (For that matter, Lenin's original program of "state capitalism" in 1917–18, before worker collectivization swept him farther into state socialism, was not so very different from Hitler's own economic policy).

Hitler's foreign policy, like his entire political career, was ultimately dictated by ideology and only partially moderated by economic considerations. The farther he went, the more complete became the extension of the Nazi system and state and the more overriding the influence of ideology. The clearest example of this was the Final Solution. Anti-Jewish policy began with not inconsiderable moderation during the initial compromise phase of the regime,[37] but accelerated ultimately as a final end in itself, an attempt to achieve a racial revolutionary goal while all else was being lost.

36. Jost Dülffer, "Der Beginn des Krieges 1939: Hitler, die innere Krise und das Mächtesystem," *Geschichte und Gessellschaft* 2.4 (1976): 443–70; and, more broadly, Timothy W. Mason, *Arbeiterklasse und Volksgemeinschaft* (West Berlin, 1975); and also *Wirtschaft und Rüstung am Vorabend des Zweiten Weltkrieges*, ed. F. Forstmeier and H.-E. Volkmann (Düsseldorf, 1975).
37. Karl Schleunes, *The Twisted Road to Auschwitz* (Urbana, Ill., 1970).

The Nazi state system was also highly peculiar and *sui generis*. It never reached maturity or full development but tended continually to shift and has always posed a problem for understanding. One of the common early approaches was the "dual state" concept,[38] "dual state" referring to the parallel between Hitler's continuation of the traditional German state and civil service apparatus and the growth of the Nazi party, its territorial organization, and paragovernmental functions. The Romanian Mihail Manoilescu, Europe's leading theorist of corporatism in the 1930s, liked to distinguish between the Russian, Italian, and German systems—the former a state run by the party, the second a state to which the party was subordinate, and the third a dual system of divided powers between party and state. More recently, considerable stress has been laid on the irrationality and confusion of the Hitler state and the proliferation, overlapping, and mutual competition of a sometimes bewildering variety of state agencies, congruent with Hitler's feudal approach to power, his emphasis on merely personal relationships and on loyalty to the leader only, and his abhorrence of rationalized central bureaucracy.[39]

This approach tends to overlook certain plans and achievements in the area of rationalization and coordination of the

38. Ernst Fraenkel, *The Dual State* (New York, 1941).

39. A classic formulation is Robert Koehl's "Feudal Aspects of National Socialism," *American Political Science Review* 54.4 (December 1960): 921–33. Its perspective is not necessarily inaccurate but is incomplete in itself. A somewhat different approach may be found in Peter Hüttenberger's "Nationalsozialistische Polykratie," (*Geschichte und Gesellschaft* 2.4 [1976]: 417–42), which may not be wrong in perceiving something of a polycratic structure to the initial phase of the regime, but extends and exaggerates the concept. There is now a fairly long bibliography on the Hitlerian party and state that has reached no fully unified conclusion. Among the main works are Dietrich Orlow, *The History of the Nazi Party, 1919–1945* 2 vols. (Pittsburgh, 1969–73); Peter Diehl-Thiele, *Partei und Staat im Dritten Reich* (Munich, 1969); Martin Broszat, *Der Staat Hitlers* (Munich, 1969); H. Mommsen, *Beamtentum im Dritten Reich* (Stuttgart, 1966); Peter Hüttenberger, *Die Gauleiter* (Stuttgart, 1969); and H. Matzerath, *Nazionalsozialismus und kommunale Selbstverwaltung* (Stuttgart, 1970).

state in the Reichsreform of 1934–36,[40] and may also under-estimate the actual role of the NSDAP in German administration. On the local level the party did tend to take over the state to some degree, and gauleiters became district state officials in a process sometimes the reverse of what happened in Italy. Moreover, local party leadership began to play an increased role during the war, so that by the final years the party leadership had indeed largely taken over the home front. Finally, the major parapolitical and administrative role of the SS steadily expanded this elite branch of Nazi power during the last phase of the regime.[41]

For much of the generation after the war, the concept of totalitarianism held vogue, likening Nazi Germany to the Soviet Union, however, much more than to Italy. The definition of totalitarianism has always been remarkably vague, and the most recent fad has been to deny that any such thing existed or exists. Since theorists of totalitarianism rarely get beyond such rudimentary and limited qualities as the single party, the use of terror, and mass mobilization, it is easy to argue either that many different kinds of regimes are totalitarian or conversely that none of them is perfectly total.

Yet the concept of totalitarianism is both valid and useful if defined in the precise and literal sense of a state system that attempts to exercise total control over all significant aspects of all major national institutions, from the economy and armed forces to the judicial system, the churches, and culture. It has been seen that in this sense the Mussolini regime was not totalitarian at all, and the Hitler system also failed to achieve full totalitarianism, though in its final phase it drew

40. See Jane Caplan, "Bureaucracy, Politics and the National Socialist State," in Stachura, ed., *Shaping of the Nazi State,* 234–56.

It might be observed in passing that *Signal,* the wartime Nazi propaganda picture magazine, liked to refer to Germany as "the most modern socialist state in the world" (S. L. Mayer, ed., *Signal: Years of Triumph, 1940–42* [London, 1978]).

41. The best study of the SS is Heinz Höhne, *The Order of the Death's Head* (New York, 1970).

nearer and nearer. Here Hannah Arendt, for one, agrees, noting that full Nazi totalitarianism equivalent to the Soviet model could have developed only after victory in the war, given Hitler's reversal of Leninist-Stalinist revolutionary priorities. For that matter, only a socialist or communist system can achieve full totalitarianism, since total control requires total institutional revolution that can only be affected by state socialism. Socialism need not be totalitarian but totalitarianism must be socialist, and National Socialism, with its mixed approach, could never establish the complete model, even had it desired, before 1945.

More recently the situation has been further confused by emphasis on irrationalities and limited autonomy within the system, which resulted in the "limits on Hitler's power."[42] This is, however, to go too far in the other direction. Hitler purposely avoided a completely centralized bureaucratic totalitarian system, but the limited autonomies that he permitted in the German state system either by design, oversight, or necessity scarcely diminished his remarkable powers of personal political dictatorship to implement his own revolutionary priorities.

The Hitler regime was so bewildering in its methods and goals that interpretation has frequently given up altogether and fallen back on sheer negatives for understanding—the "revolution of nihilism" or the overriding motivation of "antimodernism." Hitler and his crew, however repellent, were not nihilists but held tenaciously to firm and evil values. Nihilism is more nearly what came after Hitler, unless sheer hedonism is considered a value rather than the absence of values.

Since Hitlerism is atypical, it has commonly been considered antimodern in terms of a reductionist definition of modernity based on urbanism, technology, and something that is referred to as "rationality." Yet however extreme, Hitlerism was a symptomatic product of the modern world, and

42. Edward N. Peterson, *The Limits of Hitler's Power* (Princeton, 1969).

national socialism in various forms the most popular new set of political designs of the twentieth century. As indicated in chapter 2, Hitler's ideas were partly rooted in the modern scientism of German biological and zoological ideas of the late nineteenth century.[43] The Nazi leaders' keen interest in the occult was not directed toward traditional folk superstition so much as toward new modern and racial myths of the supernatural.[44] Hitler in fact rejected nearly all the formal ideas of European culture of the Medieval epoch, above all historical Christianity, and was a stern derider of premodern "superstition." As a matter of fact, Nazi racism was conceivable only in the twentieth century and at no previous time in human history. The animalistic, naturalistic, human anthropology of the Nazis was strictly a modern concept without any premodern parallels.

All of Hitler's political ideas had their origin in the Enlightenment[45]—the concept of the nation as a higher historical force, the notions of superior political sovereignty derived from the general will of the people[46] and of the inherent racial differences in human culture. These were distinct derivations from Enlightenment anthropology which rejected premodern theology and the common roots and transcendent interests of mankind. The cult of the will is the basis of modern culture, and Hitler merely carried it to an

43. Daniel Gasman, *The Scientific Origins of National Socialism: Social Darwinism in Ernst Haeckel and the German Monist League* (New York, 1971).

44. Dusty Sklar, *Gods and Beasts: The Nazis and the Occult* (New York, 1978).

45. This is largely the thesis of Marcel Déat, *Révolution française et révolution allemande* (Paris, 1943).

46. It is conveniently forgotten that the Führerprinzip is eminently Rousseauian. "In Rousseau's conception, only a leader of divine genius is able to found the state in which men are free, albeit by compulsion, and to determine what the general will is." Louis J. Halle, *The Ideological Imagination* (London, 1971), 36.

George L. Mosse formulates this in terms of the "new politics" of the nationalistic masses, stemming from eighteenth-century doctrines of popular sovereignty in which the people worship themselves as a national group or race, and are ultimately directed not by laws or parliaments but by secular national religion. *The Nationalization of the Masses* (New York, 1975), 1–20.

extreme. The very concept of National Socialism as the "will to create a new man" was possible only in the twentieth-century context as a typically modern, antitraditional idea. The same may be said of the Nazi search for extreme autonomy, a radical freedom for the German people. Hitler carried the modern goal of breaking the limits and setting new records to an unprecedented point. For no other movement did the modern doctrine of man the measure of all things rule to such an extent.[47]

This also holds with regard to social and economic programs. No ruler in modern times has gone to such lengths as Hitler to acquire, among other things, the natural resources necessary for a modern economy. Nazi *Gleichschaltung* and the effort at status revolution tended to unite German society and overcome class distinctions for the first time in German history. Though Nazi antiurbanism is said to have been inherently reactionary, radical antiurbanism has become a major trend of the late twentieth century. The most radical new communist regimes of the 1970s flaunt their ruralism and antiurbanism. In fact, though the German war economy promoted de facto urbanization and greater industrialization, rather than the reverse, an ultimate Nazi economic goal was to balance farm and industry. When sought by liberals, this is frequently deemed the height of enlightenment and sophistication. Finally, Hitler was well in advance of his times in his concern about ecology, environmental reform, and pollution.

Truly large scale genocide or mass murder is a prototypical development of the twentieth century, from Turkey to Russia to Germany to Cambodia to Africa. The unique Nazi tactic was to modernize the process, to accomplish the mass murder more efficiently and surgically than other great liquidators in Turkey, Russia, or Cambodia have done. Nor was Hitler's genocidal program any more or less "rational," since the goal of mass murder is always political, ideological, or

47. A trenchant and provocative interpretation of the problem was made by Steven Aschheim in a seminar paper, "Modernity and the Metaphysics of Nazism" (University of Wisconsin, 1975).

religious and not a matter of practical economic ends, pace Stalin or Mao Tse-tung.

National Socialism in fact constituted a unique and radical kind of modern revolutionism. This again is one of the most controverted interpretations of Hitlerism, for since many commentators hold National Socialism to have been anti-modern (normally merely meaning antiliberal), they argue that it must necessarily have been "reactionary," not revolutionary. Such an approach is held all the more tenaciously by leftist commentators because of their a priori assumption that the concept *revolution* must refer ipso facto to good revolution, revolution that is positive or creative. But of course revolutions are frequently destructive.

This problem has been approached most directly by Karl Bracher, who has identified the following revolutionary qualities of National Socialism:

1. A supreme new leadership cult of the Führer as the "artist genius"
2. The effort to develop a new Social Darwinist structure of government and society
3. The replacement of traditional nationalism by racial revolution
4. Development of the first new system of state-regulated national socialism in economics
5. Implementation of the organic status revolution for a new national *Volksgemeinschaft*
6. The goal of a completely new kind of racial imperialism on a world scale
7. Stress on new forms of advanced technology in the use of mass media and mass mobilization, a cult of new technological efficiency, new military tactics and technology, emphasis on aerial and automotive technology[48]

This list might be refined and made even more detailed, but as a general formulation it covers the main points. For devotees of colonial and minority-population "national libera-

---

48. Karl D. Bracher, *Zeitgeschichtliche Kontroversen um Faschismus Totalitarismus Demokratie* (Munich, 1976), 60–78. The list presented above constitutes my own reformulation, not an exact transcription of Bracher's.

tion" revolution, it should be pointed out that during World War II the promotion of national liberation movements among colonial and minority peoples around the world was almost *exclusively* the work of the Axis powers.[49] During his twelve years in power Hitler had a more profound impact on the world than any other revolutionary of the twentieth century, and all the more because, as Eugen Weber[50] and others have pointed out, wars constitute the primary revolutionary processes of this century.

Jacques Ellul insists,

> Informed observers of the period between the wars are convinced that National Socialism was an important and authentic revolution. De Rougemont points out how the Hitler and the Jacobin regimes were identical at every level. R. Labrousse, an authority on the French revolution, confirms that, to city only two opinions . . .
>
> The practice of "classifying," and thus dismissing, Nazism should stop, for it represents a real Freudian repression on the part of intellectuals who refuse to recognize what it was. Others lump together Nazism, dictatorship, massacres, concentration camps, racism, and Hitler's folly. That about covers the subject. Nazism was a great revolution: against the bureaucracy, against senility, in behalf of youth; against the entrenched hierarchies, against capitalism, against the petit-bourgeois mentality, against comfort and security, against the consumer society, against traditional morality; for the liberation of instinct, desire, passions, hatred of cops (yes, indeed!), the will to power and the creation of a higher order of freedom.[51]

---

49. This is not to overlook Franklin Roosevelt's vigorous opposition to west-European imperialism while acquiescing in Soviet imperialism. See W. R. Louis, *Imperialism at Bay* (New York, 1978). American support for decolonization was, however, expressed at the diplomatic, not the military level.

50. Eugen Weber, "Revolution? Counterrevolution? What Revolution?" *JCH* 9.2 (April 1974): 3–47; reprinted in Laqueur, ed., *Fascism: A Reader's Guide*, 435–67.

51. Jacques Ellul, *Autopsy of Revolution* (New York, 1971), 288. In *The Phenomenon of Revolution* (New York, 1974), Mark Hagopian concluded that "the

Main Differences between the Hitler and Mussolini Regimes

It has been suggested that the Fascist and Nazi movements and the Hitler and Mussolini regimes can be categorized together only at a very general level of abstraction. When viewed closely, the differences are frequently much more striking than the similarities, whether one looks at the question of revolutionary potential or at other aspects. A partial list of basic differences would include the following considerations:

1. The Hitlerian ideology was founded on race, that of Fascism on nationalism in a political and cultural sense. Hence Hitlerian ideology tended toward revolutionary exclusivity, while that of Fascism was more sophisticated and syncretic in formulation. Mussolini insisted that Fascism incorporated aspects of liberalism, conservatism, and socialism in a higher synthesis; Hitler aimed at a revolutionary rejection of rival doctrines. All would-be revolutionaries aim at a "new man." That of National Socialism would be a new biological as well as cultural product; Mussolini merely hoped to intensify Fascist education in the schools.

2. In structure, the Mussolini regime remained in large measure a juridical state of semipluralism and formal law. This of course placed a considerable limitation on the revolutionary potential of the Mussolini system, and also made it possible for the Duce's adversaries within the state to overthrow him. The Hitlerian *Führerstaat*, while formulating no elaborate theory of totalitarianism, was a much more complex dictatorship of one-man rule.

3. The NSDAP played a much more important role than did the PNF. Though the Hitler regime was not turned into a formal party-state theoretically (and normally in practice) run by the party, as in communist countries, a duality of party and state powers developed that Hitler

question about the revolutionary nature of fascism [in general] is not easy to answer," but "that the twelve years of the Third Reich represent a definite revolutionary thrust . . ." (363, 358).

tended to shift more and more in favor of the party or sectors thereof. The PNF, by comparison, enjoyed only a very limited autonomy and was largely transformed into a subordinate state bureaucracy. Nonetheless, the semi-pluralist and juridical structure of the Mussolini regime, being neither totalitarian nor a complete one-man dictatorship, did preserve a certain degree of formal autonomy for the Fascist Grand Council which the Council finally used to depose Mussolini.

4. Anti-Semitism of the most extreme form was central to National Socialism. By contrast, Italian Fascism was racist only in the conventional sense of early twentieth-century Europe and during its first two decades not normally anti-Semitic. Jews played a role in early Fascism disproportionate to their numbers in Italian society.

5. Hitler's foreign policy ultimately transcended traditional German expansionist and imperial aims, attempting a revolutionary racial restructuring of Europe. Mussolini's aspirations remained largely within the orbit of traditional Italian nationalist/imperalist policy, aiming at colonial expansion and the exploitation of limited conflict within the Mediterranean area.

These differences in one form or another were keenly felt by Fascists and Nazis, and were in varying forms reexpressed during the later war years,[52] which ended with one of the most sensitive and discriminating of the original Fascist leaders and Grand Council members—Giuseppe Bottai—fighting in the French Foreign Legion against Germany.

Certain Similarities between National Socialism and Communism

The inability of the Mussolini regime to overcome its rightist compromises, together with its dissimilar doctrines and origins, precluded a revolutionary convergence between the

52. Thus Himmler would reiterate to the SS in 1943, "Fascism and National Socialism are two fundamentally different things. . . . There is absolutely no comparison between Fascism and National Socialism as spiritual, ideological movements." E. Kohn-Bramstedt, *Dictatorship and Political Police*, in Hannah Arendt, *Totalitarianism* (New York, 1968), 7. Goebbels concluded that Mussolini "is not a revolutionary like the Führer or Stalin."

Mussolini and Hitler regimes. In turn the Hitler regime, in its rejection of Marxism and materialism and the formal principle of bureaucratic totalitarianism, did not take the same form as Russian communism, in spite of theories by critics about a supposed common totalitarianism. Nonetheless, there were some specific ways in which National Socialism paralleled Russian communism to a much greater degree than Fascism was capable of doing. The following list will suggest some of the similarities and parallels:

1. Frequent recognition by Hitler and various Nazi leaders (and also Mussolini) that their only revolutionary and ideological counterparts were to be found in Soviet Russia

2. The founding of both National Socialism and Russian national communism on a revolutionary action theory which held that success in practice validated ideological innovation, as the Soviet Union progressively relinquished main aspects of classic Marxist theory

3. Revolutionary doctrines of "constant struggle"

4. Rigid elitism and the leadership principle: National Socialist was someone who followed Hitler; a Bolshevik was not necessarily a Marxist but someone who followed Lenin

5. Espousal of the have-not, proletarian-nation theory, which Lenin adopted only after it had been introduced in Italy

6. Construction of a one-party dictatorship independent of any particular class

7. Major stress, not merely on a political militia (which was increasingly common in the late nineteenth and early twentieth centuries), but upon a party-army, with a regular army to be controlled by the party; by 1943 Hitler had begun to introduce "National Socialist Guidance Officers" in the regular army as the equivalent of commissars[53]

53. Robert L. Quinnett, "The German Army Confronts the NSFO," *JCH* 13.1 (January 1978):53–64.

8. Emphasis on autarchy and major (not merely partial) militarization, though the absence of a totalitarian state bureaucratic system and economy in Germany made this proportionately somewhat less thoroughgoing than in Russia; promotion of revolutionary war whenever possible as an alternative to complete and balanced internal development

9. An NEP phase of partial pluralism on the road to more complete dictatorship (common, of course, to most dictatorial systems, though more abbreviated in countries such as China and Cuba)

10. International projection of a new ideological myth as an alternative to prevailing orthodoxies, capable of eliciting a not-insignificant international response; variants of Fascist and Nazi ideologies constituted the last notable ideological innovations in the modern world after Marxism

This tentative list is not presented to propound a theory of "red fascism" or the notion that communism and nazism have been essentially the same thing. There were some fundamental differences, as previously noted, between the Russian and German systems. Nonetheless, Hitlerian National Socialism more nearly paralleled Russian communism than has any other noncommunist system.

5

Other Movements and Regimes

The emergence of Fascism stimulated radical nationalist politics in other parts of Europe and provoked several direct imitations, among them the Romanian Fascist Party of 1923 and Georges Valois's "Le Faisceau" of 1924. The advent of authoritarian government in Italy also served as a definite encouragement to the Primo de Rivera pronunciamiento in the year following the March on Rome. In general, however, the initial impact of Fascism was not great, primarily for two reasons. By the time Mussolini finally came to power, the postwar crisis had lessened and other European systems were regaining equilibrium. Secondly, unlike Germany after 1933, Italy could not—despite Mussolini's many foreign admirers—be considered a dominant or leading nation. Many of Mussolini's enthusiasts abroad cheered him in part because they felt that Fascism was appropriate for Italians but not for supposedly superior countries like their own.

Parties and movements of authoritarian nationalism during the 1920s tended toward either the radical or moderate authoritarian right more than toward the semirevolutionary new expressions of Fascism. In southwestern Europe this was much more the decade of Action Française and Portuguese Integralism (modeled on the former) than of French national socialism or Portuguese national syndicalism. Most of the new parties of the "patriotic movement" in Germany assumed a distinct rightist cast, and in the east the main new expressions of nationalism took a diffuse and populist form (the leader of the Romanian People's Party in the 1920s, General Averescu, had much in common with a Pangalos or Primo de Rivera), or a distinct right radical mode as in Hungary.

The chronology of breakdown of parliamentary government was steady throughout the interwar period: 1922–25 Italy; 1923–36 Spain; 1926 Portugal; 1926 Poland; 1926–36 Greece; 1926 Lithuania; 1929 Yugoslavia; 1933 Germany; 1933 Austria; and so on. Initially, there was an almost uniform tendency to replace parliamentary government with syncretistic, semipluralist forms of right-wing dictatorship, normally without a developed single-party system and usually without a radical new fascist-type component.

The major diffusion of putatively fascist parties and movements throughout Europe occurred in the aftermath of Hitler's triumph, even though such initiatives had not been absent either in the late twenties or the very beginning of the thirties. Moreover, after 1933 right authoritarian movements and regimes also began to adopt diverse aspects of "fascistization," assuming certain outward trappings of fascist style to present a more modern and dynamic image, and with the hope of attaining a broader mobilization and social infrastructure. By the late 1930s, as Hitler moved from victory to victory, both the fascistic movements and the right authoritarian states—though especially the former—began to undergo varying degrees of Nazification, reflecting Germany's incipient return to hegemonic status.

The characteristics of these groups varied considerably, which is not surprising for authoritarian movements structured in large measure on national voluntarism and a stress on ethnic differences. Comparative or taxonomic analysis thus becomes clearer by proceeding from country to country.

AUSTRIA

Austria presented perhaps the clearest case in Europe of the three main faces of authoritarian nationalism: a moderate right authoritarian group, the Christian Social Party; a more radical, overtly authoritarian and violent rightist group, the Heimwehr units; and revolutionary nationalists in the form of the Austrian Nazis.

Some commentators project the Heimwehren as a unique Austrian domestic variant of fascism, but the latter do not exactly fit the typology. The Heimwehren—"home guard" or military units—were organized in 1919–20 to protect the Austrian frontiers in a moment of great political and territorial flux, and secondarily to protect conservative interests from Marxism. They were thus to some extent the counterpart of the German Free Corps, but like the latter, their commitments were only to nationalism, paramilitary activism, and opposition to the left.[1] The Heimwehren never achieved either organizational unity or any specific ideology. Like the Austrian right in general, their social basis was mainly rural and small town.

The trajectory of the Heimwehren obeyed an Austrian as well as a European rhythm. Conflict between the Austrian right and maximalist Austrian Socialists first peaked in 1927, and the Heimwehren gained recruits (claiming 200,000 by 1929) as an alternative to the parliamentary system. They enjoyed support from the Hugenburg sector of the DNVP and the Stahlhelm in Germany, and more important, financial assistance from Mussolini at first channeled through the right-wing Hungarian government, another patron.

During this period an effort was made to give the rather amorphous Heimwehren central organizational unity and also an ideology. The doctrines of Othmar Spann, the chief Austrian ideologist of Catholic corporatism,[2] were propagat-

1. Horst G. W. Nusser, *Konservative Wehrverbände in Bayern, Preussen und Osterreich 1918–1933* (Munich, 1973), is the only general, comparative study.
2. On Spann, see Martin Schneller, *Zwischen Romantik und Faschismus: Der Beitrag Othmar Spanns zum Konservativismus der Weimarer Republik* (Stuttgart, 1970); and John J. Haag, "Othmar Spann and the Politics of 'Totality' " (Ph.D. diss., Rice University, 1969).

ed at various meetings and seminars, and on May 18, 1930, the main Heimwehr leaders took the famous Korneuburg Oath to transform Austria into an authoritarian corporative system. Even this was not clear-cut "fascism," and led to a new split in the movement, papered over by the selection of a new central leader, E. R. von Starhemberg, who had been dealing directly with Mussolini but soon became rather lukewarm about the Korneuburg Oath.

The significance of the Heimwehren lay only in their militia function. They were not a party as such and had scant electoral strength. In their major effort in the 1930 elections the Heimwehren front coalition registered only 6 percent of the vote, since few aside from their own militia voted for them. During 1931 the Heimwehren began to disintegrate. One radical section attempted an abortive putsch,[3] some units began to go over to the Austrian Nazis, and most clung to a steadily amorphous if authoritarian conservatism.[4]

The initiative remained in the hands of the Christian Socials, governing for most of the period since the founding of the Austrian Republic. During the 1920s, under Dr. Ignaz Seipel, the Christian Socials remained a parliamentary party, ambiguously democratic,[5] but finally moved toward a conservative brand of authoritarianism under the impact of the depression and the impasse of Austrian party politics, triangulated between Marxian Socialists, Nazis, and themselves. In 1931 they began to organize their own militia in one part of Austria. When the new Christian Social leader

3. Josef Hofmann, *Der Pfrimer-Putsch* (Vienna-Graz, 1965).
4. The best global treatment of the Heimwehren and the other authoritarian nationalist groups of Austria will be found in F. L. Carsten, *Fascist Movements in Austria from Schönerer to Hitler* (London, 1970). See also Bruce S. Pauley, *Hahnenschwanz und Hakenkreuz* (Vienna, 1972); C. E. Edmundson, *The Heimwehr and Austrian Politics, 1918–1934* (Athens, Ga., 1978); and Ludwig Jedlicka, "The Austrian Heimwehr," *JCH* 1.1 (January 1966): 127–44.
5. The principal biography is Klemens von Klemperer, *Ignaz Seipel* (Princeton, 1972), favorable to Seipel. One of the best studies of Austrian parties is the unpublished Ph.D. dissertation of Walter B. Simon, "The Political Parties of Austria" (Columbia University, 1957). See also R. J. Rath, "The First Austrian Republic—Totalitarian, Fascist, Authoritarian, or What?" in the forthcoming Larsen et al., eds., *Who Were the Fascists?*.

Dollfuss set up an authoritarian system in 1933, it was carefully differentiated from a Fascist model.[6] The new political front, the Fatherland Front, came to include the Heimwehren, but was not a state party, its functions being separated from those of the state. Rather, it was the Austrian variant of the vague, amorphous, conglomerate political fronts established at one time or another by nearly all the south-European dictatorships of the period. Italy was the main support of the Austrian regime against Nazi Germany, and in late 1933 Dollfuss promised Mussolini that he would move toward Fascism, but the new corporative state constitution of May 1, 1934, was conservative, Catholic, and virtually theocratic. It stipulated a total of seven corporations to represent Austrian society, though they were never fully organized. Starhemberg, the Heimwehr leader, negotiated on his own with Mussolini (who earlier had advised him to avoid anti-Semitism). In 1933–34 he sometimes referred vaguely to developing an "Austrian fascism,"[7] seeming to aim at the incorporation of all the more conservative aspects of the Mussolini regime, but ended up in the Fatherland Front. After the assassination of Dollfuss by Nazis, he served as vicechancellor of the Republic from 1934 to 1936 before being forced out. In the final years of the regime, from 1936 to 1938, more of the external trappings of an organized Mussolini-style dictatorship were added, with a youth group, various new front and social organizations, and a national political militia, the Storm Corps,[8] under the Fatherland Front, replacing the Heimwehren and other rightist militia. Nonetheless, neither the old Heimwehren nor the Dollfuss-Schuschnigg regime of 1933–38 ever became fascist in the fully typical sense.

By the time of Anschluss in 1938, Austrian political opinion had become triangulated between the right authoritarian

6. The main biography is Gordon Brooke-Shepherd's *Dollfuss* (London, 1961), favorable to Dollfuss.

7. In 1930 a little "Party of Austrian Fascists" was formed, but apparently quickly died.

8. This was approximately the same name that the new democratic Spanish Republic of 1931 had given to its new state police, the Assault Guards.

government, the suppressed Socialists, and the increasingly popular Nazis. National Socialism developed more slowly than in Germany, but on the basis of much the same social support[9] and with as high a proportion of blue collar workers in its SA.[10] One difference in Austrian Nazism that might be noted, however, was the existence of a momentarily important "National Catholic" sector of right-radical intellectuals, led by Artur Seyss-Inquart,[11] who were useful for the Anschluss and then largely brushed aside.

HUNGARY

Of all states in interwar Europe, Hungary probably took the prize for the largest assortment per capita of various fascist-type, semifascist, right radical, or simply authoritarian nationalist groups and movements. The penchant of Hungarian political society for radical nationalist and protofascist mobilization can perhaps be explained by the structure and situation of the country in that period. Hungary was probably the most nationally aggrieved state in all Europe because of the great proportion of its territorial and demographic losses. In addition it had been the second country to be governed briefly by a revolutionary communist dictatorship, that of Béla Kun in 1919. Third, compared with the limited development of its social structure, it had a large unemployed or underemployed national bureaucratic middle class, heavily recruited for such politics. Fourth, Hungarian culture participated in many of the same intellectual and literary processes that emphasized radical nationalism and the *völkisch* in the German-speaking world (exclusive of Switzerland). And fi-

9. According to one sample, the proportion of unskilled workers in the Austrian NSDAP (27 percent) was higher than in both the Socialist (19.8 percent) and Communist (22.5 percent) parties. Table 5 of Peter H. Merkl, "Comparing Fascist Movements," in Larsen et al., eds., *Who Were the Fascists?*

10. Gerhard Botz, "Aspects of the Social Structure of Austrian National Socialism (1918–1939)," Ibid.

11. See Wolfgang Rosar, *Deutsche Gemeinschaft: Seyss-Inquart und der Anschluss* (Vienna, 1971).

nally, the domination of politics by right nationalism and the exclusion or repression of the domestic left opened the field for radical social agitation to national socialists and revolutionary corporatists to a degree unprecedented in Europe. Nonetheless, in Hungary as in Austria and Romania, where fascist elements were also vigorous and popular, domestic fascists were completely unable to seize power. This was due not so much to the strength of liberal democracy in Hungary as to its absence. The restrictive nature of Hungarian government under Admiral Horthy concentrated power within the control of a minority and prevented any radical nationalist group from mobilizing enough mass support for a serious try at power.

Moderate conservative authoritarianism was thus represented by the Horthy regime itself, a counterrevolutionary system that aimed to restore and preserve as much as possible of the old nineteenth-century social hierarchy. The regime governed by a restrictive parliament of limited suffrage, headed by monarchy or in this case a regent (Horthy) as surrogate.[12] The regime's National Unity Party may be seen as a fairly typical government party for an authoritarian or semiauthoritarian south-European system of the time, though the limited degree of representation permitted by the regime gave this more of an electoral and parliamentary cast than in more overt dictatorships.

Right radicalism flourished in the counterrevolutionary aftermath of Béla Kun, and the officers gathered at Szeged to promote the new regime produced a number of different ultranationalist, anti-Semitic and racist societies that proposed much more radical alternatives than that offered by the new Horthy regime. Yet the "right radicals," as they were commonly known in Hungary during the 1920s, generally lacked popular support and fell short of the revolutionary aspirations of the fascist type.

12. C. A. Macartney, *October Fifteenth: A History of Hungary 1929–1945*, 2 vols. (New York, 1956–57), is still the best general account of the main period of the Horthy regime. The best comparative study of eastern Europe in this period is Joseph Rothschild, *East Central Europe between the Two World Wars* (Seattle, 1974).

More typically fascist and national socialist groups emerged in the late twenties and particularly in the early thirties, prompted by foreign example, the depression, and the stagnation and frustrations of Hungarian society. They should be divided into a least three general types, though some of the groups were perhaps not readily classifiable: (a) proponents of a kind of moderate fascism, at least partly inspired by the Italian example; (b) more radical imitations of German National Socialism, of which there were several; and (c) more highly individuated proponents of revolutionary nationalism, primarily Szalasi's Hungarist movement (Arrow Cross), at least before its Nazification after 1940.

The right radicals flourished between 1919 and 1922, then declined somewhat. They were influenced more and more by Italian Fascism, particularly after a special diplomatic relationship was established between Hungary and Italy in 1928, and in their subsequently increasingly fascist form some have been called "Szeged fascists" (referring to their point of origin in 1919). The leader of the Szeged fascists was a career army officer, Gyula Gömbös, to whom Horthy eventually offered the premiership in 1932, when the depression had created severe problems with which the official state party could not cope. As constitutional prime minister, Gömbös's path to power seemed to parallel that of Mussolini and Hitler (save that he had no organized mass movement behind him), yet in Hungary things were not so simple. The established regime forced him to moderate his program and even largely to abandon anti-Semitism before giving him the prime ministership. Once in power he worked to transform the official National Unity Party into a more radical, broadly mobilized organization, and after Hitler came to power in 1933 Nazi influence tended to replace that of Fascism among the "fascistized" sectors. Gömbös told Göring in 1935 that within three years Hungary would be reorganized into a national socialist state, but before the end of the following year he died of a sudden illness, his somewhat uncertain goals unrealized.

More radical groups were formed from about 1932 on and received further impetus from the failure of Gömbös's moderate collaborationist path. German influence was strong among most though not all of them, several of the new parties calling themselves "national socialist" with the addition of further adjectives.[13] Yet most of the new pro-Nazi national socialists seemed to be riding the German fad and were very vague about their concrete domestic goals. If all the fascistized and nazified sectors were rhetorically anticapitalist and propeasant, many of the titular national socialists were much less firm in their zeal for land reform then, for example, Gömbös and his fascistized right radical followers. Their main social support came from the bureaucratized, relatively impoverished middle classes and especially from the German (Swabian) minority (some of whom also organized their own separate Hungaro-German Nazi-like movement, the MEM).

The only significant popular force was the Arrow Cross or Hungarist movement of another career army officer, Ferenc Szalasi. The principal study of the Arrow Cross in a western language argues, to some extent persuasively, that Szalasi's movement and program cannot be merely assimilated to any preexisting foreign model.[14] Like most other radical Hungarian nationalists, Szalasi believed in Hungarian racism[15] and proposed a drastic Hungarian imperial expansion that would incorporate the greater Danube-Carpathian area. What made this unique was the proposal that regions inhabited by a strong majority (80 to 90 percent) of a single non-Magyar people would enjoy the right of autonomy. Another anomaly was Szalasi's theoretical eschewal of violence. He apparently believed (at least in the beginning) that the new Hungarism would triumph by preaching, by conviction, through conversion or acceptance. Szalasi proclaimed his movement not

13. Though not all the new "national socialist" parties were pro-Nazi. For example, Zoltan Mesko's National Socialist Agrarian Laborers' and Workers' Party was strongly anti-German and adopted a revolutionary economic program on behalf of landless peasants and workers.

14. N. M. Nagy-Talavera, *The Green Shirts and the Others* (Stanford, 1970).

15. On doctrines of Hungarian racism, see J. A. Kessler, "Turanism and Pan-Turanism in Hungary, 1890–1945" (Ph.D. diss., University of California, Berkeley, 1967).

anti-Semitic but simply "a-Semitic," advocating that all Jews leave Hungary for elsewhere. His notion of Hungarian "True Christianity" may in a sense be compared with the contemporary efforts at "German Christianity," but was perhaps less totally heretical. Finally, Szalasi advocated a revolutionary economic corporatism that would overthrow big landlords and capital in the interest of greater collective well-being. Probably the program need not be taken very seriously as a power contender, but it was no carbon copy of anyone else.

The Arrow Cross became a genuine mass movement of poor workers and peasants in the late 1930s. Since it did not run entirely on a straight-party ticket in the last elections of 1939 and since the Hungarian elections were partially manipulated, its exact electoral support is difficult to calculate, but the best indications that we have—more than 20 percent of the popular vote under such conditions[16]—would seem to demonstrate that it was for the moment the second most popular revolutionary nationalist party in Europe, second only to National Socialism.

The very absence of democracy in Hungary limited its chances, as did the visionary ineptitude and virtual schizophrenia of its own leaders. An authoritarian regime was normally able to contain any popular fascist threat against it, and the popularity of the Arrow Cross apparently declined during the war. In the process, it became increasingly Nazi-

16. In fact, the Arrow Cross–national socialist factions' electoral coalition returned forty-nine deputies in 1939, of whom thirty-one were Arrow Cross men, about 13 percent of the national total. But the evidence indicates that Arrow Cross candidates were prevented from running in some districts, and that they registered a high number of second-place votes in quite a few areas. In general, they did best in worker districts of Budapest and some of the poor peasant regions. It was clearly the leading national protest party. The main study of its social basis is Miklós Lackó, *Nyilasok, Nemzetisocialisták, 1935–1944* [*Arrow Cross Men: National Socialists 1935–1944*] (Budapest, 1966), with an English abridgement, *Men of the Arrow Cross: National Socialists 1935–1944* (Budapest, 1969); and his "The Social Basis of the Hungarian Fascist Movement," in Larsen et al., eds., *Who Were the Fascists?* On the 1939 elections, see Gyorgy Ránki, "A Case Study of the 1939 Elections in Hungary," ibid.

fied, having never lived up to the ideals of its leader, and was placed in power only briefly in 1944 as a puppet of German military intervention.

ROMANIA

The situation of Romania is analogous to that of Hungary only with respect to the considerable strength of the Legionary movement (Iron Guard) in the late 1930s. Conversely, Romania was one of the main beneficiaries of World War I, which doubled the size of the country. And despite the proverbial corruption and coercion of Romanian politics, it had a largely competitive parliamentary party system until 1938 and underwent a major land reform in the 1920s. Yet the enormous expansion of the country and the partial democratization of some institutions led to a national identity crisis by the end of the twenties and a prolonged search for viable government alternatives. As throughout southern and eastern Europe, the postwar democratic breakthrough (in Romania's case, honest elections and a democratic Peasant Party government in 1928) led to political breakdown.

As in Hungary and some other countries, three faces of authoritarian nationalism can be identified in Romania. A fascist type of revolutionary nationalism was represented by the Legionaries, a radical right emerged in the National Christian Party, devoted almost exclusively to antisemitism, and a more moderate erstwhile "legitimate" authoritarianism appeared at the end of the period in the royalist dictatorship of Carol (1938–40), followed by that of Marshal Antonescu (1940–44). The first phase of transition from liberal nationalism was represented by General Averescu's Populist Party, founded in 1919, which governed briefly several times in the 1920s and carried out much of the land reform. It was an initial effort to mobilize peasants and other sectors of the lower classes behind a reformist, quasi-authoritarian nationalism, but fell between two stools and disappeared in the 1930s.

The Legion of the Archangel Michael, commonly known as

the Iron Guard, was probably the most unusual mass movement of interwar Europe. It is generally classified as fascist
because it met in varying ways the main criteria of any appropriate fascist typology, and yet it presented undeniably
individual characteristics of its own. The Legion was founded in 1927 by C. Z. Codreanu, who came originally from the
extreme religious, right-nationalist, and anti-Semitic background that produced the National Christian Party. Codreanu, however, moved in a more revolutionary direction, ap-
pealing to radical nationalist youth and the peasantry. Those
qualities were not unique; what made Codreanu distinctly
different was that he became a sort of religious mystic. The
Legionaries identified themselves totally with their own interpretation of Romanian Orthodoxy, and their ultimate goal
was not political but transcendental—national salvation for
the community of Romanian people (the Romanian "race" as
defined ultimately by tradition) and for each individual
member thereof. The Legionaries had little in the way of
program. Codreanu pointed out that a dozen different political programs already existed in Romania. He proclaimed the
need for a new spirit instead, a cultural-religious revolution
whose goal was the *Omul nou*—the "new man." The Legionaries pointed toward some sort of organic national authoritarian political system, but never defined it, and a more national and collective or communal basis for the economy,
while abhorring Marxism and materialist socialism. They engaged in small-scale collective enterprises of their own for
public works, cooperative shops and restaurants, and so
forth. Theirs was a kind of revolutionary alliance of students
and poor peasants, the more dynamic because during the
postwar decade enrollment in Romanian universities had increased a whopping 400 percent—proportionately more than
anywhere else in Europe[17]—creating a large new unemployed intelligentsia prone to radical nationalism. The move-

17. A. C. Janos, "The One-Party State and Social Mobilization: East Europe between the Wars," in S. P. Huntington and C. H. Moore, eds., *Authoritarian Politics in Modern Society* (New York, 1970), table 6–4, p. 211.

ment was sometimes violent in the extreme, but Legionary violence was in one sense qualitatively different from that of other radicals and revolutionaries in its stress on self-sacrifice, leading to veritable immolation reminiscent of the most moralistic and idealistic of the Russian Socialist Revolutionary assassins at the turn of the century. The crusading impulse was always strong among the most fervent fascists, and Ernst Nolte is correct in saying that in terms of single-minded fanaticism of commitment Codreanu was the other European nationalist leader most like Hitler (whom he also resembled in intense personal magnetism). It must be emphasized once more, however, that the Legionary martyr complex created a degree of self-destructiveness rarely equaled in other movements.[18]

In the last regular elections, the Legionaries garnered about 16.5 percent of the popular vote. Given the degree of electoral manipulation still practiced in Romania, this may have indicated popular support equal to the 20 percent or so received by the Arrow Cross in 1939. Yet access to power was completely blocked in Romania as in Hungary, for early in 1938 King Carol established the Romanian variant of the common conservative dictatorship of eastern and southern Europe of that period. Most of the Legionary leaders were massacred in cold blood, and Carol's henchmen tried to fascistize an essentially right-wing regime by forming a new

18. The best account of the Legion will be found in Nagy-Talavera, *Green Shirts*. Eugen Weber has written two important studies: "Romania," in Rogger and Weber, eds., *The European Right*, 501–74; and "The Men of the Archangel," *JCH* 1.1 (April 1966): 101–26. T. I. Armon emphasizes the incoherence of the movement in "La Guardia di Ferro," *SC* 7.3 (September 1976): 507–44. See also Z. Barbu, "Rumania," in Woolf, ed., *European Fascism*, 146–66; articles by Emanuel Turczynski and S. Fischer-Galati in P. F. Sugar, ed., *Native Fascism in the Successor States, 1918–1945* (Santa Barbara, 1971), 101–23; and Nolte, *Die Krise des liberalen Systems*, 212–26. Carlo Sburlati, *Codreanu el capitán* (Barcelona, 1970), is a recent hagiography. Codreanu's autobiographical *Pentru legionari* has been translated into several western languages (e.g., *Guardia de Hierro*, [Barcelona, 1976]). The best treatment of Romanian affairs in general during this period will be found in Henry L. Roberts, *Rumania* (New Haven, 1951).

youth movement, and in 1940, a Party of the Nation as government front. This was accompanied by a five-year national development program featuring increased state investment. Collapse of the Carolist regime in the late summer of 1940 was caused not so much by its lack of popular support as by German expansionism, which had begun to truncate the country geographically.

The army-based Antonescu dictatorship that followed tried to come to terms with the now decapitated Legion as the most popular nationalist movement, but lasting compromise was impossible. Civil war broke out in Bucharest early in 1941, the Legion was defeated and expelled from the government with Hitler's acquiescence. During the final years of Romanian independence the country was governed by rightist dictatorship under Antonescu.

It might also be observed that during the interwar period even the former ruling party, the National Liberals, moved toward a kind of corporatism and authoritarian nationalism. Their policies of "neoliberalism" formed in some respects a rough parallel to the rightward, authoritarian, and corporatist evolution of conservative liberals in such countries as Italy, Germany, and Spain.

In Mihail Manoilescu, Romania also produced probably Europe's leading theoretician of practical, developmental authoritarian corporatism during the 1930s. Director of the national bank and later economics minister and foreign minister of the right-wing Carolist dictatorship, Manoilescu propounded corporatism as the most useful program of integrated national economics for what would later be called "delayed developing nations," but had very limited opportunity to put his theories into practice.[19]

19. Manoilescu's main publications were *Théorie du protectionnisme et de l'échange international* (Paris, 1929); *L'Espace corporatif* (Paris, 1934); *Le Siècle du corporatisme* (Paris, 1936); and *Der einzige Partei* (Berlin, 1941). He did not use the word planning, and did not propose autarchy, but argued the efficacy of national corporatism for the integration of resources and for independent development, and aimed for import substitution (even at high individual costs) and for a balanced domestic productive structure.

OTHER BALKAN CASES

There were no fascist-type movements worthy of consideration in Greece, Bulgaria, and Yugoslavia, but one emerged later in Croatia during the war, thanks primarily to German conquest and the creation of a new Croatian satellite state. By the later 1930s, the common feature of Balkan government had become right-wing royalist dictatorship (Yugoslavia, 1929–39, Bulgaria, 1935–43, Greece, 1936–41, Romania, 1938–40). These regimes are usually described as conservative or reactionary, but, though right-wing, all but the Bulgarian tried to introduce significant new procedures, and all underwent some degree of outward fascistization. The main phase of pseudofascistization under the Yugoslav dictatorship came during the premiership of Milan Stojadinović (1935–38), who tried unsuccessfully to introduce some of the outward trappings of fascism by attempting to form a new state party on a mass basis and by introducing a new corporative economic development program. Only the royalist regime of "Tsar" Boris in Bulgaria largely resisted the trappings of fascism, aiming simply at a "regime without parties" that propounded no formal doctrine or new organization.

The only successful new mass movement in these countries after World War I, and that but momentarily, was Alex-

---

Manoilescu drew a distinction between corporatism and fascism, defining the latter as an Italian phenomenon and the former as integration and representation of all the social, economic, and cultural forces of a given country, with all their national differences. Corporatism would be "totalitarian" in his lexicon, because it would include all social and economic forces, but would not be centralized or despotic because it would permit limited pluralism and decentralized autonomy within specific delimited spheres. This was the substance of what he called "pure corporatism" as distinct from Mussolini's "state" or "subordinate" corporatism. However, Mussolini and Hitler were viewed in his last work as differing aspects of modern national political and economic developmentalism, combining "Rousseau, Danton and Napoleon." The only worthwhile study is P. C. Schmitter, "Reflections on Mihail Manoilescu," in K. Jowitt, ed., *Social Change in Romania, 1860–1940* (Berkeley, 1978), 117–39.

ander Stamboliski's Bulgarian Agrarian Union, an essentially democratic peasant reform party that governed Bulgaria from 1920 to 1923.[20] The Agrarians, too, had a party militia, the Orange Guard, but so did the Bulgarian left-wing parties.

Various formally fascist or Nazi-like parties were organized in the three countries, several calling themselves national socialist but failing to achieve support. Only slightly less insignificant was the Zbor movement of Ljotic in Serbia, Dr Tsankov's Social National Party in Bulgaria during the thirties, and the later Ratnitsi (Warriors) and Legionnaire movement of Gernal Lukov in Bulgaria by the end of the decade.[21] The absence of significant fascist movements in Greece and Bulgaria is in some respects something of a mystery, for Bulgaria was one of the major losers of World War I, and Greece encountered national disaster in the war with Turkey in 1920–23. Both faced severe economic problems as well, and normally lacked stable and effective government. Absence of leadership is one explanation for the weakness of fascistic parties, but convincing explanations have not yet been developed.

Before the war, the major figure in authoritarian nationalism in the south Balkans was General Metaxas, who served as dictator of Greece under the crown from mid-1936 to 1941. He was, however, more a figure of the radical authoritarian right than a fascist revolutionary, for his only political group had been an extreme right-wing monarchist party and in power he founded no new mass movement of his own. Metaxas looked to the past more than to the future, and sought to promote a new ethnicism and nationalist culture that he called Hellenism. He proposed no drastic changes in Greece other than political and cultural ones, but did admire some

20. John D. Bell, *Peasants in Power* (Princeton, 1977).

21. See M. L. Miller, *Bulgaria during the Second World War* (Stanford, 1975); Nolte, *Die Krise des liberalen Systems,* 194–200; and articles by Dimitrije Djordjevic and Ivan Avakumovic in Sugar, ed., *Native Fascism,* 125–43.

aspects of the Italian and German regimes. Therefore a few trappings of fascism were brought in, but strictly in the conventional form of a youth movement, etc.

Metaxas employed the term *totalitarian* but gave it little institutional content beyond a general concept of national coordination under a political dictatorship. He aimed at a corporate system of economic regulation, and worked particularly to improve the financial situation of the peasantry. Various trappings, such as the Fascist salute and the emblem of the Cretan double axe (rather like the fasces) were used for the youth movement, but he failed to develop a radical and institutionalized system, lacked ambition in foreign affairs, and based his new philosophy heavily on tradition and religion. Metaxas obviously resembled Franco much more than Hitler or Mussolini.[22]

CZECHOSLOVAKIA

The major qualification normally applied to Czechoslovakia in discussions of interwar Europe is that it was the only functional democracy east of Germany. Even though both the government and economy of the country were Czech-dominated, this qualification remains formally correct. Since Germany's was the only democratic system to succumb to a fascist-type movement after Italy, little support for such movements might have been expected in Czechoslovakia, and this was indeed the case. There were two overtly fascistic Czech parties, the National Fascist Community (NOF, organized in

22. There is little material, other than Greek, on Metaxas. See Harry Cliadakis, "Greece, 1935–1941" (Ph.D. diss., New York University, 1970). Paul Hayes emphasizes the merely fascistized but less than generically fascist character of Metaxas in his *Fascism* (London, 1973), 177–89. Conversely, Cliadakis, in "Le Régime de Metaxas et la Deuxième Guerre Mondiale," (*Revue d'Histoire de la 2e Guerre Mondiale*, no. 107 [1977], pp. 19–38), argues the intrinsically fascist nature of the regime, but uses a very broad definition of fascism that might apply to diverse types of authoritarian anti-Marxist nationalism.

1926), and the Czech National Socialist Camp (Vlajka), which developed in the 1930s. In an urban, industrial setting of modern parliamentary democracy where the workers clung to socialism and most of the middle classes to variants of liberalism, these two small derivative groups had no opportunity to flourish.[23]

Much more significant was the partial fascistization of the Slovak People's Party, the principal political force in Slovakia throughout this period. It eventually became the beneficiary of Hitler's destruction of the Czech state and the creation of a separate satellite Slovakia. The Slovak People's Party was originally a moderate conservative and somewhat authoritarian Catholic populist-nationalist party oriented toward corporatism, and it never lost this primary coloring, although it was to some extent influenced by Nazification after 1938.[24]

POLAND AND THE BALTIC STATES

Like all other parts of southern and eastern Europe, Poland and the Baltic states came to be controlled by right authoritarian governments. More categorically fascist movements, of which there were a number in this area, tended to be quite weak, though the Polish regime's effort from 1936 to 1939 to

23. In English, there is an unpublished paper by Joseph F. Zacek, "The Flaw in Masaryk's Democracy: Czech Fascism, 1927–1942." (Needless to say, "fascism" was scarcely the main flow in Masaryk's democracy.) There are Czech contributions in the symposium *Fašismus a Europa* (Prague, 1969). On other extreme nationalists in Czechoslovakia, see Bedrich Lowenstein, "Il radicalismo di destra in Cecoslovacchia e la prima guerra mondiale," *SC* 1.3 (September 1970): 503–28; and Peter Burian, "Demokratie und Parlamentarismus in der Ersten Tschechoslowakischen Republik," in H.-E. Volkmann, ed., *Die Krise des Parlamentarismus in Ostmitteleuropa zwischen dem beiden Weltkriegen* (Marburg/Lahn, 1967), 85–132.

24. See primarily Yeshayahu Jelinek, *The Parish Republic: Hlinka's Slovak People's Party, 1939–1945* (Boulder/New York, 1976), and "Stormtroopers in Slovakia: The Rodobrana and the Hlinka Guard," *JCH* 6.3 (July 1971): 97–119; and also Jorge K. Hensch, *Die Slowakei und Hitlers Ostpolitik* (Köln/Graz, 1965).

set up a protofascist state party, the OZN, was pressed farther than similar efforts in the Balkan countries.

Though the Pilsudski coup d'etat of 1926, which set up the
authoritarian system in interwar Poland, was much blood-
ier[25] than the March on Rome four years earlier, Pilsudski
himself denied any ambition to create a thoroughly repressive state. The more serious students of his regime tend to
agree that it was a conservative and moderate semipluralist
system more like that of Dollfuss and Schuschnigg or Primo
de Rivera in Spain than like Mussolini's Italy.[26] The government political front (BBWR) organized in 1928 resembled
Primo de Rivera's Unión Patriótica or the Austrian Fatherland Front more than a fascist organization.

A more radical role in some respects was played by the
National Democrat (later simply National) Party of western
Poland. A mass electoral party, the National Democrats were
intensely anti-Semitic and demanded a more repressive policy against other national minorities. They tended to admire
Mussolini's Italy, like other proauthoritarian Catholic groups
of eastern Europe, but were later also somewhat influenced
by Nazi racism. Such tendencies, however, came out more
strongly among the radical National Democrat youth, who in
the 1930s split off as National Radicals and in turn gave birth
to two more explicitly fascist-like organizations, ABC and Falanga.

Falanga was probably the only clear-cut fascistic party in
Poland in the late 1930s. Its name was derived from Spanish
Falangism, but its Catholicism was more extreme than that of
its Spanish counterpart, as Falanga insisted that "God is the
highest end of man,"[27] a statement more appropriate for
Codreanu than for José Antonio Primo de Rivera. The other
unique feature of Falanga was its eventual insistence on the

25. See J. Rothschild, *Pilsudski's Coup d'Etat* (New York, 1966).
26. Compare the remarks of Frantiszek Ryszka and Jerzy Borejsza in Borejsza's "Italian Fascism and East-Central Europe, 1922–1943," in Larsen et
al., eds., *Who Were the Fascists?*.
27. E. D. Wynot, Jr., *Polish Politics in Transition: The Camp of National Unity
and the Struggle for Power, 1935–1939* (Athens, Ga., 1974), 88.

elimination of the private sector of the economy in favor of some sort of national socialism.[28]

A fundamental change in Polish government occurred with the new corporative/authoritarian constitution of 1935 and the death of Pilsudski that same year. The constitution reduced the sphere of tolerated pluralism and served as a source of some inspiration to corporative authoritarians in certain other Catholic countries, such as Brazil. Pilsudski's successors—the Colonels—realized that they would need a stronger, more mobilized organization than the defunct BBWR. The result was OZN, the Camp of National Unity, Poland's variant of bureaucratic state protofascism. Colonel Koc, its first director, came to rely disproportionately on Boleslaw Piasecki, head of Falanga, and the revolutionary totalitarian implications of this relationship led to Koc's ouster and the severing of the Falanga connection. The phrase *directed democracy* was sometimes used to describe the new system, but in fact by 1939 the new directors of OZN were pressing forward with plans for a mobilized state organization and a controlled one-party system. The political logic of a state between Nazi Germany and Communist Russia seemed inescapable to the Polish leaders, and only the outbreak of war seems to have prevented the development of a more repressive and integrated one-party system.[29]

Finally, it might be noted that, as in the case of other multinational states such as Yugoslavia and Spain, the Polish regime had to face a kind of minority-nationality "national liberation" group that had many of the qualities of fascism, the Organization of Ukrainian Nationalists, partially nazified during the 1930s.

The situations of the three Baltic states formed partial parallels. A moderate rightist dictatorship was established by military coup in Lithuania at the close of 1926, after major

28. This helps to explain why Falanga's leader, Boleslaw Piasecki (who in 1938 liked to be called "Il Duce"), could after 1945 be used as a major ally by the Communists for a kind of Catholic socialism. See Lucjan Blit, *The Eastern Pretender* (London, 1965).

29. The principal study is Wynot, *Polish Politics in Transition*.

gains by the left in domestic elections and the signing of a new treaty with the Soviet Union. The dominant figure under the new regime was President Antanas Smetona, who remained chief of state until the disappearance of Lithuania in 1940. He distinguished between corporatism and salutary authoritarianism on the one hand and totalitarianism on the other. Some degree of pluralism was retained in subsequent constitutions, but the major political force was the Tautininkai (National Union), a right radical group resting on the intelligentsia and the more prosperous peasants. It assumed a more prominent place in the late 1930s, and the system seemed to be moving toward a one-party regime in the final year of its existence.[30]

By contrast, the moderate regimes of what Georg von Rauch calls "authoritarian democracy" in Latvia and Estonia were instituted simply as preventive authoritarianism in 1934 by the moderate forces. Konstantin Päts, leader of the Farmers Party in Estonia, established a more authoritarian government mainly to check the influence of the right-radical Veterans' League (technically, The Association of Estonian Freedom Fighters), while in Latvia the new Ulmanis government was aimed against both the Communists and the Thunder Cross, a vigorous new Latvian fascist-type party influenced by Nazism (though politically strongly anti-German).

Both the Latvian and Estonian regimes tried to maintain pluralism and considerable moderation. In terms of foreign models they thought of Austria and the Italy of the early 1930s. The Estonian regime did create a political front, the National Association, but in neither case did a rigidly institutionalized dictatorship develop.[31] Their main achievement was to maintain a remarkably positive rate of economic growth in the late 1930s.

30. See Leonas Sabaliunas, *Lithuania, 1939–1940* (Bloomington, Ind., 1972); and Georg von Rauch, *The Baltic States* (Berkeley, 1974), 119–20, 161–65.

31. Von Rauch, *Baltic States*, 146–61; Tönü Parming, *The Collapse of Liberal Democracy and the Rise of Authoritarianism in Estonia* (London/Beverly Hills, 1975); Jurgen von Hehn, *Lettland zwischen Demokratie und Diktatur* (Munich, 1957).

THE NORTH EUROPEAN DEMOCRACIES

The activity of Fascist and Nazi-type parties in the north-European democracies is of interest primarily to those concerned with negative findings. None of the north-European parties ever mobilized more than 2 percent of the popular vote, with the two limited and short-lived exceptions of the Finnish IKL in 1936 and the Dutch National Socialists in 1935 and 1937. Moreover, no north-European party of this type ever found influential allies in other political sectors.

The insignificance of north-European fascistic or would-be fascistic parties is in no way surprising, since nearly all the conditions listed by most analysts as likely prerequisites for the emergence of fascist politics were lacking in northern Europe. None of the northern democracies except Ireland faced significant problems of nationalism, ethnicity, or international status. All save Ireland were highly educated, prosperous, economically developed, and socially balanced and enjoyed established modern political cultures and parliamentary constitutional traditions. There was neither space nor "need" for revolutionary nationalism.[32]

32. For a brief discussion, see my "Fascism in Western Europe," in Laqueur, ed., *Fascism: A Reader's Guide*, 295–311. The literature on fascist-type parties and movements in the north-European democracies is almost more extensive than the topic warrants. The most notorious of these groups was Vidkun Quisling's Nasjonal Samling (National Unification) in Norway, primarily because of his role under German occupation. The Nasjonal Samling's 2.16 percent of the popular vote in the 1933 elections was its high-water mark as an autonomous force. Paul M. Hayes, *Quisling* (London, 1971), is the best biography. See also Hans-Dietrich Loock, *Quisling, Rosenberg und Terboven* (Stuttgart, 1970); A. S. Milward, *The Fascist Economy in Norway* (Oxford, 1972); O. K. Hidal, "Vidkun Quisling's Decline as a Political Figure in Prewar Norway, 1933–1937," *JMH* 43.3 (September 1971): 440–67; and the much less satisfactory *Quisling* (London, 1965) by Ralph Hewins. The social basis of the Nasjonal Samling is systematically studied in the work of Stein U. Larsen, J. P. Myklebust, and others in Larsen et al., eds., *Who Were the Fascists?* References to further works in Scandinavian languages on the Nazi-type parties in Norway, Sweden, and Denmark may be found in the notes to my article cited above.

The most thorough biography of Sir Oswald Mosley, leader of the insignificant British Union of Fascists, is Robert Skidelsky's *Oswald Mosley*

The most significant partial exception is the case of Finland in the 1930s, a case explained by the aftermath of revolutionary civil war (more severe in Finland than in the better-known case of Hungary in 1919), the proximity and threat of the Soviet Union, and the existence of genuine Finnish irredentism, eastern Karelia having been retained by the Soviet Union in the 1920s. After the victory of the Whites in the Finnish civil war, Finnish traditions, institutions, and society rather easily supported the development of a fairly model parliamentary constitutionalism. The radical right in Finnish politics during the 1920s was represented by the Academic Karelia Society (AKS), which propounded doctrines of Finnish hybrid racism, military expansion into the greater Finnish east, and a more elitist, hierarchical, authoritarian government. It had considerable influence among the educated young but remained technically what its name indicated, a merely "academic" society with only a few thousand members.

A more revolutionary and fascistic kind of nationalism emerged after 1929 in the form of the Lapua movement, named for a small town that had been the target of an anti-communist uprising that year. An abortive effort to seize the government in 1932 led to the outlawing of the Lapua movement, but it was reorganized as the People's Patriotic Movement (IKL), which stood for a drastic corporative reorganization of social and economic structure to achieve a new Finnish "people's community." The influence of Hitlerism by this time was obvious, and the IKL drew 8.3 percent of the popular vote in the 1936 elections. Yet that was its highwater

---

(London, 1975). Earlier works are Colin Cross, *The Fascists in Britain* (New York, 1963); Robert Benewick, *Political Violence and Public Order: A Study of British Fascism* (London, 1969); and W. F. Mandle, *Anti-Semitism and the British Union of Fascists* (London, 1968). Maurice Manning, *The Blueshirts* (Dublin, 1970), which deals with the only possible Irish counterpart, reveals that the Blueshirts could scarecely be defined as representatives of a generic fascism.

On what little there was of a Swiss fascism, see Beat Glaus, *Die Nationale Front* (Einsiedeln, 1969); and W. Wolf, *Faschismus in der Schweiz* (Zurich, 1969).

mark, for consensus did exist in Finnish society in support of democratic parliamentary institutions, and the country was also more successful in dealing with the economic depression than were many others in Europe. The appearance of a revolutionary fascist threat led to a parliamentary closing of the ranks and a strengthening of the system once more, as in Belgium, and the IKL vote declined somewhat in the last prewar elections of 1939.[33]

A minor statistical exception to the approximate "2 percent rule" as the limit of public support for Fascist- or Nazi-like parties in north-European democracies might also technically be observed in the case of Holland, where Anton Mussert's National Socialist Movement of the Netherlands (NSB) drew 7.9 percent of the national vote in the provincial elections of 1935 and 4.2 percent in the parliamentary elections of 1937. The NSB lost most of its support in the final provincial elections of 1939, however, so that the experience seems to have been a momentary politico-statistical aberration.

Despite its title, the NSB was much more a Fascist- than Nazi-style party. It proposed a corporate system rather similar to Italy's instead of a *Volksgemeinschaft,* and upheld freedom of religion as part of Dutch national principle. It was not merely not officially anti-Semitic (though there was a radical Nazi wing) but even accepted Jewish members—in other words, a very Dutch kind of national socialism.[34] (There was also a minuscule National Socialist Dutch Workers' Party, but it was so radical, alien, and mimetic that it failed to attract support.)

33. The literature in western languages is scant. See Marvin Rintala, *Three Generations: The Extreme Right Wing in Finnish Politics* (Bloomington, Ind. 1962), and "Finland," in Rogger and Weber, eds., *The European Right,* 408–42; and A. K. Upton, "Finland," in Woolf, ed., *European Fascism,* 184–216. References in Finnish may be found in my article cited in the preceding footnote.

34. There is a brief summary in Werner Warmbrunn, *The Dutch under German Occupation* (Stanford, 1963), 83–96; in Dutch, see G. A. Kooy, *Het echec van een "volkse" Beweging* (Assen, 1964); and A. A. de Jonge, *Het national-socialisme in Nederland* (The Hague, 1968).

FRANCE AND BELGIUM

The French-speaking countries also seem to present certain exceptions to the generalization about fascism's lack of appeal in the north-European democracies, but again the exceptions are partial and limited rather than fully developed and clear-cut. Despite the pullulation of putatively fascist leagues and parties in France, no exceptions to the "2 percent rule" may be found in that country, for none of the French groups got themselves together sufficiently to break into the electoral system. Moreover, France is after all not a "north-European democracy" in terms of its institutional stability and unswerving devotion to liberal constitutional process. It shares many of the characteristics of the south-European polity in terms of repressive centralization, revolutionary rather than evolutionary patterns of change, radical adversary intelligentsia cultures, class antagonisms, and sectarian or status-seeking splinter politics. Since France has had one of the most advanced economies and highest standards of living in the world since the eleventh century, the explanations for this state of affairs presumably lie more in the realm of culture and institutions than in socioeconomic determinism. Conversely, Belgium has indeed functioned in almost every respect as a model democracy of the north-European type since the country's emergence in 1830. The main discord in Belgium stems from the ethnic division that colors much of the country's politics and is probably the primary explanation for political dissidence of the 1930s.

Zeev Sternhell has conclusively demonstrated that nearly all the ideas found in fascism and nazism first appeared in France.[35] The fusion of radical nationalism with revolutionary and collectivist or semicollectivist socioeconomic aspirations first occurred there, and in parallel fashion France was the first major country in which the main revolutionary left overtly rejected parliamentarianism while supporting a kind

35. In *La Droite révolutionnaire* and other works by Sternhell cited in chapter 2.

of nationalism. Similarly the effects of the cultural and intellectual revolution of the 1890s extended farther in France than in any other country outside the greater German and Italian cultural areas. What of course was different was simply the general situation of France compared with countries in central and eastern Europe. France was one of the oldest and always most successful of national states, a victor in World War I, a prosperous and in general socially balanced country, and one of the two dominant imperial powers in the western world. There was obviously little need or room for revolutionary nationalism.

French fascists moved toward a kind of fascism from both the right and left, but more from the latter direction, paralleling the founding Fascists of Italy (or England, for that matter). Since the main French force of the radical right, Action Française, was essentially reactionary and also profoundly nonactivist, as well as little interested in social issues or mobilization, the imitation of fascism was first essayed by Georges Valois, a young militant who left Action Française to create a modern, mobilizing revolutionary nationalist movement. His Le Faisceau, founded in 1925, may have enrolled nearly 50,000 members during the following year before going into decline. Valois's formula that "nationalism plus socialism equals fascism" was simplistic but not entirely inaccurate. His goal was to wed French syndicalism with nationalism and build a novel kind of radical movement, but his success was brief. On the one hand, he could not recruit among a well-organized left, and on the other, space was closed off by the success of French conservatism and new radical right groups.[36]

In general, right-wing authoritarian nationalism was far more popular in France than fascism. The temporary growth of the Faisceau was considerably exceeded by that of a new right radical youth movement, the Jeunesses Patriotes of

36. The best study again is by Zeev Sternhell, "Anatomie d'un mouvement fasciste: Le Faisceau de Georges Valois," *Revue française de science politique* 26.1 (February 1976): 5–40.

Pierre Taittinger. The latter were a direct outgrowth of the old Derouledist League of Patriots, whose residues survived into the 1920s, and like the Valois party, were momentarily stimulated by the leftist victory of the Cartel des Gauches in the 1924 French elections. By the same token, they declined after the moderate conservative victory in 1928. The Jeunesses were subsequently outstripped by two new rightist movements, the Solidarité Française and the Croix de Feu. Police estimates of uncertain reliability placed the following of the Solidarité Française (organized in 1933) as high as a quarter of a million in 1934, before it too went into decline.

The largest of all the new nationalist movements in interwar France was Colonel de la Rocque's Croix de Feu. Though again no reliable figures are available, it became one of the largest political forces in France during the prewar decade. The Croix de Feu seem to have drawn more extensive support from big business and finance than the other groups, for some sectors of French big business looked upon it as the vehicle for the imposition of a kind of technocratic authoritarian system.[37]

It was these rightist "leagues," financed by big business and based on the middle classes, that created the "fascist scare" in France at the time of the February 1934 riots in Paris. The result of the scare was to magnify French antifascism, which had been vocal and organized ever since 1923, before any fascist or even any new right authoritarian force existed in France. "Thus after February 6, 1934, antifascism became the dominant political fact in France, a thousand times more important than fascism."[38] This was a major element in the electoral victory of the Popular Front in 1936, which then ordered legal dissolution of the rightist leagues. The only really important one, the Croix de Feu, reorganized itself as the Parti Social Français, but this reconstitution as a

37. Klaus-Jürgen Muller, "French Fascism and Modernization," *JCH* 11.4 (October 1976): 75–107.
38. Jean Plumyène and Raymond Lasierra, *Les Fascismes français 1923–1963* (Paris, 1963), 42.

political party occurred too late to participate in the final parliamentary elections before the war.[39]

Only three new specifically fascistic parties emerged in the 1930s, and then weakly or equivocally. The first were the Francistes of Marcel Bucard, organized in 1933, in part from a tiny nucleus left over by an abortive French national socialist party organized after World War I by Gustave Hervé. They were later subsidized by Mussolini and seem to have been the most direct and instransigent fascist group in France,[40] which may help to explain their almost complete lack of support.

More significant was the neosocialism of Marcel Déat and the multiclass national socialism of Jacques Doriot. In the early 1930s Déat was a rising star in the French Socialist Party and Doriot the most popular and dynamic young leader in French Communism. Their situations were thus remarkably similar to those of Mussolini in Italian socialism in 1912 or Sir Oswald Mosley, subsequent leader of British fascism, in the Labour Party of the late 1920s. Déat broke with orthodox French Marxian socialism in the early 1930s over the issues of nationalism, economic modernization, and class sectarianism. He held that the road to well-being and development lay

39. The most extensive survey of all the French fascistic and right radical groups of the interwar is Plumyène and Lasierra, *Fascismes français*. See also Eugen Weber, "France," in Rogger and Webber, eds., *The European Right*, 71–127; René Rémond, *The Right Wing in France* (Philadelphia, 1966); Philippe Bourdrel, *La Cagoule* (Paris, 1970); Raoul Girardet, "Notes sur l'esprit d'un fascisme français 1934–1939," *Revue française de science politique*, no. 5 (1955), pp. 529–46; Zeev Sternhell, "Some Aspects of French Fascism," in Larsen et al., eds., *Who Were the Fascists?*; and a number of articles by Robert Soucy: "The Nature of Fascism in France," *JCH* 1.1 (April 1966): 27–55; "French Fascism as Class Conciliation and Moral Regeneration," *Societas* 1.4 (Autumn 1971): 287–97; "French Fascist Intellectuals in the 1930s," *French Historical Studies* 8.3 (Spring 1974): 445–58; and "France," in S. R. Ward, ed., *The War Generation* (Port Washington, N.Y., 1975), 59–103. Philippe Rudaux, *Les Croix de Feu et le P.S.F.* (Paris, 1967), is a sympathetic account by a former member.

40. Or such is the opinion of some commentators. The *Sommaire* issued by the party from time to time presented a recognizably fascist type of program but was not remarkable in any way.

through organized national planning and the integration of all productive forces, class socialism being both politically self-defeating in France and economically nonfunctional. His Socialist Party of France (1934) was not fascist but simply nationalist and directed toward class collaboration and integrated, planned economic growth. For a time it carried with it a significant minority of Socialist deputies in the chamber and nearly one-fifth of the regular party members. Only during the German occupation did Déat fully espouse a kind of genuine fascism. His Rassemblement National Populaire (1941) formed the extreme left of wartime French fascism and collaboration.[41]

The situation of Doriot was at least equally complex. By 1935 he had broken with Communism largely over the issues of Stalinism and Russian domination. The Parti Populaire Français (PPF) that he subsequently founded was organized too late to participate in the last French prewar elections of 1936, but carried a significant minority of French Communist militants with it and grew rapidly. Though the membership of nearly 300,000 that it claimed early in 1938 was several times the real figure, the PPF became far and away the largest of the French fascist groups. This momentary success was not, however, unrelated to the fact that the PPF required several years to transform itself into a fully fascist-type organization, a process that was probably completed only under the German occupation. Like Déat's new group, it occupied a kind of halfway house between economic socialism and nationalistic class collaboration, without accepting all the prin-

---

41. Déat's transition from orthodox socialism is studied in Stanley Grossman, "Neo-Socialism: A Study in Political Metamorphosis," (Ph.D. diss., University of Wisconsin, 1969).

There was considerable congruence between the economic ideas of Déat and those of the Belgian Labor Party leader Hendrik de Man, who collaborated with the German occupation but did not become a fascist by the definition employed in this study. On De Man, see Peter Dodge, *Beyond Marxism: The Faith and Works of Hendrik de Man* (The Hague, 1966); and Erik von S. Hansen, *Hendrik de Man and the Crisis in European Socialism, 1926–1936* (Ithaca, 1968).

ciples of fascist culture and politics. After Munich and with the growth of international tensions, support for the still ambiguous PPF seems to have declined rapidly.[42] It is a measure of the relative strength and consensus behind the Third Republic that at various times both French Communists and the increasingly fascistic converts of the PPF proclaimed their defense of republican constitutional institutions against each other.

More problematic would seem to be the case of Belgium, where two reputedly fascistic movements, Christus Rex and the VNV (Flemish National Federation), gained 11.49 and 7.12 percent respectively of the popular vote in the 1936 parliamentary elections, for a combined vote of 18.61. The main qualification in the case of Belgium is that neither Rex nor the VNV could be accurately described as categorically fascist in 1936. The VNV was supported by Flemish nationalists of varying doctrinal persuasions. Some of its leaders and militants were indeed fascistic in inclination, others relatively democratic, and the official line uncertain. Léon Degrelle's Rexist movement was originated by radical Catholic youth, and its original goals were a corporative Catholic reform of Belgian government that initially rejected overt authoritarianism and even proposed to introduce a limited form of women's suffrage. Only after the 1936 elections, and particularly in 1938, did Degrelle and the VNV leader, Staf de Clercq, align their policies and programs directly with fascist politics. In the process, Degrelle lost most of his support.

---

42. The authoritative study is Dieter Wolf, *Die Doriot-Bewegung* (Stuttgart, 1967). See also Gilbert Allardyce, "The Political Transition of Jacques Doriot," *JCH* 1.1 (January 1966): 56–74; and Allardyce's Ph.D. dissertation by the same title (University of Iowa, 1966).

The PPF was the party that gained the support of the main group of French fascist intellectuals (Drieu la Rochelle, Brasillach, etc.), who have attracted much attention from historians. Cf., *inter alia*, Paul Sérant, *Le Romantisme fasciste* (Paris, 1959); Tarmo Kunnas, *Drieu la Rochelle, Céline, Brasillach et la tentation fasciste* (Paris, 1972); Jacqueline Morand, *Les Idées politiques de Louis-Ferdinand Céline* (Paris, 1972); and W. R. Tucker, *The Fascist Ego* (Berkeley, 1975).

Eight of the twenty-one parliamentary deputies of Rex resigned from the movement in protest before the next elections in 1939. Whereas Degrelle had gained 19 percent of the
vote in the presidential elections of 1937, his movement
dropped to 4.43 in the 1939 contest; the VNV, relying on
Flemish nationalism, gained a total of 8.27 percent. In the
case of both groups, as in those of Déat and Doriot, the transition to a completely fascist position was not made until after 1940.[43]

WARTIME COLLABORATORS AND SATELLITES

Movements and regimes that took on a fascist or semifascist
form as collaborators or satellites of Germany during the war
form a different grouping. Nazification or Nazi collaboration
after 1939 as a result of German conquest was primarily a
circumstantial affair, not a development of indigenous political forces. German occupation completed the fascistization of
forces already tending toward some form of fascism, as in

43. The only general treatment of the Belgian movements is an unpublished doctoral dissertation by Ronald Chertok, "Belgian Fascism" (Washington
University, 1975), which employs an extremely flexible definition of fascism.
The best study of the early years of Rex is Jean-Michel Etienne, *Le Mouvement
rexiste jusqu'en 1940* (Paris, 1968), which concludes that Rex could not be
characterized as categorically fascist in the early period. See also the articles
by Luc Schepens and Daniele Wallef in Larsen et al., eds., *Who Were the
Fascists?*; and Jean Stengers, "Belgium," in Rogger and Weber, eds., *The European Right*, 128–67.

A more convincing candidate for an early Belgian fascism would have
been the small Légion Nationale, organized of veterans in the 1920s. It exhibited most of the characteristics of generic fascism, but failed to generate
support. Yet another was Joris Van Severen's Verdinaso (which stood, approximately, for Federation of Low Countries' National Solidarity), sometimes described as the most directly fascist movement in Belgium. Verdinaso was a clear-cut movement of political authoritarianism, but it is very
doubtful that it could be described as categorically fascist. Van Severen
stood for hierarchy, aristocracy, morality, and a cultural revolution that
would bind together Holland, Belgium, and Luxemburg. Though he paid
some lip service to Mussolini, his main inspirations were Maurras and to
some degree Salazar. Cf. R. Baes, *Joris Van Severen* (Antwerp, 1961).

France and Belgium, though few foreign fascists or fascisti-zers deliberately worked as fifth-column agents to sabotage their country's war effort *before* German conquest. Fascism after all is extreme nationalism, and postconquest collabora-tors functioned as "patriotic traitors," with the exception of one or two like Quisling who assisted the foreign conquest and offered a new name for national ignominy. Yet only Pol-ish fascists continued to resist the Germans for some time after conquest; in general the allure of Nazification became too great to resist.

In most cases, nonetheless, Hitler found it more satisfac-tory to deal with conservative right-wing authoritarians as satellites, for they were more compliant and less challenging. Even in the conquered lands he was reluctant to hand limited power to a Quisling or a Mussert as head of occupation gov-ernment, and so in general the domestic fascists and nazis of conquered lands derived less advantage from the German conquest than might have been thought. The most favored were those like Degrelle who largely abandoned national pol-itics to devote themselves to the Waffen SS.[44]

The first satellite government to emerge, that of auton-omous Slovakia, remained a Catholic right authoritarian system with a limited semipluralism, though under one-par-ty government. Hitler vetoed a fully corporate *Schuschniggiade*

44. The most complete catalog of collaborationist and nazified groups in western occupied Europe is David Littlejohn, *The Patriotic Traitors* (London, 1972). See also Norman Rich, *Hitler's War Aims* (New York, 1974), vol. 2 *The Establishment of the New Order*. Special numbers on "occupation fascism" and the satellites have appeared in *La Revue d'Histoire de la 2me Guerre Mondiale,* nos. 56 ("Vichy et la jeunesse"), 62 ("La Hongrie dans la 2me Guerre Mon-diale"), 66 '(Sur le fascisme"), and 70 ("Sur la Roumanie en guerre"). Two key economic studies are Alan Milward's *The New Order and the French Econo-my* (London, 1970); and *The Fascist Economy in Norway* (London, 1972). John Armstrong, "Collaborationism in World War II: The Integral Nationalist Variant in Eastern Europe" (*JMH* 40.3 [September 1968]: 396–410), views the Slovak People's Party, the Ustashi, and the Organization of Ukrainian Na-tionalists as integral nationalists rather than generically fascist. The last days of the Arrow Cross regime in Budapest receive some attention in Peter Goz-tony, *Endkampf an der Donau* (Vienna, 1969).

based on the former Austrian system (of Dollfuss and Schuschnigg) on the one hand, and the main leaders of the Slovak People's Party resisted direct Nazification on the other. The second satellite, Antonescu's Romanian regime, was initiated in 1940 as a "Legionnaire state" formed as a coalition of the army and Iron Guard. When it broke down early in 1941, Hitler did nothing to prevent the complete suppression of the Legionnaires by Antonescu's army.

The most important satellite was Vichy France, because it governed the most advanced country. Pétain's regime was distinctly rightist and authoritarian but never fascist. Even the relatively moderate Parti Social Français (formerly Croix de Feu), with its 350,000 members perhaps the largest political movement in France, was dissolved, and soon nearly all overt French fascists were concentrated in the northern German-occupied zone. Vichy had no party and no fully unified ideology. Its "national revolution" was by no means merely a reactionary hoax, as it is often made out to be, for the wartime regime seriously promoted corporative regulation, reorganization, and limited aspects of technocracy, some of which survived into the Fourth and Fifth Republics.[45]

By far the most radical satellite regime was the Croatian Ustasha state. Beginning in the 1920s as the radical youth wing of extreme Croatian nationalism, the Ustashi ("Insur-

45. The literature on Vichy France is extensive; the best one-volume synthesis is R. O. Paxton, *Vichy France* (New York, 1972). Roger Bourderon in "Was the Vichy Regime Fascist?" (reprinted in John Cairns, ed., *Contemporary France* [New York, 1978], 200–27) argues that the answer is yes, citing the degree of authoritarian rule, ideological coincidences of the Vichy "new order," state economic controls, the growing stringency of police power, and the final radicalization of Vichy under German domination. Yet his argument seems to me to exaggerate and to blur distinctions. There was no genuine state party under Vichy, and economic regulations were more nearly technocratic than fully statist. Major aspects of Vichy's "new order" blended Catholicism and even progressivist republican corporatism in greater measure than direct Nazi or Fascist ideas. Also, a more German-controlled late Vichy should be distinguished from the earlier autonomous Vichy.

The real French fascists presented their wartime programs in Déat's *Le Parti unique* (Paris, 1942) and Doriot's *Refaire la France* (Paris, 1944).

gents") came increasingly under Nazi racist and ideological influence in the late 1930s. During the years 1941–44 they embarked upon a program of genocide against Orthodox Serbs, a program of truly Hitlerian proportions, given the size of Croatia and the means at their disposal. In this sense the Ustasha state was the most Nazified of all satellite regimes, and yet in their internal structure and policy even the Ustashi leader Pavelić did not impose an unalloyed one-party totalitarian system, for some compromises had to be made with the Catholic church and with peasant Catholic opinion.[46]

All the satellite groups and regimes drew on tendencies and initiatives endemic to their own countries, antedating the German conquest, yet none could be said to have been autonomous and spontaneous, with the possible exception of the Slovak regime. They were all primarily if not exclusively creatures of Nazi expansion, and their history is essentially a phenomenon of Hitler's Europe rather than of the genuine political evolution of their own lands. Though much more diversified and much less institutionalized than the subsequent People's Democracies of eastern Europe, they were similarly products of imperial conquest and hegemony.

46. The only study, though inadequate to the topic, is Martin Broszat and Ladislas Hory, *Der kroatische Ustascha Staat, 1941–1945* (Stuttgart, 1964).

6
Post-fascist Survivals: Spain and Portugal

The long-lived Spanish and Portuguese dictatorships, which survived until 1974–75, have constituted another problem for students of generic fascism and the national authoritarian states of Europe. Though fairly typical products of the new politics of the fascist era (or in the case of the Portuguese Estado Novo, technically antedating the main period of fascism), they survived its termination by three decades, and in the process had to make some fundamental adjustments to the postwar communist and social democratic period of European history.

Most rigorous analysts do not claim that either the Franco or the Salazar regimes were ever fully or even intrinsically fascist, and some deny that they had anything to do with fascism at all. A major fascist-type component in the Franco regime during its first decade seems fairly obvious, however, and indicates that the Spanish case is complicated.

Both Spain and Portugal were among the first countries to introduce more authoritarian forms of government in the twentieth century. Portugal, in fact, led the way, beginning

139

with the royalist semidictatorship of João Franco in 1907–8, the extraparliamentary government of General Pimenta de Castro in 1915, and the short-lived insurrectionary, plebiscitary effort at a presidential regime under Sidónio Pais and his República Nova in 1917–18.

The comparisons in the cases of Spain and Portugal should of course be made with Italy and not with Germany or even with east-European countries. In fact, generalizing on a broader level, it is probably correct to state that Spain and Italy have shown more points of similarity during the modern period than have any other two large European countries. Though the modern national state was not established in Italy until the middle of the nineteenth century, nearly two generations after the inception of the modern liberal system in Spain, problems and sequences of national development, particularly in politics, tended to follow parallel courses. Per capita income levels seem to have been roughly similar in the 1860s, and Italy pulled significantly ahead only during the main spurt of industrialization after 1900. By the 1920s, of course, Italy was more than an entire generation ahead of Spain in economic development.

Several major differences stand out nonetheless. Italy's political and economic leadership during the main liberal period (1860–1922) was a more concerted one than Spain's and provided greater stimulus and direction to both national policy and economic development. Secondly, nationalism was frequently a major catalyst in Italy, whereas Spain has experienced less organized and aggressive nationalism than any other large country in modern Europe.[1]

Breakdown of the liberal system occurred at approximately the same time in Spain, Italy, and Portugal—during the era of World War I and its immediate aftermath. When direct

1. For further discussion of the similarities and differences in Spanish and Italian political development, and the weakness of nationalism in Spain, see my articles "Spanish Fascism in Comparative Perspective" (*Iberian Studies* (2 [1973]; 3–12, reprinted in H. A. Turner, Jr., ed., *Reappraisals of Fascism* [New York, 1976]; and "La derecha en Italia y España," *Boletín de Ciencia Política,* nos. 13–14 (August-December, 1974), 65–82.

authoritarian systems were inaugurated, however—in Spain in 1923, in Portugal in 1926—they emerged under pretorian leadership. Mass politics entered Spain with the Second Republic in 1931 and Portugal only with the revolution of 1974. Hence there was no question of organized mass movements coming to the fore in the Iberian countries during the 1920s.

SPAIN

The Primo de Rivera dictatorship (1923–30) was an essay in moderate authoritarianism. It failed completely to generate a theory or ideology, above all because the erstwhile dictator himself was uncertain about his ultimate goals. Miguel Primo de Rivera thought of himself (to some extent correctly) in the tradition of nineteenth-century Spanish pretorian figures who temporarily intervened *manu militari* in the liberal political process, not to overthrow liberalism but simply to establish limits and introduce reforms.

There was nonetheless another side to *primorriverismo*. While disclaiming any desire to imitate Fascism, the Spanish dictator stressed his admiration for and interest in the Italian regime. Alfonso XIII and his prime minister, whom he introduced as "my Mussolini," were the first official state visitors of the Mussolini government. In addition to establishing authoritarian rule, Primo reimposed centralism in Spain, established a government political association—vague and amorphous though it was—and initiated a new propaganda campaign to glorify the leader. His labor minister, Eduardo Aunós (the "white Lenin"), visited Rome in 1926 to observe the initial phases of Italian national syndicalist corporatism with a view to future Spanish policy.[2]

Yet very little came of all this. There was no serious effort

---

2. Shlomo Ben-Ami, in "The Dictatorship of Primo de Rivera: A Political Reassessment," *JCH* 12.1 (January 1977): 65–84, stresses the new authoritarian and parafascist style introduced by Primo. Though Ben-Ami may exaggerate these points, his emphasis on Primo de Rivera's role in the destruction of constitutional conservatism in Spain is quite correct.

at a Spanish corporatism, but only a modest program of state syndical arbitration during the last years of the decade. The only political alternative that the Spanish dictatorship could conceive was to propose an increase in the powers of the state executive council and selection of half the members of parliament through indirect corporative elections. Primo de Rivera had his own doubts even about these proposals and finally scrapped them himself before resigning in bewilderment and frustration.[3]

Mussolini nonetheless viewed the Primo de Rivera regime as part of the nationalist, authoritarian, and at least semi-corporativist (if not fascist) new order in southern Europe, and was disturbed by its sudden and complete collapse in the winter of 1930. According to De Felice, the conclusions that he drew from this were that the leading right-wing institutions—monarchy and church—merited little confidence, and that the future depended on some sort of accentuation of fascist authoritarianism.[4]

Primo de Rivera failed completely to overcome the political, ideological, and cultural environment of liberalism, even within his own thinking, and his downfall greatly radicalized Spanish politics, leading to the inauguration of mass democracy. Within five short years the Spanish Republic produced hyperpoliticization, revolutionary competition, and multiple political breakdowns, horizontal and vertical, without parallel in the history of peacetime western politics during the twentieth century. Only during the Second Republic did the main Spanish variants of authoritarian nationalism—moderate, right radical, and fascist—finally take belated form.

---

3. For a more extensive discussion and further references, see "Primo de Rivera: La búsqueda de una alternativia política," in my *Ejército y sociedad en la España liberal 1808–1936* (Madrid, 1977), 311–28. An early analysis that defined some of the fundamental differences between Primo de Rivera and Mussolini is Wolfgang Scholz, *Die Lage des spanischen Staates vor der Revolution (unter Berücksichtigung ihres Verhältnisses zum italienischen Fascismus)* [sic] (Dresden, 1932).
4. Renzo de Felice, *Mussolini il Duce* (Turin, 1974), 129–131.

Moderate, technically legalistic, corporative authoritarianism in Spain emerged as mass political Catholicism in
the CEDA (Spanish Confederation of Autonomous Rightist
Groups), which flourished briefly as the country's largest
single political party between 1933 and 1936 before being totally eclipsed by the Civil War. The ultimate goals of the
CEDA were always vague. Though it was committed to legal,
nonviolent parliamentary tactics in practice, the CEDA's
cherished aim of constitutional revision seemed to point toward a more authoritarian and corporative Catholic republic.
Like all but the most moderate and liberal groups in Spain,
the CEDA organized its own youth movement and shirt formation. After 1933 the latter (JAP) underwent a certain vertigo of fascistization, like so many other right nationalist
groups elsewhere, but the ambivalence of the JAP and the
entire CEDA was symbolized by the half-fascist salute that
was officially adopted—raising the right-arm only halfway
and bending it at the elbow back across the chest.[5]

The radical right in Spain was composed of two different
sectors: the neotraditionalists of a revitalized Carlism (the
Traditionalist Communion, CT) and the more modernistic
Alfonsine monarchists (supporters of the former king). By
the early 1930s Carlist doctrine had been influenced by Catholic corporatist theories, and presented a program of corporatist neotraditionalist monarchism that eschewed extreme
statism and tried to clearly differentiate itself from fascist
radicalism and dictatorship.[6] The outbreak of Republican
and leftist anticlericalism provoked a sudden upsurge of
Carlist support, and yet neotraditionalism could never directly rally more than 3 or 4 percent of Spain's population.

The neoauthoritarian *alfonsino* monarchists were in part an

5. The chief general account of the Spanish right under the Republic is R.
A. H. Robinson, *The Origins of Franco's Spain* (London/Pittsburgh, 1970); and
of the CEDA, José Luis Montero, *La CEDA* (Madrid, 1977). There is an important memoir by the top CEDA leader, Jose Ma. Gil Robles, *No fue posible la
paz* (Barcelona, 1968).

6. There is an excellent study by Martín Blinkhorn, *Carlism and Crisis in
Spain 1931–1939* (Cambridge, Mass., 1975). See especially the chapter "Carlism and Fascism," 163–82.

offshoot of the activist right-wing of the old monarchist Conservative party, their evolution being similar to that of part of the historic "Destra" of conservative liberalism in Italy. Only after the triumph of Republican radicalism did the Spanish monarchists turn to overt authoritarianism, under the twin influences of Action Française and the right (Rocco/ Nationalist) wing of Italian fascism. For several years their journal, *Acción Española*, patterned after the Action Française, elaborated an intellectual and theoretical basis for authoritarian neomonarchist government.[7]

The main spokesman of Spain's radical right was José Calvo Sotelo, ex-Conservative and former finance minister under Primo de Rivera, who was not converted to clear-cut authoritarianism until his Parisian exile during 1931–32. Winning a seat in parliament in the 1933 elections enabled him to return to Spain, where he became the key leader of the small monarchist Spanish Renovation party and organized a broader right nationalist grouping, the National Bloc, in 1934–35. During the final weeks before the Civil War he became the main spokesman for the rightist opposition in parliament, and his murder by leftist police agents became the signal for the start of the Civil War.

In Spain as in Italy, the underlying doctrine and structure for institutionalized authoritarian government stemmed not from radical fascism but from the more right-wing authoritarianism. Calvo Sotelo proposed not the restoration but the "installation" (*instauración*) of an authoritarian new monarchy, which would have to be preceded by an indeterminate period of dictatorship. He understood clearly that this was unlikely to come about through political mobilization but would probably require forcible intervention by the military. Parliament would have to be replaced by an indirect corporate chamber representing social and economic interests, and a strong government would then be in a position to stimulate the economy through state regulation and reflationary policies.

7. Luis Ma. Ansón, *Acción Española* (Zaragoza, 1960).

Calvo Sotelo admired Italian Fascism, attempted to join the Falange in Madrid in 1934, and did not object if critics referred to his goals as fascist. But his project was much nearer to Rocco or Maurras than to Mussolini, Panunzio, or the Spanish Falangists. He had no interest in promoting a revolutionary mass party or demagogical national syndicalism, and preferred to rely on traditional elites rather than a new nationalistic militia. Though he had been liquidated by the time the Civil War began, the somewhat vague blueprint outlined by Calvo Sotelo and the *Acción Española* ideologues more nearly approximated the structure and policies of the subsequent Franco regime than the revolutionary "national syndicalist state" posited by the fascistic Falangists.[8]

More categorically fascist politics were introduced into Spain in several stages, all unsuccessful, before the outbreak of the Civil War in 1936. The initial champion of the fascist idea was the avant-garde esthete Ernesto Giménez Caballero ("the Spanish D'Annunzio"), who publicly announced his fascism in 1929 and was soon almost completely ostracized by the predominantly liberal Spanish cultural establishment, becoming what he himself called "a literary Robinson Crusoe." Giménez Caballero's fascism was derived directly from Rome (his wife was Italian) and was unusual in being avowedly international in scope and structure. He predicated fascism on Latin Catholic culture, and saw it as the main hope for cultural renewal of the heartlands of historic Latin Christendom. By the same token, Giménez Caballero's fascism was opposed to the Protestant north and to Nazism

---

8. Though several hagiographic biographies exist, there is no adequate study of Calvo Sotelo and his influence. For an introduction, see Robinson, *Origins of Franco's Spain;* and also his "Monarchist Myth of the Franco Regime," *Iberian Studies* (1973); as well as my "1936: Calvo Sotelo y la Gran Derecha" *Nueva Historia* 2.20 (September 1978): 88–95. There are two preliminary accounts in Spanish: Manuel Pi y Navarro, *Los primeros veinticinco años de Calvo Sotelo* (Zaragoza, 1961); and Julián Soriano Flores de Lemus, *Calvo Sotelo ante la Segunda República* (Madrid, 1975). Calvo Sotelo outlined some of his economic ideas in *El capitalismo contemporáneo y su evolución* (Madrid, 1935).

(at one point he saw war between Fascism and Nazism as inevitable).[9]

Giménez Caballero was not a political organizer, however, and the first facist political grouping in Spain was created by Ramiro Ledesma Ramos, an underemployed university graduate who had specialized in mathematics and philosophy. Here again the inspiration was primarily Italian, his little band being named "Juntas de Ofensiva Nacional-Sindicalista" (a rather equivalent term to "Fasci Italiani di Combattimento") and their weekly publication *La Conquista del Estado* ("The Conquest of the State," the title of a sometime publication directed by the leading Fascist writer Curzio Malaparte). Yet, though Ledesma drew his inspiration from Italy (and also in part from Germany, temporarily affecting an Hitlerian hairstyle), he soon became keenly aware of the need to avoid, or at least avoid the appearance of, imitating Italian Fascism or other foreign movements. The official program of the JONS, aiming at a "national syndicalist state," might be read as a carbon copy of the ideas and goals of Italian Fascism, yet Ledesma preferred to avoid the label, realizing that it was counterproductive in the generally left-liberal Spanish atmosphere.[10]

The JONS remained totally isolated at the small-sect level. Relying mainly on university and secondary students, they were a typical product of radical intelligentsia politics and

9. Giménez Caballero has been studied by Douglas Foard in "Ernesto Giménez Caballero and the Revolt of the Aesthetes" (Ph.D. diss., Washington University, 1972), of which a bowdlerized version was translated by the elderly Giménez Caballero for publication in Madrid in 1975; and more briefly in Foard's article "The Forgotten Falangist: Giménez Caballero," *JCH* 10.1 (January 1975); 3–18.

10. As the organizational—and to a large degree ideological—founder of Spanish fascism, Ledesma has been the subject of two recent full-length biographies, both entitled *Ramiro Ledesma Ramos*. The first, by Tomás Borrás (Madrid, 1972), is descriptive, superficial, and hagiographic. The second, by Jose Ma. Sánchez Diana (Madrid, 1975), has somewhat greater analytic depth.

during their two and a half years of independent existence (1931–34) failed to have the slightest impact on Spanish affairs.

A more vigorous, better-financed attempt at a Spanish fascism was essayed by sectors of the right in 1933.[11] The triumph of Hitler stimulated interest in Spain also, not so much among potential fascists—of whom there seemed to be so few in the peninsula—but among right radicals or potential right radicals, who were distinctly more numerous. Basque financiers went shopping during the summer of 1933 for the leader of a potential counterrevolutionary, demagogic Spanish fascism. Though they provided a trickle of support to Ledesma and the JONS, the latter were deemed to be both too radical and too unimportant to merit major support.

The main leader of a would-be Spanish fascism who came to the fore in the summer and autumn of 1933 was José Antonio Primo de Rivera, eldest son of the late dictator. He first evolved from conservative authoritarian monarchism to a more radical brand of nationalist authoritarianism that was not entirely unlike Calvo Sotelo's new ideas. By 1933 the younger Primo de Rivera—soon to be known generally as José Antonio—had become interested in something rather like fascism (Italian style) as the vehicle for giving form and ideological content to the national authoritarian regime attempted so uncertainly and unsuccessfully by his father. Unlike Ledesma, who had greater initial experience and insight in such matters, José Antonio was not averse to using the

11. For taxonomic purposes, it might be pointed out that a tiny right-radical Spanish Nationalist Party had been organized by a physician named Albiñana in 1930. Albiñana early adopted more than a few of the trappings of fascism, stressing imperial expansion on the one hand and a broad, economically reformist state syndicalism on the other. He organized his own minuscule "Legion" for street battle and at one point apparently hoped to develop a mass movement. After 1933 he dropped his most fascistic overtones in favor of a more orthodox and conservative right radicalism. The only pertinent study is in Manuel Pastor, Los orígenes del fascismo en España (Madrid, 1975), 38–61.

label *fascist*, though it was eventually decided to call the new movement that he founded with a group of colleagues in October 1933 by the more original title of Falange Española (Spanish Phalanx).

The Falange began with much more financial support from big business prone to the radical right than had the JONS, prompting the JONS to merge with it in early 1934 (the resulting organization being called Falange Española de las JONS). During the next two years, and indeed all the way down to the beginning of the Civil War, the Falange was distinguished primarily by its insignificance. Like the Romanian Iron Guard, it relied at first on its student clientele, but unlike the Romanian movement, completely failed to generate any broader lower- or middle-class support.

The only advantage of this period in the wilderness was that it did give the movement's leaders some time to reflect on what they were about. After a year or so, José Antonio Primo de Rivera began to move "left," as the national syndicalism of the Falangists took on more socially radical overtones. There was a somewhat belated reaction to the danger of mimesis, and before the close of 1934 most Falangists were denying that they were fascists. By 1935, the criticism of Italian corporatism as too conservative and capitalistic, a criticism fairly common among the more radical types of fascists and Nazis abroad, was being echoed by some Falangist leaders, including Primo de Rivera.

It was all somewhat bewildering to Italian Fascists. During the "universal fascism" phase of the mid-1930s, the Italian taxonomists somewhat inconclusively decided that Falangists were indeed fascists because of their belief in "authority, hierarchy, order" and their antimaterialist Falangist "mysticism."[12] José Antonio, for his part, recognized that all the "nationalist renewal" movements opposing Marxism, liberalism, and the old conservatism had some things in common but also exhibited pronounced national differences. The

12. Ledeen, *Universal Fascism*, 100, 110–11.

Spanish right having ceased to support a more radical fascism, the Falange figured on the foreign payroll of the Italian regime for approximately nine months in 1935–36.[13]

Unlike many other fascist movements, the Falange did develop an official program, the Twenty-Seven Points, before the close of 1934. These exhibited all the main points of fascistic doctrine, and in the economic sphere called for the development of a complete national syndicalist state. Though most property was to remain in private hands, banking and credit facilities were to be nationalized and large landed estates expropriated and divided. Despite Falangist criticism of the inadequacies of Italian corporatism, however, no detailed blueprint of the "national syndicalist state" was ever developed.[14]

That Falangism exhibited certain distinct characteristics of its own is undeniable, but these did not prevent it from sharing nearly all the general qualities and characteristics that would compose an inventory of generic fascism. As hypernationalists, all fascist groups by definition revealed certain distinct national traits. In the Spanish case, Falangism differed somewhat from Italian Fascism in its basic Catholic religious (if politically anticlerical) identity, for this was central to Falangism and only marginal to Fascism (even if stressed during the Fascist/National Socialist polemics of 1933–34). The Falangists' concept of the "new man" thus incorporated nearly all the qualities of the traditional Catholic hero, while fusing them with twentieth-century components. Yet this

13. John F. Coverdale, *Italian Intervention in the Spanish Civil War* (Princeton, 1975), 50–64.

14. The most lengthy attempt to elaborate this program was José Luis de Arrese's *La revolución social del nacionalsindicalismo* (Madrid, 1940), which was either suppressed or confiscated by police in 1936 and appeared only in 1940 after the Civil War. The "social revolution" of national syndicalism consisted of an assortment of limited proposals, such as for profit-sharing, vague workers' councils in factories, a family wage, restoration of municipal patrimonies for communal support, and the aforementioned nationalization of banking and credit. In general this did not go so far toward "semi-socialism" as the original proposals of German national socialists and Italian national syndicalists.

distinction still seems relative rather than absolute. One other presumably fascist movement, the Romanian Iron Guard, was considerably more thoroughgoing and fanatical in its religious identity, and Boleslaw Piasecki's Polish "Falanga," whose name was derivative, was also more extreme and pronounced in its Catholicism.

José Antonio Primo de Rivera remained a highly ambivalent figure, perhaps the most ambiguous of all European national fascist leaders. Major personal characteristics—such as a fastidious estheticism combined with a genuine if sometimes contradictory sense of moral scruple, a cultivated intellectual sense of distance and irony, and, for a Spanish politician, a remarkably limited spirit of sectarianism and group rivalry—may have disqualified him for successful leadership. There is abundant testimony that he considered abandoning the project at several points, but could not escape the commitment imposed by the deaths and sacrifices of other movement members.

Of all national fascist leaders, he was probably the most repelled by the brutality and violence associated with the fascist enterprise. He stopped using the term *fascist* before the end of 1934 and the term *totalitarian* before the end of 1935. He would occasionally refer to rightist conspirators as "fascist windbags" (*fascistas llenos de viento*). Yet however diffident and differential may have been his approach, he never renounced the fascist goals in politics. In the post-fascist era his admirers have made much of José Antonio's "humanism," his opposition to total dictatorship, his stress on the individual personality and "man the bearer of eternal values," and his Catholicism.[15] Yet in the Joseantonian formulation these do not necessarily contradict fascism; fairly similar formulations might be found by some nominally leading members of the PNF.

Large sectors of the Spanish right were becoming "fascis-

15. The most systematic analysis along these lines is that of Adolfo Muñoz Alonso, *Un pensador para un pueblo* (Madrid, 1969). Cf. Cecilio de Miguel Medina, *La personalidad religiosa de José Antonio* (Madrid, 1975).

tized," as Ledesma aptly put it, in one or more superficial senses, but the erstwhile fascist movement itself was worse than anemic. Antifascism had been strong among the left from 1932 on, but it was precisely the latter who registered, as Ledesma commented ironically, the only truly "fascist" activity in Spain in terms of violence and direct action. Malaparte's *Technique of the Coup d'Etat* exerted its main influence during 1931–33 on the direct-action proponents of Spanish anarchism (FAI),[16] who engaged in various abortive putsches. In its first phases, Falangism seemed so fastidious, rhetorical, and averse to direct action that rightist critics labeled it "franciscanism" rather than fascism. After Ledesma broke with Primo de Rivera and the Falange, the question mark that he placed in the title of his memoir *¿Fascismo en España?* seemed fully appropriate. In the final elections of 1936 the Falange registered only 44,000 votes in all Spain, about 0.7 percent of all ballots cast, revealing fascism as weaker in Spain than in any other large continental European country.

The profound debility of fascism, so long as the regular Spanish political system existed, had several causes. The absence of any strong sense of Spanish nationalism deprived fascism of that key rallying point. In Spain mobilized nationalism was inverted—it was expressed through the intense "regional nationalism" of Catalans and Basques, directed against the unified Spanish nation-state. Another key factor was the limited secularization of rural and provincial society in much of Spain, particularly in the north. There, as in Slovakia and Austria, the most obvious and attractive cross-class alternative to liberal or leftist politics was political Catholicism. Moreover, the nominal electoral success of the CEDA from 1933 down to early 1936 gave this tactic the appearance of victory. Fascism enjoyed much less cultural reinforcement in Spain than in central Europe, for the cultural and intellectual revolution of 1890 had achieved less resonance in the peninsula. There was a rightist/Catholic culture

16. Cf. Fidel Miró, *Cataluña, los trabajadores y el problema de las nacionalidades* (Mexico City, 1967), 54–55.

of considerable force, but not a secular/vitalist/Darwinist cultural environment of any vigor. Finally, as far as political revolutionism was concerned, the left seemed able to enforce a monopoly of its several brands; it enjoyed greater political success and support in Spain than in any other country in the world during the 1930s. There remained less of an outlet for fascism as the consummation of a frustrated, deviant revolution than in central Europe.

The fascist movement in Spain could not immediately profit from the breakdown of the Spanish polity, because one of the last effective legal measures taken by the Republican government in the spring of 1936 was the suppression of the Falange. Though disillusioned rightists—primarily the young—began to flock to the clandestine, partially disarticulated movement, the collapse of political order erased the very concept of political victory in the Italian or German senses, and even Falangists had never seen that as a practical possibility.

Civil War produced a polarized revolutionary/counterrevolutionary conflict in which leadership passed completely into the hands of the insurgent Nationalist military who created the Franco regime. Growth of Falangist membership to several hundred thousand during the first year of the Civil War was not in itself decisive, for death in battle and execution had decapitated the movement, while military dictatorship in the Nationalist zone totally subordinated it.

The subsequent decision by Franco to take over the movement in April 1937 and create a syncretic, heterogeneous state party on the basis of Falangism was fully logical and practical. From the moment that he became dictator (October 1, 1936), he was concerned to avoid what he termed the "Primo de Rivera error," that is, the failure to transcend a Latin American–style personal military dictatorship without doctrine or structure. By that time the majority of continental European states were in the process of converting themselves into syncretic national authoritarian systems, some of them following the Italian example of creating a state party and introducing corporative economic regulations.

The entity that Franco elevated into *partido único* in April 1937 was not, however, integral Falangism, but a union of Falangists, Carlists, and all other members of various rightist and other groups who were willing to join. Though the Falangist program—now the Twenty-Six Points—was raised to official state doctrine, Franco specifically announced that this was to be understood merely as a point of departure and would be modified or elaborated depending upon future requirements.

For the next decade and more the Franquist state was normally taken, outside Spain, to be a "fascist regime." It is doubtful, however, that one can speak of a fascist regime unless it is dominated and constructed by generic or categorical fascists, and this was hardly the case with Franquism. Core Falangists, the *camisas viejas* (lit. "old shirts"), played only a small role in the new state and held only a small minority of positions in the new system. They did not even control much of the administration of the new state party, the Falange Española Tradicionalista. Addition of the last adjective, reflecting the nominal fusion with the Carlists, underscored the major right-wing limitations to the fascism of the new regime. That early Franquism contained a major component of fascism is undeniable, but it was so restricted within a right-wing, pretorian, Catholic, and semipluralist structure that the category of "semifascist" would probably be more accurate.

Of course, the same adjective might be applied not inaccurately to Mussolini's Italy, and the similarities between the latter regime and early Franquism are rather greater than is sometimes thought. Both used subordinated state fascist parties that were merged with and subsequently incorporated unindoctrinated nonfascist elements. Both permitted limited pluralism in national society and institutions under executive dictatorship. In neither case was the institutionalization of the regime developed primarily by revolutionary fascist ideologues, but more commonly by monarchist theoreticians of the radical right, together with fascistic moderates. Though Franco enjoyed much more complete executive authority than did Mussolini, he eventually converted the juridical form of his regime into that of monarchy, retaining the powers of regent for life. In both cases the challenge of militant fascist national syndicalism was soon faced and thoroughly subordinated (the *sbloccamento* of Rossoni's national syndicates in 1928; the suppression of Salvador Merino's attempt at a more integral and autonomous national syndicalism in 1940).

The sequences of development of the two regimes were also somewhat parallel, finally diverging radically at the level of foreign policy. In both cases, an early coalition phase without official institutional structure (Italy, 1922–25; Spain, 1936–37) was followed by an institutionalization phase (Italy, 1925–29; Spain, 1937–42) succeeded by a period of equilibrium. That is of course a fairly common pattern for new systems. Foreign policy and international context marked the sharpest points of divergence, for the ultimate structure of the Franco regime was largely dependent on world affairs. Whereas Mussolini tried to play a major independent role from 1933 on, Franco had no illusions that he need not wait on events. Had Hitler won the war, there seems little doubt that Franquism would have become less conservative and rightist and more radical and overtly fascist in form. Acceptance of the term *fascist* was fairly common though never official during the first year of the Civil War, and Franco employed the term *totalitarian* in several of his early speeches. All the trappings of "Franco! Franco! Franco!" in the early years were simply imitations of Italian Fascism (or occasionally National Socialism), as were numerous agencies and institutions of the party and regime, such as the directorate of popular culture (MinCulPop) or the "Auxilio de Invierno" (Winterhilfe).

Nonetheless, there was always strong antifascist opinion among various rightist and Catholic sectors of the regime. As a result of this, but above all as a result of international events, the regime began to move in the opposite direction, starting as early as 1942. The doctrine of *caudillaje*, the Spanish equivalent of *ducismo* and the *Führerprinzip*, had always been more restrained than some leadership theories in Germany, and was not emphasized in the second half of World War II. Even before the tide turned in Russia, a major theoretical article by a sometime Falangist leader distinguishing the Spanish state from the totalitarian regimes had gone into press.[17] From the end of 1942 on, this became a general trend.[18] By the close of 1945, Spain was well into the process of transition from a partially mobilized, semifascist state to a corporative, nonmobilized "bureaucratic authoritarian" regime.

Defascistization proceeded in two general phases. The intermediate phase spanned the period 1942 to 1957–59. The last elements of opposition against Franco within the FET faded away during 1941–43 (momentarily revived by Nazi intrigues to pressure the Spanish government on entry into the war).[19] After 1943 the FET had been reduced to an even more completely subservient bureaucratic instrument than the PNF under the Mussolinian state. Though it ceased to mobilize or play as active a role in state services as during the first years of the regime, it survived officially throughout the history of the Franco regime, primarily because even though Franco preferred to discourage political mobilization, it was deemed preferable to have some sort of state political organization rather than none at all.[20]

By the 1950s it was officially known more commonly as the Movimiento Nacional, the vague and abstract appellation appearing less offensive in the new social democratic era of western Europe. Theoretically, more than 900,000 members

17. Alfonso García Valdecasas, "Los Estados totalitarios y el Estado Español," *Revista de Estudios Políticos* 2.5 (January 1942): 5–32.

18. The chief theoretical reformulation by a Falangist was Arrese's *El Estado totalitario en el pensamiento de José Antonio* (Madrid, 1944).

19. Klaus-Jörg Ruhl, *Spanien im Zweiten Weltkrieg* (Hamburg, 1975). The most serious Falangist conspiracy against Franco in 1940–41 is recounted in Armando Romero Cuesta, *Objectivo: Matar a Franco* (Madrid, 1976).

20. The best analysis of the "Movement" phase of the FET is Juan J. Linz, "From Falange to Movimiento-Organización," in S. P. Huntington and C. H. Moore, eds., *Authoritarian Politics in Modern Society* (New York, 1970), 128–203.

were carried on the rolls of various Movimiento organizations into the 1960s,[21] but this largely represented a refusal to
prune the lists of inactive members.

The final turning point, inaugurating the second and more
complete phase of defascistization, began in 1956. After a fatal incident involving activists at the University of Madrid,
old guard Falangist leaders presented a proposal to Franco
that would constitutionalize one-party Movimiento control
of much of the political processes of the regime. This was
vetoed by the military and opposed by the church hierarchy.
Consequently in 1957 Franco made his final decision in favor
of further depoliticization and strictly bureaucratic authoritarianism. A new cabinet of erstwhile "technocratic" ministers was introduced who dismantled the remains of national
syndicalist autarchy that still regulated and controlled much
of the economy, opening Spain to economic neoliberalism,
massive foreign investment and tourism, and the spectacular
boom of the 1960s. The Twenty-Seven Points of Falangism
were quietly buried, replaced in 1958 by a list of ten anodyne
"Principles of the Movement" that embraced such values as
unity, justice, well-being, and so forth.

The Movement still survived as a strictly bureaucratic resi-
due. From time to time there were outbursts by small circles
of neo-Falangist radicals, and several attempts to organize a
"revolutionary," opposition Falangism. In the new climate
of hedonism, materialism, and growing influence from west-
European democracy, none of these prospered. Neofascism
could not be effectively stimulated in a land where fascism
had been weak even before the passing of the fascist cultural
era, and had expanded only under the dire stimulus of total,
revolutionary civil war. The Movement was finally officially
dissolved in April 1977, in the democratization carried out
by King Juan Carlos after the death of Franco. Several neo-
Falangist groups competed for support in the Spanish elections of 1977—most of them quite radical in their socioinsti-

21. See Joaquín Bardavío, *La estructura del poder en España* (Madrid, 1969),
117–18.

tutional formulations—but altogether garnered only about 1 percent of the vote, scarcely better than in 1936 and much less than the neofascists of the MSI in Italy.

PORTUGAL

The case of Portugal is different and simpler. The forty-eight-year dictatorship that governed from 1926 to 1974 was essentially of the interwar east-European type, corporative, institutionalized, systematically authoritarian, but not viciously repressive, and without any direct fascist party component. There were several different, much more moderate forms of authoritarianism before the advent of the Salazarian *Estado Novo*. The "legal dictatorship" of João Franco in 1907–8 and the presidential República Nova of Sidónio Pais in 1917–18 have both been mentioned. A new Nationalist Party in the last years of the monarchy seemed to point in much the same direction. A more radical kind of pretorian authoritarianism was introduced by the leaders of the Republican Guard (GNR) during the last years of the parliamentary regime, particularly by the Octobrists of 1921 under a GNR commander, Manuel Coelho, who carried out a bloody if short-lived coup d'etat. Finally, a clear-cut radical right emerged during the last decade of the First Republic in the Integralist movement, a direct imitation of the Action Française, that agitated for an authoritarian corporative new system, with or without a monarchy.[22]

There is considerable analogy between the Portuguese military dictatorship of 1926–28 and the Primo de Rivera regime of 1923–30, the difference being that the Portuguese regime found and rather grudgingly accepted a leader capable of developing and institutionalizing it. Dr. António de Oliveira Salazar, the Coimbra professor who became finance minister and finally prime minister and leader of the regime, derived his inspiration mainly from right-wing Catholic corporative doctrine. His "New State" corporative constitution of 1933

22. Carlos Ferrão, *O Integralismo e a República*, 2 vols. (Lisbon, 1964–65).

was designed to create the first complete authoritarian corporative state in the world, more thorough than the contemporary Italian system, at that point still in transition from partial national syndicalism to corporatism. Salazar also introduced a state political organization, the National Union, but this was the equivalent of Primo de Rivera's formalistic Patriotic Union, not a radical new mass movement or even a true *parti unique*. [23]

A real fascist movement did develop briefly in Portugal, the blue-shirted National Syndicalists of Rolão Preto, who claimed to be expanding into a mass movement in 1934–35. Like Valois and a number of young fascist leaders in France, Preto was a former monarchist Integralist, disillusioned with the reactionary slant and lack of dynamic new social content in the latter movement. Salazar exiled Preto in 1934, denouncing the National Syndicalists' fascistic "exaltation of youth, and the cult of force through direct action, the principle of the superiority of state political power in social life, the propensity for organizing masses behind a single leader." [24] In 1935 the National Syndicalists attempted a revolutionary coup against the regime in conjunction with the Portuguese anarchosyndicalists—proving that the allies of fascism might be found on the extreme left as well as the extreme right—but were easily crushed. [25]

Yet despite Salazar's attempt at a clear-cut differentiation from fascism, one of the keenest students of the Estado Novo, Manuel de Lucena, insists that in form and structure the Portuguese regime more nearly resembled that of Mussolini than did any other in Europe, and that it was in fact "a

23. The two lengthiest treatments of the development of Portuguese corporatism are Howard J. Wiarda, *Corporatism and Development: The Portuguese Experience* (Amherst, 1977), and Manuel de Lucena, *A evolução do sistema corporativo português* (Lisbon, 1976), 2 vols. Important briefer studies will be found in L. S. Graham and H. M. Makler, eds., *Contemporary Portugal* (Austin, Tex., 1979), and Philippe C. Schmitter, *Corporatism and Public Policy in Authoritarian Portugal* (Beverly Hills, Calif. 1975).

24. Jacques Ploncard d'Assac, *Salazar* (Paris, 1967), 107.

25. Material on the National Syndicalists has been collected by João Medina, *Salazar e os fascistas* (Lisbon, 1979).

fascism without a fascist movement."[26] Lucena recognizes the ambiguity of any rigorous definition of fascism, but insists correctly that no extended empirical comparison can be made of the program or goals of the original Fascist movement because "pure Fascism never became a regime."[27] Fascism therefore, in terms of regime type, refers to the formal structure of the Mussolini state, even though the latter was not dominated by the Fascist party or the latter's original program. The parallelisms that he points to are (1) a dictator who functioned as prime minister without being head of state, (2) development of a corporative economic structure and finally a full corporative chamber, (3) an authoritarian police state, (4) a bureaucratized, nonautonomous, essentially nonrevolutionary state political organization, (5) semipluralist autonomy for influential sectors of society under the system, and (6) an imperialist foreign policy.[28] At the same time, Lucena recognizes some limits to the analogy, particularly in the continuing tension with the revolutionary aspects of Fascism and the greater dynamism of the regime in Italy.

Up to a point, the analogy is well taken, for the failure to complete a fascist revolution or create a totalitarian system in Italy meant that the Mussolini regime was simply the most radical and dynamic of the new semipluralist authoritarian national regimes in Europe. Though Salazar's doctrines were largely rightist in inspiration, the formal parallels with Fascist Italy do exist, though they are obviously far from complete and are contradicted by other factors. The very precept of "a fascism without a fascist movement" indicates that we are dealing with a different phenomenon. The Salazar regime was, in fact, one of the most fully institutionalized of all the interwar authoritarian regimes (partly explaining its longevity), for its structure, partly paralleling that of Italy, was more thoroughgoing than that of the Balkan or east-European regimes.

26. Lucena, 1:23.
27. Ibid., 1:35.
28. Ibid., 1:35–51.

Moreover, the Portuguese regime was definitely influenced by Italy, though it is a moot point how direct and extensive that influence was before 1936. What is much clearer is Salazar's participation in the general "fascistizing" tendency in the Iberian peninsula and in southern and eastern Europe during the years of the Spanish Civil War. During 1936–39 the regime became more overtly authoritarian, expanded the National Union and set up a new political militia, the National Legion, to supplement the police, and organized a national youth movement. Both the latter organizations employed the fascist salute. Yet this tendency was somewhat arrested by the outbreak of the war, posing a danger from central Europe, and began to be reversed at the time that the first phase of defascistization began in Spain. After 1945, the Salazar regime moved much more fully and rapidly than the Franco regime into a nonmobilized bureaucratic authoritarianism, though the Legion was never completely disbanded until the eventual overthrow of the regime in 1974.

The Salazar regime did not contain a major fascist component from the start as did that of Franco. Developing in a partially illiterate, still not mobilized society, its goal was depoliticization from the very beginning. Yet it too was influenced by the fascist vertigo and the trappings of fascism in the late 1930s, so that in the proper circumstance it too might have taken a more overtly fascist form.

7

Fascism Outside Europe?

JAPAN

Whether or not political forces with the primary characteristics of European fascism have emerged to any significant
degree elsewhere has been problematic for some analysts,
though it has posed no problem for the observer who as-
sumes that any form of anti-Marxian authoritarianism is intrinsically fascist. The dilemma has been most acute in the
case of Japan, because of its aggressiveness in World War II
and its association with Germany and Italy. The existence of
"Japanese fascism" was detected by Soviet writers as early as
1934,[1] and most Marxist commentators have applied this interpretation to Japanese government and institutions in the
1930s ever since.[2] A slightly different formulation has been

1. O. Tanin and E. Yohan [pseuds.], *Militarism and Fascism in Japan* (New
York, 1934).
2. Cf. references in George M. Wilson, "A New Look at the Problem of
'Japanese Fascism,' " in Turner, ed., *Reappraisals of Fascism*, 199–214; and Tet-
suo Furuya, "Naissance et développement du fascisme japonais," *Revue
d'Histoire de la 2me Guerre Mondiale*, no. 86 (April 1972) pp. 1–16.

made by certain western social scientists, who point to the growing bellicosity and authoritarianism of the Japanese regime during those years and argue that fascism is a valid concept with which to label or define regimes that become aggressive and authoritarian during the industrialization of a non-state-socialist system.[3]

The most cogent reexamination of the problem has been made by George M. Wilson,[4] who argues convincingly that the concept of "Japanese fascism" is mistaken, insofar as no political movement arose to seize power and formal Japanese constitutional and institutional authority remained essentially intact, while parliamentary pluralism and elections continued to exist. This argument appears to be essentially correct, though it may be worthwhile to expand and modify it somewhat.

The main pressure to change the Japanese system came from radical elements of the military and from small radical nationalist circles. None of the ultranationalist societies transformed themselves into significant parties or movements, but some of their spokesmen and theorists might be generally described as national socialists (though not "Nazis"). Kita Ikki, Japan's leading radical nationalist ideologue of the 1930s, had in his youth been a Marxian socialist who later followed something of the same course as Mussolini. Kita and some of the other nationalist revolutionaries were opposed to capitalism. They demanded nationalization of selected major industries (together with some limited degree of worker control), with profit-sharing and state regulation for the remainder of industry that would be left under

3. This approach takes diverse forms in such scholars as Robert A. Scalapino, *Democracy and the Party Movement in Prewar Japan* (Berkeley, 1953); Richard Storry, *The Double Patriots* (Boston, 1957), and "Japanese Fascism in the Thirties," *Wiener Library Bulletin* 20.4 (Autumn 1966): 1–7; and Maruyama Masao, *Thought and Behavior in Modern Japanese Politics*, ed. Ivan Morris (London, 1963). Ivan Morris has edited a compendium of some of the main diverging interpretations of the problem under the title *Japan 1931–1945: Militarism, Fascism, Japanism?* (Boston, 1963).

4. Wilson, "A New Look at the Problem of 'Japanese Fascism.' "

private ownership. Under an organic, authoritarian new imperial government (with controlled universal male suffrage), this was to be accompanied by a drastic land reform that would introduce a more communal, partially collectivist agrarian system. An ultimate goal was the construction of a great new East Asian empire abroad.[5]

The main support for Kita and other revolutionary nationalists came from the younger field officers in the army's Imperial Way faction. Some of the latter referred to more conservative authoritarians of the so-called Control group on the general staff as fascists because the latter rejected revolutionary changes in favor of merely expanding governmental authority under existing institutions. To Imperial Way revolutionaries, status quo authoritarianism that fostered increased industrialization within a largely capitalist framework was simply fascism and destructive to the national society.[6] Conversely, there was also a reactionary "Japanist" right wing within nationalist opinion that rejected all foreign institutions and proposed to revive a purely autochthonous, largely agrarian-oriented society.[7]

Despite the assassinations, ultranationalist hysteria, and radical pressures of the 1930s, the Japanese constitution remained almost unchanged and the political party system itself was altered comparatively little.[8] When the Imperial Rule Assistance Association was finally created in 1940, it was little more than an agglomeration of most of the existing parties (even though the latter were technically in process of dissolution). Pluralism was never entirely destroyed, and patri-

5. George M. Wilson, *Radical Nationalist in Japan: Kita Ikki, 1883–1937* (Cambridge, Mass., 1969), and "Kita Ikki's Theory of Revolution," *Journal of Asian Studies* 26.1 (November 1966); 94–96. An extract of Kita's theory is presented in Morris, *Militarism, Fascism, Japanism?*, 20–25.

6. Cf. James Crowley, *Japan's Quest for Autonomy* (Princeton, 1966), 172–77, 251–79.

7. Aspects of this are treated in T. R. H. Havens, *Farm and Nation in Modern Japan: Agrarian Nationalism, 1870–1940* (Princeton, 1974).

8. This is demonstrated by G. M. Berger, *Parties Out of Power in Japan, 1931–1941* (Princeton, 1977). The restraint exercised in one aspect of Japanese repression is described in R. H. Mitchell, *Thought Control in Prewar Japan* (Ithaca, 1976).

otic nongovernment forces won 39 percent of the vote in the 1942 parliamentary elections. The changes in Japanese policy during the 1930s, which came about more by accretion than by drastic reversals, were not the result of any takeover by a fascism, military or otherwise, but stemmed from a broad consensus among most political opinion to support intense nationalism and a forward policy abroad. These changes were sometimes provoked by military factions but never determined by the latter alone.

By comparison with aggressive European regimes, Imperial Japan on the eve of World War II in many ways resembled Germany's Second Reich more than it did the Hitler system. Japan was a much less industrialized country than the Germany of the 1930s and had never achieved a fully democratic mass political mobilization. The executive authority of the emperor reigned *de jure* if not *de facto*, and institutions remained highly elitist within a deferential society.[9] Thus imperial expansion was carried out under a traditionalist and monarchist system without a radical new structure or a new independent mobilization. The culture ethos promoting expansion represented a radicalization of the traditional samurai or bushido spirit rather than a direct reflection of the cultural and social norms of the intellectual revolution of 1890 that inspired European fascism. The goal of creating a "new man," common to fascism and all thoroughgoing revolutions, was lacking. Though Japanese militarism, nationalism, and expansionism, joined with the bushido spirit, may have seemed a functional equivalent of fascism, this was so only at a very high level of abstraction. Both in structure and in ideas or ethos it specifically differed from European fascism. The closest analogy is thus probably with late Wilhelmian Germany.[10]

9. A somewhat different interpretation is presented by Kentaro Hayashi, "Japan and Germany in the Interwar Period," in J. W. Morley, ed., *Dilemmas of Growth in Prewar Japan* (Princeton, 1971), 461–88.

10. As a final note, it might be observed that the only notable attempt to directly copy central-European fascism within the Japanese Empire was the All-Russian Fascist Party of Russian exiles in Manchuria. See John J. Stephen, *The Russian Fascists* (New York, 1978).

CHINA

Most of China was governed during the fascist era by Chiang Kai-shek's Kuomintang (KMT), which is normally classified as a multiclass populist or "nation-building" party but not a fitting candidate for fascism (except by old-line Marxists). Recently, however, Lloyd Eastman has drawn attention to the Chinese "Blue Shirts" (so-called), whose official title was the Regenerationist Society, organized by radical KMT army officers in 1932. The Blue Shirts were inspired in part by European one-party states and believed that China could be unified, modernized, and developed only by a one-party system of ruthless authority that was more revolutionary than current formulations of the KMT. Their goal was said to be a highly militarized and also technocratic society of extreme nationalism that would nationalize many of the means of production. By 1934 they gained the favor of Chiang, who granted them temporary control of political indoctrination in the Chinese army and partial control of the general educational system, before pressures of civil war, internal conflict, and the struggle with Japan finally aborted the organization.[11]

Yet it appears that the significance of this group is easily exaggerated. They were not a distinct party or movement. The name Blue Shirts appears to be an invention of Japanese military intelligence; their own nickname was more nearly "Cotton-Cloth People." Not only is their discrete identity somewhat in doubt, but so is the fascist character of their ideas. Sun Yat-sen, the founder of the KMT, believed in a one-party system of guided democracy and in state-directed industrialization and modernization. Thus it would seem that the Blue Shirts, or less dramatically, Cotton-Cloth People, represented no more than a temporarily radicalized

11. Lloyd E. Eastman, *The Abortive Revolution: China under Nationalist Rule, 1927–1937* (Cambridge, Mass., 1974); "Fascists in Kuomintang China: The Blue Shirts," *China Quarterly* 49.1 (January 1972): 1–31; and "The Kuomintang in the 1930s," in C. Furth ed., *The Limits of Change* (Cambridge, Mass., 1976), 191–210.

variant of original KMT doctrine,[12] the militaristic thrust of their proposals reflecting the climate of the times—facing an aggressive Japan—and their own professional identity.

SOUTH AFRICA

Of all countries outside Europe, the Afrikaner society of South Africa may have registered the greatest degree of popular support for something approaching European-type fascism during the middle and late 1930s. Reasons for the appeal of radical nationalism to the Afrikaner population are in some respects obvious: recent memories of foreign conquest in the Boer War, constraints of the British imperial system (mild though they were), and the strong sense of minority status within the British system politically and among the South African population racially.

The Grey Shirt movement, founded by L. T. Weichardt in 1933, was probably the most clearly typologically fascist. Its main inspiration was German, not Italian, and, using a variety of names (South African Christian National Socialists, for example), tried to recruit from the entire white population, lasting in one form or another down to 1950. It was both black/white racist and anti-Semitic as well. The main limitation on its fascist orientation was the need to pay lip service to Christianity.

A much larger movement, but rather more rightist in character, was the Ossewa-Brandwag (Ox Wagon Sentinel), founded in 1938 by Dr. J. F. K. van Rensburg. It soon claimed a nominal membership of nearly 200,000 in a Boer population of less than 2,000,000, but seems to have included many cases of dual membership with the main conservative Afrikaner nationalist party, the United National Party of Malan. It went through a radical direct action phase in 1940–41, but by 1943 with the decline of the Axis had become more moderate and lost support. Pro-Nazi and anticapitalist, at its

12. Here I am drawing on unpublished research by Maria Chang of the University of California, Berkeley.

zenith it proposed a sort of syncretic racist "Calvinist" corporative republic. Some of its members seem to have taken their Calvinism seriously, and this created not inconsiderable internal tension.

There was also a right authoritarian study and pressure group, the Nuwe Orde (New Order) of Oswald Pirow, which split off from the majority Malan Afrikaner Party in 1942. It had earlier organized a 12,000-man paramilitary force in the 1930s, but its model of a conservative and religious authoritarian republic seems to have been more nearly Portugal than Germany.[13]

LATIN AMERICA

The region where continental European politics have been most copied is Latin America. Given the frequently authoritarian character of Latin American government and the rise of nationalism there between the wars, it might have seemed the most likely locale for the emergence of significant non-European fascisms. Such was not, however, the case. Only a few specifically fascistic movements appeared in Latin America, and the only one to enjoy success was the equivocal phenomenon of Peronism.

Several reasons may be advanced for the weakness, indeed virtual absence, of categorical fascism in Latin America: (1) the generally low rate of political mobilization, a generation or more behind even the most backward countries of Europe; (2) the noncompetitive nature of nationalism in most Latin American countries, which are not threatened with direct foreign domination and conquest or wars; hence war and competitive nationalism have been largely absent as catalysts or mobilizing factors; (3) as a corollary of the first factor, the

13. My sole source on fascism and authoritarian nationalism in South Africa is a Master's thesis by Steven Uran, "Fascism and National Socialism in South Africa" (University of Wisconsin, 1975). For background see T. D. Moodie, *The Rise of Afrikanerdom* (Berkeley, 1975). There is a discussion of Apartheid "fascism" in A. James Gregor, *Contemporary Radical Ideologies* (New York, 1968).

customary elitist/patronal domination of political processes, and hence the capacity of dominant and less-radical groups, as in eastern Europe, to suppress revolutionary nationalism; (4) the multiracial composition of many Latin American societies, which blurs radical nationalist identity and usually creates internal divisions and complexes that fortify the status quo; (5) political dominance of the military, who choke off other violent political manifestations; (6) weakness of the pre-1960 revolutionary left, which could thus not serve as a stimulus; (7) the tendency of Latin American nationalists after 1930 to reject both Europe and North America, turning either to populist nativism or some variant of the Hispanic tradition; (8) the inappropriateness of the national socialist/ national syndicalist economics of autarchy to countries so dependent on the world economy as those of Latin America; and (9) the development of a rather distinct Latin American mode of radical multiclass nationalism in the form of populist movements, such as the Peruvian APRA and the Bolivian MNR (some might add the Mexican PRI).[14]

Though several overtly mimetic little fascist groups in Latin America, such as the Argentine Fascist Party (founded in 1938), were totally insignificant, there were a few movements corresponding in whole or in part to European fascist parties that merit brief consideration. The largest of these was the Ação Integralista Brasileira (AIB) of Plínio Salgado, founded in 1932 and inspired in considerable measure by Italian Fascism. It tried to blend an Italian type of corporatist authoritarianism with native Brazilian culture. Though the term *totalitarian* was frequently used in its propaganda, its meaning was as vague and limited as in the Italian and Spanish contexts. Salgado himself was semimystical and his movement strongly identified with Catholicism and also with the sanctity of the family. Though the Integralists generated more pop-

14. A somewhat different list of factors, on which I have drawn in part, is offered by Alistair Hennessy, "Fascism and Populism in Latin America," in Laqueur, ed., *Fascism: A Reader's Guide*, 255–62. On Latin American populism, see Grant Hilliker, *The Politics of Reform in Peru: The Aprista and Other Mass Parties of Latin America* (Baltimore, 1971).

ular support in the mid-1930s than any other fascist-type party in Latin America, this was restricted, as in the case of nearly all other Brazilian groups, to the middle classes, and featured those of German and Italian background disproportionately.[15]

Brazil, like most other countries in Latin America (or southern and eastern Europe), was governed by a more conservative, semicorporatist authoritarian regime under Getulio Vargas, an *estado novo* ("New State") following Portuguese not Italian terminology. The Integralists met the same fate at the hands of Vargas as their Portuguese counterparts under Salazar: when they finally rose in an attempted coup against the regime in 1938, their movement was crushed, never to rise again.[16]

One of the interesting minor cases was that of the National Socialist Movement (MNS), or *Nacis* as they were called for short, in Chile. Founded by the Hispano-German Jorge González von Mareés in 1932, *nacismo* was in part inspired by German National Socialism but developed its own distinctive Chilean characteristics. González von Mareés appears to have been an abstractly moralistic idealist who liked to emphasize political pedagogy for the nation. His movement stood for social corporatism and strong government with great central authority, but in 1937 its leader publicly criticized Hitler for having become a tyrant. By 1938 he rejected ties or comparisons with Nazism or Fascism and declared the movement to be democratic. Though formally anti-

15. The best study is Helgio Trindade, *Integralismo* (Sao Paulo, 1974). See also J. Chasin, *O Integralismo de Plínio Salgado: Forma de regressividade no capitalismo hiper-tardio* (Sao Paulo, 1978); Jarbas Medeiros, *Ideologia autoritária no Brazil 1930–1945* (Rio de Janeiro, 1978); E. R. Broxson, "Plínio Salgado and Brazilian Integralism" (Ph.D. diss., Catholic University, 1973); and S. Hilton, "Ação Integralista Brasileira," *Luso-Brazilian Review* 9.2 (December 1972): 3–29.

16. The most pertinent study of the Vargas regime in this period and its relations with the Integralists is Robert M. Levine, *The Vargas Regime: The Critical Years, 1934–1938* (New York, 1970). It might be noted that after 1945 the Integralist movement reemerged in more moderate form, and several ex-Integralists assumed key roles in the military regime that was established in 1964.

Semitic, González admitted that there was no "Jewish problem" in Chile and theoretically espoused freedom of religion. In the parliamentary elections of 1937 the Nacis gained only a little over 3 percent of the popular vote, but did well in the worker districts of some of the larger cities. They faced the usual problem of most fascist-style movements: how to break in from the outside as a third force against both right and left. González von Mareés rejected violence for its own sake but advocated it as a "defensive necessity." An attempted coup against the rightist government of Alessandri was easily repressed, and over fifty captured Nacis were then massacred in cold blood in much the same way that the rightist regime in Romania was dispatching Legionnaires. At this point the Nacis decided to support Aguirre Cerda, the presidential candidate of the Chilean Popular Front, and gave him the margin of votes needed for a very narrow victory. There seems little doubt that a movement originally inspired by German Nazism—if always nonracist and antiimperialist (neither of which need necessarily be nonfascist)—had evolved into something different. Theoretical anti-Semitism was dropped, and the movement even featured one Jewish leader by 1938. By 1941 the MNS had been reconstituted as the Popular Socialist Vanguard but was already in decline, having failed to find room for growth in Chilean political society, and no longer offering so distinct an alternative as before 1938.[17]

Various attempts at the formation of violent nationalist or radical antileftist mass movements were made in Mexico during these years, but they had the characteristics of the radical right more than of European fascism. The Gold Shirts of General Nicolás Rodríguez, organized in 1934, were violent, anti-Semitic, antileftist, and authoritarian, and directly aped German and Italian styles, but their goals were essentially counterrevolutionary and rightist. They were easily controlled by a government that was itself developing into a

17. The chief study is a doctoral dissertation by Michael Potashnik, "Nacismo: National Socialism in Chile, 1932–1938" (University of California, Los Angeles, 1974).

one-party, semicorporatist system. Only one Mexican president, Plutarco Elías Calles in the early 1930s, seems to have toyed with the idea of fascistizing the Mexican regime. An auxiliary force that he encouraged, Acción Revolucionaria Mexicana (ARM), was identified with the Gold Shirts in an abortive revolt against the subsequent administration in 1938 (the Cedillo rebellion). The main counterrevolutionary mass movement was, however, that of the Cristeros, a major Catholic peasant force that became the largest single popular movement in twentieth-century Mexico, somewhat reminiscent of the Spanish Carlists.[18]

A likely candidate for a "fascist situation" during the 1930s was Bolivia, the only Latin American country during the period to have engaged in and decisively lost an international war, the Chaco conflict with Paraguay from 1932 to 1935. Bolivia's national frustration brought to power an unstable new radical coalition under Colonel David Toro in 1936, composed of radical officers, war veterans organized subsequently as a "Legion," and small socialist and labor groups. Toro's goal was "military socialism," which aimed at corporate economic organization, a new system of national syndicalism, and a partially corporate parliament. Toro fell from power in 1937, but his successors developed a new social constitution (1938) and a prosyndical Labor Code. All this was much less than a Bolivian fascism, but the influence of Italian ideas on military socialism is accepted by the most authoritative scholar in the area.[19] Military socialism set the background for the rise of the nationalist populist left in Bo-

18. Jean Meyer, *La Cristiada*, 3 vols. (Mexico City, 1973); and more broadly, for a general study of diverse forces, see Hugh Campbell, "The Radical Right in Mexico, 1929–1939" (Ph.D. diss. University of California, Los Angeles, 1968).

19. Herbert Klein has published two articles in the *Hispanic American Historical Review*: "David Toro and the Establishment of 'Military Socialism' in Bolivia" 45.1 (February 1965); 25–52; and "Germán Busch and the Era of 'Military Socialism' in Bolivia" 47.2 (May 1967): 166–84; and a general political history, *Parties and Political Change in Bolivia 1880–1952* (London, 1969), especially 228–402.

It might be noted that there is a "Falange" in Bolivia, the Falange Socialista Boliviana. Despite its name, which implies either fascism or socialism,

livia, the Movimiento Nacionalista Revolucionario (MNR). The MNR formed an alliance with a subsequent organization of radical officers, RADEPA, which was pro-Axis in orientation and came to power briefly by coup at the end of 1943. The MNR, however, developed into one of the two outstanding Latin American pluralist populist parties, and finally achieved power on its own in 1952 to begin a Bolivian populist revolution. Though the experiences of the 1930s did serve to radicalize and mobilize portions of Bolivian politics, they encouraged a "typically Latin American" form of national radicalism.

In any consideration of putative fascism in Latin America, by far the greatest attention has been focused on Argentine Peronism. A discussion of "Peronist fascism" necessarily refers to the years of Perón in power (1946–55), not to the subsequent history of the Peronist party as a mass syndical opposition group. It should be noted first of all that the first effort to introduce the style and a little of the substance of Italian Fascism was made under the short-lived military dictatorship of Uriburu between 1930 and 1932, a proposal too radical for most of the Argentine elite. During World War II, however, the Argentine government—which had extensive and hegemonic designs of its own—was more sympathetic to Germany and Italy than was any other major government in the Western Hemisphere. A number of small fascist or profascist groups had already been formed during the 1930s, and a profascist military group, GOU (Grupo de Oficiales Unidos), seized control of the Argentine government in 1943, imposing temporary dictatorship and a policy initially more favorable to the Axis than Argentina had had.[20]

---

the FSB is a right authoritarian corporatist and Catholic movement. Originally founded in 1937, it formed the main political opposition to the MNR revolution, and more recently has been a principal collaborator of the military regime in the 1970s. The program of the FSB is to some extent set forth in Rodolfo Surcou Macedo, *Hacia la revolución integral* (La Paz, 1961); and in *Conozca Falange Socialista Boliviana* (La Paz, 1972).

20. The politics of the Argentine army in this period has been ably studied by Robert Potash in *The Army and Politics in Argentina, 1928–1945* (Stanford, 1969); and more generally by Martin Goldwert in *Democracy, Militarism and Nationalism in Argentina, 1930–1966* (Austin, 1972).

Perón emerged as a leading figure in GOU, and took office as elective president of the Republic in 1946. The uniqueness of Peronism is that its main support stemmed from the mass organization of Argentine labor fomented by his government. The Peronist regime of 1946–55 was a personal government of limited authoritarianism that tolerated a considerable degree of pluralism. Its twin pillars were nationalism and social reform, encouraging industrial development on the one hand and income redistribution on the other, with the ultimate goal of making Argentina the dominant power in South America. Perón had been a military attaché in Fascist Italy and later admitted that he had been influenced by Fascism, but after 1945 strove to create an independent position. The ideology of the regime was termed *Justicialism*, and attempted a synthesis of the four principles of idealism, materialism, individualism and collectivism. Perón defined European fascism as an exaggerated combination of idealism and collectivism that excluded individualism and a salutary materialism, a definition that as far as it goes is not necessarily inaccurate. At one point he declared, "Mussolini was the greatest man of our century, but he committed certain disastrous errors. I, who have the advantage of his precedent before me, shall follow in his footsteps but also avoid his errors."[21]

Most analysts of the Peronist case have concluded that Peronism in power did indeed have most of the characteristics that they variously impute to fascism, even though its military-syndical base made it an unusual example.[22] The regime was of course like nearly all new Latin American systems ec-

21. George Blanksten, *Perón's Argentina* (Chicago, 1953), 279.
22. Blanksten regards Peronism as nearer to being fascist than nonfascist, and S. M. Lipset, in *Political Man* (New York, 1969), terms it a "fascism of the left" (see chap. 5). The fascist categorization is largely accepted by Paul Hayes, *Fascism* (London, 1972); and by H. U. Thamer and Wolfgang Wippermann,, *Faschistische und neofascistische Bewegungen* (Darmstadt, 1977). On the other hand, Gino Germani distinguishes (in my opinion correctly) between European fascism and Argentine "national populism," even though he fails to define their full typological or morphological differences in his *Authoritarianism, Fascism, and National Populism* (New Brunswick, N.J., 1978).

lectic; one of Perón's advisers, speechwriters, and syndical theorists was José Figuerola, a Spaniard who had earlier served as labor advisor to the Spanish dictator Primo de Rivera in the late 1920s.

Though the Peronist political party was organized in 1949 with announced aspirations of becoming a *partido único*, Perón never established a complete and rigid dictatorship. He relied on the support of organized labor, middle-class nationalists, much of the industrialist class, and a significant part of the army officer corps. Having displaced and alienated the formerly dominant landlord class, he had to balance the appeals and discontents of various sectors to sustain his power. Inflation, corruption, and economic slowdown, together with his demagogic and distributive social policies, eventually united the upper classes against him. A feud with the church and mounting national and institutional frustrations turned most of the military against the regime and led to Peron's overthrow in 1955.[23]

A careful assessment reveals that Peronism had most but not all the characteristics of European fascism. It was for a long time not an organized political movement and even after Perón was in power could not define a new system. Perón did express the fascist negatives, and to a certain degree built on cultural and philosophical values akin to European fascist movements, with expansive goals in foreign affairs. The aim of a single-party regime was conceived but never effectively implemented. Perón's "leftist" demagogy and worker mobilization scarcely made him unfascist, as some naively contend, but he did not project the fascist insistence on an or-

23. The literature on Peronism is now extensive. See particularly, in addition to Blanksten's *Perón's Argentina*, R. J. Alexander, *The Perón Era* (New York, 1951); Pierre Lux-Wurm, *Le Péronisme* (Paris, 1965); Peter Waldmann, *Der Peronismus 1943–1955* (Hamburg, 1974); and, on the historical background, M. Falcoff and R. H. Dolkart eds., *Prologue to Perón* (Berkeley, 1976). For the social base, Peter H. Smith, "The Social Base of Peronism," *Hispanic American Historical Review* 52.1 (February 1972): 55–73; and "Social Mobilization, Political Participation, and the Rise of Juan Perón," *Political Science Quarterly* 84.1 (March 1969); 30–49.

ganic new national hierarchy that could effectively discipline society. The ways in which Perón fell short of a complete model of European fascism stemmed from his personal, national, and historical circumstances. In military-dominated Latin American political society, abrupt changes were produced only by the army, and a radical new movement had to be developed from the top downward. Rising to prominence after 1945 and with only limited power at his disposal, Perón purposefully moderated the extent of his ambitions as well as their timing and does not seem to have conceived a full-scale European fascist model as feasible in a country like Argentina after World War II. The crucial use of feminist leadership (Dōna Evita), central to the entire mobilization process, was also a serious deviation from fascist style.

GENERIC FASCISM: A UNIQUELY EUROPEAN PHENOMENON

Thus it seems that the full characteristics of European fascism could not be reproduced on a significant scale outside Europe. The specific preconditions encountered in Europe but not present or not jointly present in other continents were (1) intense nationalist/imperialist competition among newer nations, formed mostly in the 1860s; (2) liberal democratic systems nominally in place in the same countries, but without deep functional roots on the one hand or a dominant elite or oligarchy on the other; (3) opportunity for mobilized nationalism on a mass basis as an independent force not restricted to elites or an institutionalized oligarchy; (4) a new cultural orientation stemming from the cultural and intellectual revolution of 1890–1914.

Japan was intensely nationalist/imperialist, and one of the new states emerging in the 1860s and striving to break into the imperial order, but lacked the opportunity for radical new social and political mobilization, given the limitations of her political development. In addition, her culture remained semitraditionalist and not receptive to the radical new ideas associated with fascism. Latin American nationalism was considerably weaker, and the Latin American polities were normally subject to oligarchic domination. With the partial exception of Argentina, the cultural attitudes and values accompanying fascism had received little exposure. South Africa had a much more fully European type of polity and distribution of power within the white population. However, its international problems were in process of resolution and its culture less secularized. The large black majority perhaps deflected the utility of a national socialist approach to radical nationalism, so that a more prudent and conservative kind of nationalism remained dominant.

It is consequently doubtful that a typology derived from European fascism can be applied to non-European movements or regimes with any specificity. As the two most assiduous students of fascism, Ernst Nolte and Renzo de Felice, have insisted, it was an historical phenomenon primarily limited to Europe during the era of the two world wars.

8

Theories of Fascism

Ever since the March on Rome, political analysts have tried to formulate an interpretation or theory capable of explaining the phenomenon of European fascism. As the only genuinely novel form of radicalism emerging from World War I, and one that seemed to involve multiple ambiguities if not outright contradictions, fascism did not readily lend itself to monocausal explanation or a simple unified theory. For more than half a century the debate has gone on, and there is still no consensus regarding an explanatory concept.[1]

The principal theories or interpretations of fascism have been directed primarily toward a definition of the underlying nature of this supposed species of politics, toward its overall significance, or more commonly, toward its principal sources or causes. The main interpretations may for convenience's sake be summarized in twelve categories, though with the understanding that these concepts are not always

1. The principal studies of the interpretations of fascism are Renzo de Felice, *Interpretations of Fascism* (Cambridge, Mass., 1977); Gregor, *Inter-*

mutually exclusive but in some cases may draw on each other:

1. A violent, dictatorial agent of bourgeois capitalism
2. A twentieth-century form of "Bonapartism"
3. The expression of a unique radicalism of the middle classes
4. The consequence of unique national histories
5. The product of a cultural or moral breakdown
6. A unique metapolitical phenomenon
7. The result of extreme neurotic or pathological psychosocial impulses
8. The product of the rise of amorphous masses
9. A typical manifestation of twentieth-century totalitarianism
10. A revolt against "modernization"
11. The consequence of a certain stage of socioeconomic growth or a phase in the development sequence
12. The denial that any such general phenomenon as generic fascism can be defined

Before briefly considering each of these interpretations, it should be pointed out that few of those who attempt to develop a causal theory or explanatory concept of fascism define exactly what they mean by the term or specifically which parties or movements they are trying to interpret, beyond a primary reference (normally to German National Socialism). The very absence of an empirical definition of what is meant by fascism and an understanding of precisely the groups to which the term is thought to refer has been a major obstacle to conceptual clarification.

---

pretations of Fascism; and Wolfgang Wippermann, *Faschismustheorien* (Darmstadt, 1976). In addition, De Felice has written and edited a more extensive combined commentary and anthology, *Il fascismo: Le interpretazioni dei contemporanei e degli storici* (Bari, 1970); and Ernst Nolte's compendium, *Theorien über den Faschismus* (Köln, 1967), is also useful; as is Gerhard Schulz, *Faschismus Nationalsozialismus: Versionen und theoretische Kontroversen, 1922–1972* (Berlin, 1974).

FASCISM AS A VIOLENT, DICTATORIAL AGENT OF BOURGEOIS CAPITALISM

The notion that fascism is primarily to be understood as the agent of "capitalism," "big business," "finance capital," the "bourgeoisie," or some conceivable combination thereof is one of the oldest, most standard, and widely disseminated interpretations. It was formulated to some extent even before Italian Fascism was formally organized (to explain Mussolini's defection from orthodox socialism) and began to be given general currency, with primary reference to Italy, as early as 1923 in the formulations of the Hungarian Communist Gyula Šaš[2] and the German Clara Zetkin.[3] This became the standard Third International interpretation of fascism, and was also adopted by some non-Communists as well. Leading western exponents of the concept were R. Palme Dutt[4] and Daniel Guérin.[5] Some of the notable recent exponents of the Marxist concept of fascism are Reinhard Kühnl,[6] Nikos Poulantzas,[7] Boris Lopukhov,[8] Alexander Galkin,[9] and Mihaly Vajda,[10] though the last two have in-

2. Gyula Šaš, *Der Faschismus in Italien* (Hamburg, 1923), reprinted in De Felice, *Il facismo*, 68–80; and in the same vein, German Sandomirsky, *Fashizm*, 2 vols., (Moscow-Leningrad, 1923).

3. Clara Zetkin, "Der Kampt gegen den Faschismus," *Protocols of the 1923 Comintern Conference*, reprinted in Nolte, *Theorien*, 88–111.

4. Rajani Palme Dutt, *Fascism and Social Revolution* (London, 1934).

5. Daniel Guérin, *Fascisme et grande capital* (Paris, 1936). For a discussion of other early exponents of the Marxist concept, see De Felice, *Interpretations*, 30–54; and John Cammett, "Communist Theories of Fascism, 1920–1935," *Science and Society* 31.2 (Spring 1967): 149–63.

6. Reinhard Kühnl, *Formen bürgerlicher Herrschaft* (Hamburg, 1971). On expressions of the Marxist theory of fascism in East Germany, see Wippermann, *Faschismustheorien*, 19–37.

7. Nikos Poulantzas, *Fascisme et dictature* (Paris, 1970).

8. Boris Lopukhov, *Fashizm i rabochoe dvizenie v Italii 1919–1929* (Moscow, 1968).

9. Alexander Galkin, "Capitalist Society and Fascism," *Social Sciences: USSR Academy of Sciences* 2 (1970): 128–38, discussed in Gregor, *Interpretations*, 163–68.

10. Mihaly Vajda, *Fascism as a Mass Movement* (London, 1976), and "The Rise of Fascism in Italy and Germany," *Telos* 12 (1972): 3–26, discussed in Gregor, *Interpretations*, 166–70.

troduced serious modifications in the concept (see below). In general, those who follow the Marxist interpretation either do not distinguish, or reject the significance of any distinction, between the core fascist groups and forces of right authoritarianism.

FASCISM AS A TWENTIETH-CENTURY FORM OF "BONAPARTISM"

The inaccuracy of the mere "agent" theory became clear to more perceptive and objective observers, including some Marxists, during the first years of Italian Fascism. In 1930 the dissident German Communist August Thalheimer suggested that instead, fascism should be seen as a contemporary equivalent of "Bonapartism," that is, an autonomous form of authoritarian government independent of specific class domination.[11] In this interpretation, fascism was the product of a political and social crisis in which traditional forms of class domination were not only no longer effective but had produced a situation of relative class equilibrium, allowing a new form of dictatorship to free itself of class domination. Though fascism might benefit certain social sectors more than others, it served, itself, as a political force above all, and could enjoy a transitory independent success until the weight of social and economic factors eventually shifted against it. Some of the more recent Communist theorists such as Galkin and Vajda have incorporated aspects of the Thalheimer explanation, viewing fascism as an atypical crisis produced by certain variants of capitalist society in which the fascist regime manages to some extent to free itself of capitalist domination, at least temporarily.[12]

11. August Thalheimer, "Ueber den Faschismus," *Gegen den Strom*, nos. 2–4 (January 1930), reprinted in De Felice, *Il facismo*, 272–95. For further discussion, see Wippermann, *Faschismustheorien*, 42–48; and the critique by Jost Dülffer, "Bonapartism, Fascism and National Socialism," *JCH* 11.4 (October 1976), 109–28.

12. Samuel Farber, in *Revolution and Reaction in Cuba, 1933–1960* (Middletown, Conn., 1977), applies the Bonapartist concept to the Castro revolution, not altogether unconvincingly.

FASCISM AS THE EXPRESSION
OF A UNIQUE RADICALISM
OF THE MIDDLE CLASSES

A different social-class concept of fascism has been suggested by several observers and scholars who do not see fascism as the agent of a bourgeoisie but rather as the vehicle of sectors of the middle classes, previously denied status among the national elite, to forge a new national system that will give them a more salient role. This interpretation was first suggested by Luigi Salvatorelli in his *Nazionalfascismo* (1923), when he underscored the role of the "humanistic petite bourgeoisie"—civil servants, the professionally educated— seeking to restructure the Italian state and society against both the higher capitalist bourgeoisie and the workers. His interpretation has drawn considerable support from the leading student of Italian Fascism[13] and also from the most official historian of that movement.[14] It largely coincides with the thesis of Seymour Lipset about fascism as the "radicalism of the center."[15]

This approach explains the social recruitment of part of the base of certain major fascist parties and also accounts for certain aspects of the fascist program. Yet it is limited in its explanatory ability, for it fails to account for the numbers of fascist supporters outside the middle classes in such diverse countries as Germany, Hungary, and Romania. Nor is it able to explain the full nature and extent of radical goals among leaders so different as Hitler, Déat, Piasecki, and Codreanu. The "radicalism of the middle classes" thus accounts for one of the most important strands of fascism, but is inadequate to provide a general theory of fascism.

13. De Felice, *Interpretations*, 130, 174–92, and *Fascism: An Informal Introduction to its Theory and Practice* (New Brunswick, N.J., 1976).

14. Gioacchino Volpe, *Storia del movimento fascista* (Milan, 1939), 46–47.

15. Lipset, "Fascism—Left, Right and Center," chapter 5 of his *Political Man* (New York, 1960).

FASCISM AS THE CONSEQUENCE
OF UNIQUE NATIONAL HISTORIES

Various writers and historians have tried to portray Fascism[16] and Nazism[17] as essentially unique Italian and German diseases, stemming from defective cultural and social values and institutions rooted in the earlier histories of these countries. Though such an approach cannot by any means be totally discounted, its proponents have increasingly lost support because of the superficiality of their analyses of the two national histories involved, analyses which failed to make adequate comparisons with other countries that had similar factors and problems, whether or not to a lesser degree. This has been recognized as leading to an unhistorical and unempirical reductionism.

FASCISM AS THE PRODUCT
OF A CULTURAL OR MORAL BREAKDOWN

Historians of culture in Germany and Italy, led by such figures as Benedetto Croce[18] and Friedrich Meinecke,[19] have seen fascism as the product of cultural fragmentation and moral relativism in European values from the late nineteenth century on. In this view, the crisis of World War I and its aftermath, producing intense economic dislocation, social conflict, and cultural anomie, resulted in a kind of spiritual collapse that permitted novel forms of radical nationalism to

16. For example, D. Mack Smith, *Italy: A Modern History* (Ann Arbor, 1959).

17. This literature, somewhat simple-minded in focus, flourished especially during World War II. Leading examples are Edmond Vermeil, *Doctrinaires de la révolution allemande* (Paris, 1939); W. M. McGovern, *From Luther to Hitler: The History of Fascist-Nazi Political Philosophy* (New York, 1941); and Peter Viereck, *Metapolitics: From the Romantics to Hitler* (Boston, 1941).

18. References to and evaluations of Croce's writings on fascism will be found in Gregor, *Interpretations*, 29–32.

19. Selections from Meinecke, Hans Kohn, and Gerhard Ritter in this vein are presented and discussed in De Felice, *Il fascismo*, 391–437.

flourish. One of the most cogent contemporary statements of this approach was made by Peter Drucker.[20]

The weakness of the cultural or moral-crisis approach alone is that it only tries to explain which conditions permitted fascist movements to develop, without accounting for their specific ideas, values, forms, or goals. By contrast, A. James Gregor in his *The Ideology of Fascism* (New York, 1969) argues that Italian Fascism developed a coherent ideology that was not the product of nihilistic collapse but rather the consequence of specific new cultural, political, and sociological ideas developed in western and central Europe during the late nineteenth and early twentieth centuries.

FASCISM AS A UNIQUE METAPOLITICAL PHENOMENON

The most renowned student of facism, Ernst Nolte, interprets fascism in a manner quite different from any of the foregoing theories, for he dismisses most of the factors advanced by other interpreters as either secondary or tending to irrelevance. Nolte views fascism primarily as a metapolitical phenomenon, that is, as the product of certain political, cultural and ideological aspirations arising out of liberal democracy and aiming to create a radically new order, with new values and doctrines of its own, rejecting existing projects of "transcendence," and seeking an alternate kind of revolution of the right. For him, fascism is a product of the era of world wars and of Bolshevism, seeking to counteract the latter by adopting some of its forms and techniques.[21]

Though few scholars have accepted Nolte's exact formulations, other leading figures have suggested metapolitical interpretations of their own. Before Nolte's first book was published, Eugen Weber suggested that fascism was a unique and specific revolutionary project in its own right,[22] while

---

20. Peter Drucker, *The End of Economic Man* (New York, 1939).
21. Ernst Nolte, *Three Faces of Fascism* (New York, 1966).
22. Eugen Weber, *Varieties of Fascism* (New York, 1964).

George Mosse, the leading historian of Nazi and pre-Nazi culture,[23] interprets fascism as a revolution of the right with transcendental goals of its own and specific, not merely reactive or opportunistic, cultural and ideological content.[24] Somewhat similarly, the Catholic philosopher Augusto del Noce sees fascism as the revolutionary form of certain European nationalisms during the "first age of secularization," when modern secularism was still capable of projecting idealistic and semitranscendent goals and before the complete victory of materialism and consumerism. He interprets Italian Fascism as the competitor of Leninism and the more radical German National Socialism as the competitive counterpart of Stalinism, thus constituting two different phases of twentieth-century radicalism.[25]

FASCISM AS THE RESULT
OF EXTREME NEUROTIC
OR PATHOLOGICAL PSYCHOSOCIAL IMPULSES

This approach is more intuitive than empirical, but flourished in some quarters during and immediately after the fascist era. Its most widely read theorists have been Erich Fromm, Wilhelm Reich, and Theodor Adorno and his colleagues. Fromm's *Escape from Freedom* (New York, 1941, 1965)

23. George L. Mosse, *The Crisis of German Ideology* (New York, 1964), *Nazi Culture* (New York, 1968), *Germans and Jews* (New York, 1970), *The Nationalization of the Masses* (New York, 1975), and "The Genesis of Fascism," *JCH* 1.1 (April 1966): 14–26.

24. George L. Mosse, *Nazism: A History and Comparative Analysis of National Socialism* (New Brunswick, N.J., 1978). Mosse's review of Nolte, probably the best critique of the latter, appeared in the *Journal of the History of Ideas* 27.4 (Oct.–Dec., 1966); 621–25. J. P. Stern, in *Hitler: The Führer and the People* (Glasgow, 1975), tends to agree with Mosse.

25. Augusto del Noce, *L'Epoca della secolarizzazione* (Milan, 1970), 111–35; and "Per una definizione storica del fascismo," in *Il problema storico del fascismo* (Florence, 1970), 11–46.

Peter Merkl, in "Comparing Fascist Movements" (Larsen et al., eds., *Who Were the Fascists?*), adds another variant by concluding that "the evidence for generational revolt as the one great motivating force all these diverse fascist movements have in common appears to be strong indeed."

contended that facism should be seen as the product of decaying central-European middle-class society, but differed from the standard Marxist approach by laying the main emphasis on feelings of isolation, impotence, anomie, and frustration.

A more extreme Freudian approach was exemplified by Wilhelm Reich's *The Mass Psychology of Fascism* (New York, 1930, 1946, 1970), which propounded a psychosexual explanation. Reich viewed fascism as a combination of sexual repression and sadomasochistic compensatory and aggressive impulses, and as the natural consequence of a "bourgeois society" grounded on sexual repression.

A different but not unrelated approach may be found in the work by Theodor Adorno et al., *The Authoritarian Personality* (New York, 1950). This study suggested that fascism could be understood as the prime expression of certain "authoritarian personality" traits that tended toward rigidity, repression, and dictatorship, and might be most commonly expected among the interwar central-European middle classes.

The weakness of these theories is in the unverifiably speculative content of the concepts of Fromm and Reich and the peculiarly reductionist nature of the latter's sexual ideas, which cannot be rendered methodologically applicable to the main dimensions of the problem. The "authoritarian personality" inventory is more specific and empirical, but subsequent investigation has been unable to substantiate any clear assumptions about middle-class or central-European personality traits in this period, and one empirical study not surprisingly found communist personalities as "authoritarian" as those of fascists.

FASCISM AS THE PRODUCT OF THE RISE OF AMORPHOUS MASSES

Another concept of fascism considers it the product of unique qualitative changes in European society, as the traditional class structure gave way to large, undifferentiated, and atomized populations—the "masses" of urban, industrial society. This idea was first advanced by José Ortega y Gasset,[26] and in varying ways has been reformulated by Emil Lederer,[27] Talcott Parsons,[28] and Hannah Arendt,[29] and perhaps most cogently by William Kornhauser.[30] It emphasizes the irrational, antiintellectual, and visceral nature of the fascist appeal to "mass man," and thus to some extent complements the "cultural breakdown" theory.

This approach tends, however, to obfuscate the extent to which practical ideological content and cogent appeals to tangible interests figured in the programs and practices of fascist movements, as well as the extent to which many of their supporters were still identified and definable as members of structured social or institutional sectors. Moreover, it fails to distinguish between the nature of "mass society" in the German context as distinct from any other industrialized country.

FASCISM AS A TYPICAL MANIFESTATION OF TWENTIETH-CENTURY TOTALITARIANISM

In the immediate aftermath of World War II, when the specter of a Europe dominated by Hitlerism was replaced by that of one dominated by Stalinism, a new line of interpretation developed among some western political theorists which suggested that fascism in general, but more specifically National Socialism, did not constitute an absolutely unique category or genus but was merely one typical manifestation of the much broader and even more sinister general phenomenon of twentieth-century totalitarianism, which would endure long after the specific fascist movements had expired.[31] This concept enjoyed considerable vogue during the 1950s

26. José Ortega y Gasset, *The Revolt of the Masses* (New York, 1932).

27. Emil Lederer, *The State of the Masses* (New York, 1940).

28. Talcott Parsons, "Some Sociological Aspects of the Fascist Movements," in his *Essays in Sociological Theory*, rev. ed. (New York, 1949).

29. Hannah Arendt, *The Origins of Totalitarianism* (New York, 1951).

30. William Kornhauser, *The Politics of Mass Society* (New York, 1959).

31. The key statement of this approach is Carl J. Friedrich and Zbigniew Brzezinski, *Totalitarian Dictatorship and Autocracy* (New York, 1956). Also *Totalitarianism*, ed. Carl J. Friedrich (New York, 1954).

but later drew increasing criticism. Hannah Arendt excepted Mussolini's Italy from the whole category of totalitarian systems, undercutting the concept of generic fascism as totalitarianism. Later still, in a major article, Wolfgang Sauer drew attention to common features of Fascism and National Socialism and the differences from Communist systems,[32] casting further doubt on any common identity as generic totalitarianism. Western theorists have encountered increasing difficulty in defining totalitarianism—even though this may merely be due to perverseness and simplism—[33] and some doubt its existence as a continuous, comparable category at all.[34]

FASCISM AS RESISTANCE TO MODERNIZATION

The old argument that fascism was merely irrational and incomprehensible in normal terms has been given a new twist by some western scholars in recent years who have interpreted it as an expression of resistance to "modernization"—however variously defined. They see fascist movements as primarily opposed to central features of western liberal society such as urbanization, industrialization, liberal education, rationalist materialism, individualism, social differentiation, and pluralist autonomy, and so categorize fascism as inherently opposed to modernization "itself." Henry A. Turner, Jr., has provided the most succinct, direct statement of this point of view.[35] Wolfgang Sauer interprets fascism as the political movement of "losers" in the modernization process, while Barrington Moore, employing a highly elastic

32. Wolfgang Sauer, "National Socialism: Totalitarianism or Fascism?" *AHR* 73.2 (December 1967): 404–22.

33. For example, Hans Buchheim, in *Totalitarian Rule* (Middletown, Conn., 1968). comes up with such fatuities as "The concept of totalitarian rule cannot be determined by purely logical means" (p. 11), and "The essence of fascism is rebellion against freedom" (p. 23), and so on.

34. Cf. Herbert Spiro, "Totalitarianism," *International Encyclopedia of the Social Sciences* (New York, 1968), vol. 16.

35. Henry A. Turner, Jr., "Fascism and Modernization," *World Politics* 24.4 (July 1972): 547–64, reprinted in Turner's *Reappraisals of Fascism*, 117–39.

definition of fascism, believes that it was the product of an aberrant modernization process controlled by martial, rural elites.[36] Ernst Nolte has argued that fascism was, among other things, the expression of resistance to modern "transcendance," a philosophical concept that seems to be not unrelated to that of modernization in the social sciences. Alan Cassels, however, offers a major qualification to the antimodernist thesis by his concept of "two faces of fascism," suggesting that in some underdeveloped countries fascism was a modernizing force, but turned against the modernization process in countries like Germany that were already industrialized.[37] The antimodernity thesis has been vigorously combatted by a few scholars, some of whom argue an interpretation that is diametrically opposed.[38]

FASCISM AS THE CONSEQUENCE OF A CERTAIN STAGE OF SOCIOECONOMIC GROWTH OR PHASE IN THE DEVELOPMENT SEQUENCE

Most of the preceding interpretations were "classical concepts," formulated originally in the 1920s and 30s in terms of the fundamental interests or impulses of European society or its economic structure. A different approach emerged twenty years after the defeat of Nazi Germany, and was influenced by general ideas about the structural and political imperatives of economic modernization and the recent experiences of newly emerging "Third World" countries.

The stages of growth concept holds that the process of modernization and industrialization has frequently tended

36. Barrington Moore, Jr., *Social Origins of Dictatorship and Democracy* (Boston, 1966).

37. Alan Cassels, "Janus: The Two Faces of Fascism," *Canadian Historical Papers 1969*, 166–84, reprinted in Turner, ed., *Reappraisals of Fascism*, 69–92; and Cassels's textbook, *Fascism* (New York, 1974).

38. See, for example, A. James Gregor, "Fascism and Modernization: Some Addenda," *World Politics* 26.3 (April 1973): 370–84; and also Ludovico Garruccio [pseud.], *L'industrializzazione tra nazionalismo e rivoluzione* (Bologna, 1969).

to produce severe internal conflict as the balance of power shifts between or threatens various social and economic groups. Those who lean toward this approach differ from the Marxists in not reducing the conflict to a capital versus labor struggle but defining it more broadly in terms of a large range of social/structural forces and national interests.

Two leading exponents of this approach have been A. F. K. Organski and Ludovico Garruccio (pseud.). Organski[39] has suggested that the potential for fascism arises at the point at which the industrial sector of the economy first begins to equal in size and labor force that of the primary sector, creating the potential for severe conflicts that also serve to elicit aggressive nationalism and authoritarian government. The trouble with this concept is that its author did not refine it sufficiently to make it uniquely applicable to Italy and other countries undergoing a "fascist" experience, and as such it cannot be applied to Germany (nor does its author attempt to do so). Most countries passing through that stage of growth have never experienced anything that could be called fascism.

Perhaps the most serious effort to understand fascism in terms of broad comparative patterns of modernization is Ludovico Garruccio's *L'industrializzazione tra nazionalismo e rivoluzione*. It suggests that what was known as fascism was the central-European variant of a common experience of crisis, normally issuing into authoritarian government, that has accompanied the effort of modern nations (or, in the case of Russia, empires) to establish their identity and power on a modern basis, overcome internal conflict, and complete their social and economic modernization. This concept is extremely suggestive, and may help to explain the relationship of fascism to communism and to Third World development dictatorships, but fails to identify or explain the unique historical features of European fascism.

39. A. F. K. Organski, *The Stages of Political Development* (New York, 1965), and "Fascism and Modernization," in Woolf, ed., *The Nature of Fascism*, 19–41. This line of interpretation was to some degree foreshadowed by Franz Borkenau in his 1933 article "Zur Soziologie des Faschismus," reprinted in Nolte, *Theorien*, 156–81.

A. James Gregor has in some respects expanded this approach by arguing that fascism in diverse manifestations is, more than communism, the typical revolution of the twentieth century, for it was the first to introduce new techniques and concepts of national revolution and integrated dictatorship.[40] Italian Fascism is specifically identified as a prototype of the mass mobilizing development dictatorship designed to achieve a broad threshold of modernization,[41] though this concept is not specifically applied to other presumed fascisms.

THE DENIAL THAT ANY SUCH GENERAL PHENOMENON AS GENERIC FASCISM CAN BE DEFINED

There are, finally, a few keen analysts of a nominalist turn of mind who have concluded that generic fascism is a projection of the imagination and that the various putative fascist movements are too dissimilar to form a distinct category. Depending on how rigidly or uniformly the category of generic fascism is defined, they may well be right. The most direct statement of this position has been made by Gilbert Allardyce,[42] but in varying degrees it has been supported by Karl D. Bracher (who does not deny the possibility of constructing an abstract "fascist minimum" but doubts its utility), John Lukacs, and others.

40. A. James Gregor, *The Fascist Persuasion in Radical Politics* (Princeton, 1974).
41. In Gregor's forthcoming study of Italian Fascist policy.
42. Gilbert Allardyce, "What Fascism is Not: Thoughts on the Deflation of a Concept," *AHR* 84.2 (April 1979), 367–88.

9
Generic Fascism: A Conclusion

It has been amply demonstrated that few problems in recent European history have generated more controversy than the interpretation of fascism. The controversy centers mainly on two issues: one is the search for adequate theories or interpretations that can "explain" fascism and its causes, as surveyed in the preceding chapter; the other involves the question of whether or not a generic fascism, as distinct from a variety of sometimes basically different radical and authoritarian nationalist movements and regimes, can be demonstrated to have existed with any degree of unity or similarity.

Most of the theories that have been mentioned can be easily shown to lack general or even specific validity. They tend toward the monocausal or reductionist and can be either disproven or shown to be inadequate with greater or lesser ease. Moreover, most of those who try to deal with the theory of fascism are not primarily concerned with a common or comparative category of diverse movements and regimes but refer either exclusively or primarily to German National Socialism, which drastically reduces the scope and application of their arguments.

The original Fascists and Nazis, like scholars and polemicists of a later day, themselves went back and forth on the issue of a common "generic" fascism. Even before Mussolini came to power, the term *fascist* was occasionally being extended to other nationalist and authoritarian groups by Communists, who encountered in the Italian Fascists a new phenomenon, the first example of a successful new violent multiclass anticommunist force, a unique and formidable enemy who used some of the Communists' own weapons. This was a development never predicted nor easily explained in the classic Marxist schema. Nevertheless, the label was quickly recognized by Communists as a useful polemical device, and within a few years its application had been stretched out of any conceivably recognizable content, as Communists began to apply it (accompanied by all manner of hyphenated adjectives) to virtually every noncommunist movement. This was the primary origin of the rhetorical and polemical use of the term which has predominated since. By the same token "antifascism" became an equally broad and vague concept and was taken up in some countries before any fascism existed to combat.

Conversely, Italian Fascists were at first wont to deny any intrinsic similarity between their movement and new authoritarian nationalists in Germany or elsewhere. Mussolini, rather typically, failed to adopt a firm and consistent position one way or the other. As early as 1921 he suggested to a Romanian admirer that like-minded activists might form a Romanian equivalent of Fascism (and in fact an ephemeral Romanian Fascist Party was formed in 1923), and in 1923 he responded to the flattery of his first formal state visitors, the King of Spain and the Spanish dictator Primo de Rivera, by suggesting that Fascism did present a series of generalizable characteristics that might be reproduced elsewhere. But when Mussolini visited Germany that same year, he found it politic to deny any fundamental similarity between Fascism and the German authoritarian nationalist groups. In 1925 Giuseppe Bastianini presented an enthusiastic report to the Fascist Grand Council that there were already groups in forty different countries which either called themselves fascist or were so termed by others. Yet in the following year Mussolini denied any real similarity to or connection with those who were sometimes called Hungarian fascists, and so it went. In March 1928 he made his famous statement, "Fascism is not for export."[1]

In effect Mussolini always wavered between the notion that Fascism had developed a new style, a new set of beliefs, values, and political forms that might constitute the basis of Italian hegemony in a broader European fascism, and his realization that such ambitions were imprudent, would be difficult to achieve, and would always face conflict and contradiction with would-be fascists elsewhere who would press their own national interests and exhibit marked national idiosyncracies.

Hitler's approach, at least vis-a-vis Italy, was more firm, practical, and consistent. He is abundantly on record as having become convinced, at least from the time of the March on Rome, that Fascism and National Socialism shared a common destiny. Though not at all considered identical in the sense of point-by-point similarity, they were deemed historical equivalents in their respective countries. While Hitler remained firm in that general conviction from beginning to end, he did not try to develop a worldwide concept of generic national socialism, and would not normally call National Socialism "fascist." Since the core of Nazism was race, the most specific counterparts of Nazism were to be found less in political forms and characteristics than in the most firm supporters of the Aryan racial principle and Aryan racial revolution, wherever they might be. In the process of Europe-wide racial revolution, Hitler however soon became convinced that a combination of political characteristics and national interests dictated that Italy would be the most natural immediate ally of a National Socialist Germany. If this conclusion was in one sense contradictory, Hitler proved fully consistent in its prosecution and for some time even respected Ital-

---

1. See especially Meir Michaelis, "I rapporti tra fascismo e nazismo prima dell' avento di Hitler al potere (1922–1933)," *Rivista Storica Italiana* 85.3 (September 1973): 544–600.

ian control of the Alto Adige (a northeastern corner of Italy inhabited by German-speaking people). This position was much appreciated. By 1928, if not before, the NSDAP was one of several authoritarian nationalist groups being subsidized by the Italian state.[2]

Hitler's unswerving admiration for Mussolini and by extension (but more weakly) for Fascism was not necessarily shared by other leading Nazis. The ideologist Rosenberg was interested in an international association of kindred movements, but increasingly deprecated the racial confusion and intermittent philosemitism of the Fascists. Some of the more radical Nazis rejected the Mussolini regime for other reasons, especially for being too conservative or allegedly capitalistic, aversions shared in varying ways and degrees by Gregor Strasser, Goebbels, and Himmler. (This conviction that Fascist corporatism was too capitalist or conservative would be a common criticism later among national syndicalists or national socialists in Spain, France, Japan, and elsewhere.) Strasser also considered the *Führerprinzip* to have been pioneered by Mussolini (in a sense that was correct) and resented it as a "fascist" foreign import.[3]

In general, nonetheless, Mussolini and certain other Fascist leaders turned increasingly, if not unswervingly, toward contact with and support for other nationalist groups abroad. Subsidies in the late 1920s were one aspect of this policy, the strongly pro-Nazi stance of the anti-Semitic Fascist journal *Il Tevere* another. The new Fascist review *Antieuropa*, founded in 1929, was directed especially toward the universality of fascist-type radical nationalism, but at first harbored no illusions as to absolute generic identity or a fascist international. The hypernationalism of parallel groups, if nothing else, would bring them into mutual conflict so that "they could not be friends."[4]

The collapse of the Spanish regime of Primo de Rivera was something of a blow to Mussolini, but he hailed the big elec-

2. Ibid., 597–600.
3. Ibid., 582–83.
4. Ibid., 575, 584–86.

toral victories of Hitler that began in 1930. While Hitler declared that National Socialism marked a "fascistization" of
Germany (admittedly not his normal terminology), Mussolini applauded the advance of what he eventually termed
"German fascism" and its victory in 1933,[5] despite an earlier
preference for the more conservative Stahlhelm.

By 1934 the Italian regime was promoting "universal fascism" on the one hand, however, while increasingly dis-
sociating itself from German National Socialism. That year
marked the peak of a war of words in which all the negative
features of Nazism and the differences between itself and
Fascism were underscored and sometimes exaggerated. Mussolini put all this behind him with the formation of the Axis,
but lesser Nazi leaders remained scornful of Fascism for its
limitations, conservatism, and lack of full revolutionary potential.[6]

In sum, the top Fascists and Nazis realized that they had a
lot in common and seemed to represent a new departure
compared with previous political groups, but they were uncertain just how far any mutual identity extended, and remained conscious of major, some thought decisive, differences between themselves. As indicated in chapter 4, the
original Fascists were unable to solve the political and conceptual problem of generic fascism, even when they made a
specific effort to affirm and define it in the 1930s

My own conclusion, after two decades of examining various and manifold forms of fascistiana, is that a rigorous "ei-
ther-or" approach toward the problem of generic fascism is
fundamentally misleading. That is, the common reduction of
all putative fascisms to one single generic phenomenon of
absolutely common identity is distortive and inaccurate,
while a radically nominalist approach which insists that all
radical nationalist movements of interwar Europe were inherently different, though correct in the ultimate sense that
none was a carbon copy of any other, has the opposite defect
of ignoring distinctive similarities. Even some of the most

5. Ibid., 572–77.
6. Cf. the quotations in Arendt, *Totalitarianism*.

distinguished critics of the concept of generic fascism, such as Karl Bracher and Renzo de Felice, admit that it is analytically possible to define certain common characteristics that would compose a "fascist minimum," while denying that such generic identity is capable of specifying what was most significant and historically decisive about any presumably fascist movement. Thus the typology of fascism presented in chapter 1 has been used throughout this book as a touchstone to demarcate the type of movement classified as fascist, but without assuming that the generic typology could define all the most important features of any individual movement.

LIMITATIONS OF THE GENERIC CONCEPT: THE VARIETIES OF FASCISM

As stated earlier, the suggested typological description of common features of a generic fascism is useful only for limited purposes of comparison and distinction. On occasion the differences between fascistic movements—whether political or ideological—seemed almost as important as the similarities. When employing an inductive inventory of characteristics of generic fascism, individual movements should be understood to have potentially possessed (depending upon cases) further beliefs, goals, and characteristics of major importance that did not necessarily contradict the common features but went beyond them. For these reasons, the typological description may serve as an analytical or heuristic device but should not be used as a monolithic, reified taxonomic category.[7] It may help us to understand the common traits of the most radical forms of a generation of Euro-

7. Hence the term *generic* has been used simply for general illustration and in conformity with verbal convention. To try to apply exact taxonomic language, which is usually derived from biological references, would probably lead to greater uncertainty and confusion, since we do not have sufficient understanding of political movements to demonstrate that they conform to or differ from each other with the taxonomic regularity or distinctness observable in the biological world. The term *generic fascism* is used only in a tentative sense, and is not intended to indicate that fascistic movements constituted a specific, delimited "genus" altogether distinct from other pos-

pean nationalism, conditioned by unique cultural, political, and social influences, but cannot provide the full historical definition of each of these movements. It may, however, serve to underscore the historical uniqueness of fascism if we are able to conclude that neither before 1919 nor after 1945 have significant political movements existed sharing the full cluster of fascist characteristics.

Some scholars perceived early that European fascism was not uniform but included a variety of distinct subtypes. They have defined this problem diversely. Eugen Weber distinguished two general subtypes or tendencies among fascist movements, the "fascist" proper or Italian, and the "national socialist," contending that the Italian type was pragmatic (and hence more moderate, even conservative) and the national socialist type more theoretically motivated and fanatical, hence more radical and destructive. More recently, Alan Cassels has suggested a kind of dichotomy between southwest-European fascists and central-European national social-

---

sible "genera" of political movements, or that there was a necessarily direct and identifiable genetic relationship between them.

If a tentative and limited identification of generic fascism is to be categorized in comparison with other nonparliamentary parties, then it might be identified as one of the major types of revolutionary mass movements that have emerged since the 1790s, of which at least six general types can be identified:

1. Jacobin (1792–1871 or 1917), leading to the radical republican movements of southern Europe in the nineteenth and early twentieth centuries
2. Anarchist (1835–1939)
3. Socialist (1868–1939) (R. Luxemburg, Mensheviks, PSI, Austro-Marxists, PSDE)
4. Leninist (1903–)
5. Fascist (1919–45)
6. Populist (1890–)

The latter is the most amorphous genus of the entire family, presumably embracing the Russian SRs, the Stambuliski peasant party, the early Mexican PRI or its immediate antecedents, APRA, the Bolivian MNR, the early Kuomintang, and probably a number of other Third World movements.

One might possibly add a seventh category of mass counterrevolutionary movements with some radical goals of their own, most notably the Spanish Carlists.

ists in terms of modernizing and regressive tendencies.[8] Wolfgang Sauer distinguished between three different "subtypes of fascism": the "original Mediterranean"; the "various and not too long-lived regimes" of east-central Europe as "a mixed, or not full-fledged variation; and German Nazism as a special form."[9]

There is substance to most of these distinctions, especially in the case of Weber's basic duality, but none of them is sufficiently detailed to make allowance for all the major subtypes. Since fascism was grounded in extreme nationalism, national movements sensitively reflected institutional, cultural, social, and spiritual differences in their own countries, producing many national variations. A minimum of six varieties can be identified (though some might make the list considerably longer):

1. Paradigmatic Italian Fascism, pluralistic, diverse and not easily definable in simple terms. Forms to some extent derivative appeared in France, England, Belgium, Austria, Hungary, Romania, and possibly even Brazil.

2. German National Socialism, sometimes defined as the most extreme or radical form of fascism, the only fascistic movement to achieve a total dictatorship and so to develop its own system. Somewhat parallel or derivative movements emerged in Scandinavia, the Low Countries, the Baltic States and Hungary, and more artificially, in several of the satellite states during the war. The Italian and German types were the two predominant, but not the only, forms of fascism.

3. Spanish Falangism. Though to some extent derivative from the Italian form, it became a kind of Catholic and culturally more traditionalist fascism that was more marginal.

4. The Romanian Legionary or Iron Guard movement, a mystical, kenotic form of semireligious fascism that repre-

---

8. Cassels, *Fascism*. Andrew Janos has also drawn a distinction in an unpublished paper, "Two Faces of East European Fascism."

9. Wolfgang Sauer, "National Socialism: Totalitarianism or Fascism?," *AHR* 73.2 (December 1967), 404–22.

sented the only notable movement of this kind in an Orthodox country, and was also marginal.

5. Szalasi's "Hungarist" or Arrow Cross movement, somewhat distinct from either the Hungarian national socialists or Hungarian proponents of a more moderate and pragmatic Italian-style movement, and for a short time, perhaps, the second most popular fascist movement in Europe.

6. Abortive undeveloped fascisms attempted through bureaucratic means by right-wing authoritarian regimes, mainly in eastern Europe during the 1930s. None of these efforts, however, produced fully formed and complete fascist organizations.

Since fascist politics was a novel and late-blooming form, a large proportion of fascist leaders and even ordinary activists began their political careers in association with nonfascist groups, usually either of the radical left or Catholic or authoritarian right. The transformation that issued into fascist politics and organization was rarely instantaneous and complete. Sometimes a long evolutionary period of five years and more was required for the transformation into fascism, and sometimes that metamorphosis was never complete, stopping short at the boundary of a kind of partial protofascism. Thus amid the tensions of the 1930s many groups and movements were denounced as fascist, when they did not fully exhibit the characteristics of generic fascism but were simply moving toward certain aspects of fascist doctrine or style; or they may have merely begun to exhibit a few of the external trappings of fascist organizations, as was frequently the case with rightist groups, without actually adopting the radical spirit, doctrines and goals of generic fascism. The undeniable vertigo produced by fascist politics during the depression decade induced displays of window-dressing in marginally related groups that was frequently accepted for the real thing. Not only did it confuse analysts and historians of a subsequent generation, but it also confused the original fascists themselves, when Mussolini's regime began to move toward a broader doctrine of "universal fascism" and then was faced with the problem of identifying kindred fascist or sympathetic and fascistizing or fascistizable elements in other countries.[10]

THE DISTINCTION BETWEEN
FASCIST MOVEMENTS AND REGIMES

Another major source of confusion in defining generic fascism has stemmed from the failure to distinguish between fascist movements and regimes. Most fascist parties failed to develop beyond the movement stage, and even in Italy the Fascists as a movement never assumed full power to develop a complete regime-system. One of the many paradoxes of fascist movements was that though they aspired to destroy the liberal political system (or more exactly, its residues) and introduce a peculiarly apolitical style of militarized politics, they were nonetheless constrained to function in large measure as a regular political force within liberal or semiliberal political systems. This was due in part to their need to rely on portions of the middle classes, and to the fact that such mobilized national-integrative movements could develop only in countries that had already achieved a not-inconsiderable degree of social and political development, which brought with it electoral parliamentary systems of comparatively long standing that had to be coped with. Thus fascist movements were never able to function as revolutionary-insurrectionist forces in the Leninist-Maoist style—the means whereby all independent communist parties that established their own regimes have come to power. The fact that fascist movements were forced to work out their militarized style of politics largely within a middle-class parliamentary framework exposed them to major contradictions and normally made it difficult for them to work with existing parliamentary groups. Even in the most favorable situations, radical authoritarian movements or coalitions aiming at a

10. See Ledeen, *Universal Fascism;* and De Felice, "I movimenti fascisti nel mondo," *Mussolini il Duce,* appendix 8.

new dictatorship have great, normally insurmountable, difficulty in passing the "40-percent barrier," and this is true of such diverse movements as German National Socialism, Austromarxism, parliamentary communism in southwestern Europe, or the Allende coalition in Chile. Fascist movements, at any rate, were always dependent on allies in the final drive for power. Most of them failed to find effective allies, and the majority of those who did were in varying ways overwhelmed by their allies, whether the more conservative right, or during the war, the maximal fascist regime of Germany.

Thus in the absence of a plurality of generically fascist regimes and systems, it is possible to refer only to a number of semifascist or would-be-fascist regimes, while in turn distinguishing between the character and structure of each type and subtype both among themselves and in comparison to diverse kinds of conservative (or at least nonsocialist) nonfascist authoritarian regimes. In general, the genus to which these refer is not that of fascist systems but rather of syncretic or mixed national authoritarian regimes of the twentieth century, of which the prototototalitarian National Socialist regime in Germany may be considered the most extreme or atypical variation.

Rather than an anomaly, as Anglo-American theorists long considered it, the syncretic national authoritarian system has become the most common new political form of the twentieth century and is more numerous than either liberal parliamentary or totalitarian socialist systems, though the latter will presumably grow in number in the future. Within this general group at least seven different types may be identified:

1. The Hitler regime as the most extreme expression of generic fascism and the only completely fascist regime-system. It moved toward the elimination of all pluralism and by its last year of life had nearly achieved that. The fact that the Hitler regime represented the only fully fascist-controlled system, however, should not be interpreted as a demonstration that it realized the inherent tendencies of

all fascist movements, for it represented only one specific form of fascism.

2. The Mussolini regime, created in large measure on the basis of the Fascist movement, but in fact established and developed as a more limited and even semipluralist dictatorship in which the party was largely subordinated to the state and system rather than merely to the leader. The state itself completely failed to realize its own theoretical aspirations toward totalitarianism (and in fact gave a less-than-total meaning to the term), as many analysts have recognized.

3. Satellite fascist or semifascist regimes established by or through the Nazi imperium during World War II. As satellite and semicolonial regimes they largely lacked authenticity or independent political significance. Their actual structure was mostly of the more syncretic type mentioned in categories four and five, with the possible exceptions of the Szalasi and Quisling governments. The Croatian Ustasha regime had to water down aspects of its newfound fascism because of the need to ally with other, especially Catholic, groups, and the Slovak regime remained rooted in political Catholicism and limited pluralism. The Vichy regime, at most, never harbored more than a modest component of generic fascism. Hitler normally preferred to deal with either conservative right-wing elements or the more moderate sectors of foreign fascist groups. Extreme maximal fascists abroad who verged on the national socialist type—or conversely varied too widely from it—were themselves too radically nationalist, competitive, and hard to deal with.

4. Syncretic dictatorships based on a nonfascist leadership principle, usually derived from military command and a semipluralist national coalition but combining a significant fascist party component. The chief examples would be Spain from 1937 to 1945 and Romania from 1940 to 1944.

5. Syncretic, semipluralist authoritarian regimes lacking a mass-based government or a distinctive new state system

which strove to develop a semibureaucratic fascist movement from the top downward but normally failed in the
enterprise. Examples would be Poland, 1937–39; Romania, 1938–40; Hungary, 1932–40 (somewhat intermittently); and to some extent Yugoslavia, 1935–39, and
Greece, 1936–41. The case of Peronist Argentina bears
some slight analogy with this type.

6. Conservative or bureaucratic-nationalist authoritarian regimes that were semi-pluralist and eschewed radical new
forms of mass mobilization. Examples would be Spain,
1923–30 (and in a partial sense again after 1945); Portugal
under the Estado Novo (1926/33–1974); Brazil under Vargas; Poland under Pilsudski; Hungary during most of
Horthy's regency, save for the Gömbös and Imredy minis-
tries; and probably also Austria under the Dollfuss-
Schuschnigg regime, for Schuschnigg's policy was more
to downgrade and defascistize the Heimwehr than to
fascistize the regime. However, a case can be made that
the Austria of the Fatherland Front belonged to category
5.

7. Strictly pretorian syncretic or semipluralist regimes that
do not attempt significant new political mobilization.
Aside from the Greece of the Colonels (1967–74), the examples are mainly Latin America (Argentina under Onga-
nía, Brazil since 1964, "military socialism" in Bolivia and
Peru—at least in their initial phases—and Chile since
1973). Other examples of regimes that roughly correspond
to categories 6 and 7 may be found in various parts of the
Third World.[11]

Given these limitations to the scope of analysis, it is
doubtful that fascism can be generically defined in terms of a
regime structure that was typically and fully fascist. Even the

11. No doubt this taxonomy might be further extended, particularly in the
Third World. For example, a lower category of primitive pretorian regimes
that lack sufficient civic structure might also be recognized, particularly in
the Caribbean and Africa. For a more extensive classification, see Juan J.
Linz, "Totalitarian and Authoritarian Regimes," in F. Greenstein and N.
Polby, eds., *Handbook of Political Science*, (Reading, Mass. 1975), 3: 175–411.

Hitler regime—the only one fully dominated by a fascist-type party and its leader—failed to last long enough to achieve a complete and finished structure.

The concept "fascist regime" may therefore be employed only in a very loose and general sense in terms of analogies to the new style of dictatorship introduced by Mussolini. Thus many prefer to call fascist any non-Marxist authoritarian system based on a single party and attempting to regulate a mixed economy. Within this very loose framework of definition one may identify a considerable number of "fascist regimes" both before and after World War II. Few of them, however, have had much to do with fascist movements or the historic culture of fascism.

TOWARD AN HISTORICAL UNDERSTANDING OF FASCISM

The sources of fascism cannot be grasped by reference to a demonic social class or any sociological or philosophical abstraction. Fascism can only be understood in terms of the particular historical contexts of greater central Europe in the years following World War I. Its success obviously depended on specific national historical circumstances and key variables that either were not present or were not present with sufficient force in most countries.

The chief cultural variables were the doctrines of intense nationalism, militarism, and international Social Darwinism in the forms that became widespread among the World War I generation in greater central Europe, coupled with the contemporary philosophical and cultural currents of neo-idealism, vitalism, and activism and the cult of the hero. Such trends might have been found in most European countries before 1914, but outside greater central Europe were largely counterbalanced by opposing cultural influences. These particular strands, however, were most strongly developed in the German- and Italian-speaking worlds and their cultural hinterland (such as the regions of Austria-Hungary).

The main political variable was not primarily the breakdown of established liberal democracy—none of the fully established liberal democratic systems (those of northern Europe and the lands of the former British empire) broke down—but was the impact of military defeat and severe national frustration or status deprivation reacting on political systems where the transition to mobilized liberal democracy had just gotten underway. Conversely, fascism could not make much headway in preliberal democratic systems, for the latter did not permit mobilization, challenge, and fully free elections. Rather, the two successful movements took advantage of systems just making or just having made the transition to liberal democracy while faced with a national crisis heavily influenced by foreign relations and a sense of international restrictions.

The main social variables seem to have had to do with an expanding or expanded series of middle sectors not yet adjusted to a modern, industrial, and liberal democratic framework of economy and government. Fascism was not a temptation for fully developed countries (those with industrial economies and rooted liberal democratic systems established for a generation or more) or for backward, agrarian, underdeveloped lands. Concretely, it affected seriously only the new countries of the 1860s—Germany, Italy, and Austria-Hungary. It was a consequence of the frustrations of national, imperial, and to some extent structural intermediacy in the early twentieth century, dependent on a peculiar culture of activism, overt authority, organic community, will power, and violence. Its most dangerous manifestations were due to the fact that down to 1945 a country of only high intermediate strength like Germany, not possessing genuine continental-imperial resources, could threaten the peace of the world and conquer most of Europe.

Characteristic fascist movements were primarily restricted to interwar Europe and even more specifically to central and east-central Europe and Civil War Spain. To call the entire period 1919–45 an era of fascism may be true in the sense that fascism was the most original and vigorous new type of radical movement in those years, and also in the sense that Germany for a time became the dominant state in Europe. It is inaccurate, however, if taken to imply that fascism became generally dominant politically, since comparatively few Europeans were directly converted to fascism. In the overwhelming majority of cases fascistic parties were quite unsuccessful and drew few votes. Antifascism (often as a Communist-organized doctrine) preceded fascism in many European countries, and among Italian Socialists—in their opposition to Mussolini's "social chauvinism"—it almost preceded the original fascism itself. Before 1939, antifascists, both voters and activists, always outnumbered fascists in Europe as a whole.

Crises and semirevolutionary situations do not long persist, and fascist movements lacked any clear-cut class or interest basis to sustain them. Their emphasis on a militarized style of politics, together with their need for allies, however fissiparous the association, greatly restricted their opportunities and their working time, requiring them to win power in less than a generation and in some cases within only a few years. The drive of a fascist movement toward power threatened the host polity with a state of political war (though not insurrectionary civil war) quite different from normal parliamentary politics. No system can long withstand a state of latent war, even if a direct insurrection is not launched. It either succumbs or overcomes the challenge. In the great majority of cases the fascist challenge was repelled, though sometimes at the cost of establishing a more moderate authoritarian system. At any rate, the 0.7 percent of the popular vote won by the Falange in the final Spanish elections of 1936 was much nearer the norm than the 38 percent won by the Nazis in 1932.

If fascism was partly a cultural phenomenon and partly a matter of the outworking of the imperialist-nationalist politics of the new states of the 1860s, it is unlikely to recur again in a form recognizable as generic European fascism. There are at least two primary reasons for this. One is that the imperialist pretensions and dynamics of the new states of the 1860s were destroyed in 1945 and are not likely to be revived. Secondly and more important, the cultural underpinnings of generic fascism have been completely eroded in the post-

1945 era, particularly since about 1960. All competing ideological forces now share a common humanist materialism, to the exclusion of either the older idealism or vitalism. The trend is accentuated by the general crisis of authority, broadly accepted concepts of equality (socially, racially, internationally), the all-consuming march of bureaucracy, and the acceleration of social atomization.

Despite the likelihood that extinct specific forms cannot recur, fascism was central to twentieth-century radicalism and nationalism, so that many of its characteristics and influences endure. Thus it is easy to play the game of defining contemporary "fascisms," since many nationalist authoritarian regimes have some of the characteristics of fascism (just as all communist regimes have some of the characteristics of fascism), even though close analysis always fails to substantiate the typology. A favorite case is, or was, the Nasser (now Sadat) regime in Egypt, with its *Führerprinzip*, "Arab socialism," a state sector of the economy approaching 40 percent, bellicosity against Israel, and presumed antisemitism. Yet the Nasserite regime had no very specific philosophy or culture and no coherent one-party movement behind it other than the amorphous Arab National Union. It was never consistently anticommunist, or for that matter very coherent in any form.[12] In its latest phase under Sadat, it has turned out to be the very opposite of bellicose or ferociously anti-Jewish.

The game can be played with Israel as well. In fact, I have been personally acquainted with a few European fascists who admire Israel as the perfect "representative fascist" state, with relative internal democracy but external integral nationalism and exclusivism. Israel is indeed in some respects a product of central-European integral nationalism, is ethnocentric, ultranationalist, militarist, and expansive, seeking Lebensraum and operating on the basis of a *Herren-*

12. Cf. Jean Lacouture, *Nasser* (London, 1973). On the profascist leanings of Nasser's generation, see James P. Jankowski, *Egypt's Young Rebels: 'Young Egypt,' 1933–1952* (Stanford, 1975).

volk and *Untermenschen* theory of sorts for the Holy Land. It is also a genuine functioning democracy, at least for its Jewish population, and functions as a *Rechtsstaat*, with constitutional scrupulosity, in its dealings with Muslims. No fascism there.

A much better case might be made for the Libyan dictatorship of Muammar el Qaddafi. Though riding a wave of oil, Qaddafi is a fanatical Muslim antimaterialist who is trying to establish a quasi-revolutionary system of state semi-collectivism, a sort of national socialism. His interest in violence, militarism, and international expansion is obvious. Moreover, Qaddafi has written a book (the *Green Book*, translated into various languages) to spread his gospel of the *Führerprinzip*—the bonds between the leader and a united people of all classes, creating a "true democracy" on organic principles, which sounds for all the world like Fascist Italy or Franco's Spain. And yet Qaddafi, in his system of state-controlled popular assemblies and syndicates, seems more likely to reproduce a radical, expansionist kind of "bureaucratic authoritarianism" (the phrase refers to Latin America) than a mass-mobilizing, revolutionary, single-party fascism. At any rate, he comes nearer the style and typology than anyone since Perón.

The communist peasant-nationalist regimes of Asia, relying on the *Führerprinzip*, extreme ethnocentric nationalism, and racism (and the ultimately grotesque in antimodernism in the case of the Cambodia of the Khmer Rouge) seem to some to represent the fascistization of communism. There is no doubt that, as discussed earlier, fascism and communism share many fundamental characteristics, and Russian spokesmen delight in applying the same words to China as to Nazi Germany: "petit bourgeois" policy, "bourgeois nationalism," "military-bureaucratic degeneration," "subservient obedience" of the masses, "anti-intellectualism," "voluntarism," "subjectivism," "autarchic" policies that try to place "surplus population" on "foreign territories," concluding that "the Maoist approach in no way differs from fascism."[13] Parallel lists for Cuba by more serious analysts would include the pragmatic development a posteriori of an ideology through practice, emphasis on peasantism, and extreme nationalism, government by charisma and the leadership principle, and military adventurism. Accurate though most of these technical comparisons are, they do not define doctrines and regimes that in the majority of respects are generally similar to fascism. All communist regimes—with the sole exception of Yugoslavia—have remained faithful to the Leninist-Stalinist principles of complete state bureaucracy, almost total state collectivism (with minor exceptions), and philosophical materialism. These are cardinal principles absolutely opposed to fascism.

Though the various little fascistic movements founded in the United States in the 1930s failed to prosper, the fascist characteristics of radical minority movements in the United States have also sometimes been pointed out. Marcus Garvey claimed to have invented fascism,[14] while the Black Panthers with their racism, violence, and authoritarianism, exhibited certain prime characteristics.[15] A book on the César Chávez "La Raza" movement cites[16] five "Nazi" characteristics of Chicano nationalism: (1) deification of leaders; (2) exaltation of an *Ubermensch* or "Great Race" group which must be collectivized and made a slave to itself to take its proper place in history; (3) a greater Reich or Lebensraum to be conquered in which the Great Race will reside in collective glory; (4) a vague utopian socialism specifically for the Great Race; and (5) absolute rejection of individualism and individual and property rights in favor of the collective. Detailed though the inventory is, it fails to convince one that we are dealing here with a fascist movement, both because the inventory distorts the characteristics of European Nazism and because other

13. These terms are taken from A. Malukhin, *Militarism—Backbone of Maoism* (Moscow, 1970), p. 33 and *passim*, cited in an unpublished manuscript by A. James Gregor.
14. Gregor, *Fascist Persuasion*, 360–75.
15. Cf. Ibid., 375–88.
16. Patty Newman, *Do It Up Brown!* (San Diego, 1971).

characteristics of the Chávez movement, such as its Catholic orientation and relative aversion to violence, disqualify it.

Student revolutionaries were also made prime candidates in the 1960s and early 1970s for the role of neofascists. Among their supposedly fascist characteristics were the formation of ideology through action rather than theory, anti-intellectualism, nonrationalism, voluntarism and activism, attempt to transcend both liberalism and Marxism in search of a new futurism, infatuation with myths and heroes, recruitment through a "class generationism," use of violence, hatred of plutocracies, espousal of proletarian-nation doctrines on behalf of Third World or Communist nationalisms, and the support of extreme militarism among the latter. The inventory was not unimpressive, but it left out at least as many points in which the student radicals differed fundamentally from fascism.

One of the prime group of candidates for contemporary fascism has been the new African dictatorships of the past generation. Such qualities as extreme nationalism, racism, ethnocentrism, nominally one-party systems, elaborate use of myths and national religiosity, charismatic leadership, and various forms of "African socialism" have seemed to approximate the fascist typology.[17] Closer inspection of the nature of African dictatorships, however, casts grave doubt on the "African fascism" typology. Paul Hayes has put it fairly accurately: "Many of the characteristics of European fascism may be found in certain of the African countries, though it is rare for any number to be found at the same time in one country."[18] The leadership principle there more nearly re-

17. For a more specific formulation, see A. James Gregor, "African Socialism and Fascism: An Appraisal," *Review of Politics* 29.3 (July 1967): 353–99; *Fascist Persuasion*, 406–9. A broader application may be found in Anthony J. Joes, *Fascism in the Contemporary World* (Boulder, 1978), "Fascism: The Past and the Future," *Comparative Political Studies* 7.1 (April 1974): 107–33, and "The Fascist Century," *Worldview* 21.5 (May 1978): 19–23.

18. Hayes, *Fascism*, 208. Maurice Bardèche, the only noteworthy fascist intellectual to make an effort at defining fascism after the passing of the fascist era, insists convincingly that so-called Third World fascisms are "false fascisms." The differences that he emphasizes are above all cultural. *Qu'est-ce que le fascisme?* (Paris, 1961).

sembles *caudillaje* in the Caribbean than in either Italy or Germany. The single parties normally do not turn out to be much in the way of organized parties, and the political economy falls short of any organized national syndicalism or state-regulated economy in the central-European senses.[19] Finally, the specific philosophical culture of Fascism and Nazism is largely lacking. About all that one can say is that the Fascist example of a one-party nationalist dictatorship may have been the original precedent for such regimes, but any specific and complete typology of European fascism has not been reproduced. Moreover, the new wave of African dictatorships of the 1970s has been overtly Leninist/Stalinist, seeking to implement Russian-derived norms of complete state buraucracy and a state collectivism as nearly total as circumstances permit These are regime goals quite distinct from fascism.

Fascism was after all the only major new ideology of the twentieth century, and it is not surprising that a variety of its key features reemerge in radical movements and national authoritarian regimes in later times and other regions,[20] even though the profile of the new groups is on balance distinct from the generic European fascisms. A number of these features may be specified:

1. permanent nationalistic one-party authoritarianism, neither temporary nor a prelude to internationalism
2. the charismatic leadership principle, incorporated by many communist and other regimes as well
3. the search for a synthetic ethnicist ideology, distinct from liberalism and Marxism
4. an authoritarian state system and political economy of corporatism or syndicalism or partial socialism, more limited and pluralistic than the communist model
5. the philosophical principle of voluntarist activism, unbounded by any philosophical determinism

---

19. Arnold Hughes and Martin Kolinsky, " 'Paradigmatic Fascism' and Modernisation: A Critique," *Political Studies* 24.4 (December 1976): 371–96.
20. The most thorough presentation is Gregor's *Fascist Persuasion*.

In these respects the fascist experience was fundamental to revolution and authoritarian nationalism in the twentieth century. To that extent the influence of fascism will continue to be felt for years to come, not least among some of the most vociferous formal antifascists.

REFERENCE
MATTER

A Bibliographical Note

Though an early literature on Fascism and National Socialism, some of it of considerable value, appeared well before World War II, global and comparative treatments of fascism did not emerge for an entire generation afterward. Only with the recession of the period into historical perspective did it become possible to study fascism as a more general and historical phenomenon rather than an immediate political or military problem. The two principal works that initiated the "fascism debate" in contemporary historiography and theory were Ernst Nolte's *Der Faschismus in seiner Epoche* (Munich, 1963), translated as *Three Faces of Fascism* (New York, 1966), and Eugen Weber's *Varieties of Fascism* (New York, 1964). Both had the force of originality and a new comparative approach, examining fascism as a unique historical phenomenon with diverse manifestations.

During the decade or so that followed, a number of general descriptive accounts and symposia on manifold aspects or manifestations of fascism appeared, led by the *Journal of Contemporary History*'s special number "International Fascism 1920–1945" (1966), edited by George L. Mosse and Walter Laqueur, followed by a second special number ten years later (the two subsequently published together as *International Fascism* [London, 1979]); and Nolte's *Die Krise des liberalen Systems und die faschistischen Bewegungen* (Munich, 1968).

These were followed by two composite volumes edited by Stuart J. Woolf: *The Nature of Fascism* (London, 1968) and *European Fascism* (London, 1969).

Of general surveys, Alan Cassels's *Fascism* (New York, 1975) is the most useful as a descriptive text, while Otto-Ernst Schüddekopf's *Fascism* (New York, 1973) is the best illustrated, and H. R. Kedward's *Fascism in Western Europe, 1900–1945* (New York, 1971) is the most superficial, not to say inaccurate. F. L. Carsten, *The Rise of Fascism* (Berkeley/Los Angeles, 1967), describes the growth of Fascism and National Socialism and surveys fascist movements elsewhere. An account of some of the background ideas and cultural influences is the subject of Paul Hayes, *Fascism* (London, 1972).

Much more useful is Walter Laqueur ed., *Fascism: A Reader's Guide*, (Berkeley/Los Angeles, 1976), a rich collection of studies and interpretive and analytic work, in which Juan J. Linz's "Notes Toward a Comparative Study of Fascism in Sociological Historical Perspective" stands out as the best introductory comparative sociology of fascism available. Much information will also be provided by the collective work Stein U. Larsen et al., eds., *Who Were the Fascists?* (Oslo-Bergen, forthcoming).

Explicit comparative studies of fascist movements are very few. N. M. Nagy-Talavera, *The Green Shirts and the Others: A History of Fascism in Hungary and Romania* (Stanford, 1970), is probably the most vivid example, but the broadest and most systematic is H.-U. Thamer and Wolfgang Wippermann, *Faschistische und neofaschistische Bewegungen* (Darmstadt, 1977). Others are W. Schieder, ed., *Faschismus als soziale Bewegung* (Hamburg, 1976); Jean Plumyène and Raymond Lasierra, *Les Fascismes français, 1923–1963* (Paris, 1963); Michael Ledeen, *Universal Fascism* (New York, 1972); and Manuel de Lucena, *A evoluçao do sistema corporativo portugués* (Lisbon, 1976), 2 vols. P. F. Sugar ed., *Native Fascism in the Successor States, 1918–1945* (Santa Barbara, 1971), deals with eastern Europe, and Hans Rogger and Eugen Weber, eds., *The European Right* (Berkeley/Los Angeles, 1965), provides comparison and contrast with the right. Finally, there are studies that deal with diverse elements of fascism and the authoritarian right within the same country, such as René Rémond, *The Right-Wing in France from 1815 to De Gaulle* (Philadelphia, 1969); Francis T. Carsten, *Fascist Movements in Austria: From Schönerer to Hitler* (London, 1976); Richard A. Robinson, *The Origins of Franco's Spain* (Pittsburgh, 1970); and Edward D. Wynot, Jr., *Polish Politics in Transition* (Athens, Ga., 1974).

The two best synthetic analyses of the principal theories that have been advanced to explain fascism are A. James Gregor, *Interpretations of Fascism* (Morristown, N.J., 1974), and Wolfgang Wippermann, *Faschismustheorien* (Darmstadt, 1975). Also important are Renzo de Felice's *Interpretations of Fascism* (Cambridge, Mass., 1977) and his massive anthology and commentary *Il fascismo: Le interpretazioni dei contemporanei e degli storici* (Bari, 1970), and Nolte's anthology *Theorien über de Faschismus* (Cologne, 1967). Henry A. Turner, Jr., ed., *Reappraisals of Fascism* (New York, 1976), represents some recent reinterpretations, and mention should also be made of De Felice's interpretive interview-essay *Fascism* (New Brunswick, 1977) and George L. Mosse's *Nazism: A History and Comparative Analysis of National Socialism* (New Brunswick, 1978).

The most trenchant attempts to place fascism within a general context of contemporary radicalism and revolutionism are A. James Gregor, *The Fascist Persuasion in Radical Politics* (Princeton, 1974), and Ludovico Garruccio, *L'industrializzazione tra nazionalismo e rivoluzione* (Bologna, 1969). Anthony J. Joes, *Fascism in the Contemporary World* (Boulder, 1978), makes sweeping comparisons. An original and provoctive comparison between Italian Fascism and Communism may be found in Domenico Settembrini, *Fascismo controrivoluzione imperfetta* (Florence, 1978).

Index

ABC, 123

Academic Karelia Society (AKS), 127

Ação Integralista Brasileira (AIB), 168–69, 169*n*

Acción Revolucionaria Mexicana (ARM), 171

Action Française: synthesis of integral nationalism, 27; and Camelots du Roi, 27; attitude towards militia, 27–28; as example of neomonarchist authoritarian nationalism, 27–29; attitude towards religion, 28; political economy of, 28; foreign influence of, 28–29; mentioned, 12, 37, 106, 130, 144, 157

Adorno, Theodor, 184, 185

Africa: significance of defeat for Italy, 85; fascist doctrine of racism, 85–86; fascism in, 210–11; socialism in, 210–11; mentioned, 98

Aguirre Cerda, Pedro, 170

AIB. *See* Ação Integralista Brasileira (AIB)

AKS. *See* Academic Karelia Society (AKS)

Albiñana: physician who organized Spanish Nationalist Party, 147*n*

Alessandri, Jorge, 170

Alfonso XIII, King of Spain: visits Mussolini, 141; and Alfonsine monarchists, 143–44

Alianca Popular Revolucionaria Americana (APRA), 168, 197*n*

Allardyce, Gilbert, 190

All Russian Fascist Party (of Russian Exiles in Manchuria), 164*n*

ANI. *See* Italian Nationalist Association (ANI)

Anti-Semitism: and German radical right, 31, 31*n*; Barresian view of, 37; DAP, 38; Italian Fascism, 53,

219

COMPOSED BY BYRD PRESS, RICHMOND, VIRGINIA
MANUFACTURED BY THE NORTH CENTRAL PUBLISHING CO.
ST. PAUL, MINNESOTA
TEXT AND DISPLAY LINES ARE SET IN PALATINO

Library of Congress Cataloging in Publication Data
Payne, Stanley G
Fascism, comparison and definition.
Bibliography: p.
Includes index.
1. Fascism. 2. Fascism—History. I. Title.
JC481.P374   320.5'33   79-5415
ISBN 0-299-08060-9